Health Care in
New Communities

New Communities Research Series

Shirley F. Weiss and *Raymond J. Burby, III*, series editors
Center for Urban and Regional Studies,
The University of North Carolina at Chapel Hill

- Access, Travel, and Transportation in New Communities by Robert B. Zehner

- Economic Integration in New Communities: An Evaluation of Factors Affecting Policies and Implementation by Helene V. Smookler

- Health Care in New Communities by Norman H. Loewenthal and Raymond J. Burby, III

- Indicators of the Quality of Life in New Communities by Robert B. Zehner

- Recreation and Leisure in New Communities by Raymond J. Burby, III

- Residential Mobility in New Communities: An Analysis of Recent In-movers and Prospective Out-movers by Edward J. Kaiser

- Schools in New Communities by Raymond J. Burby, III and Thomas G. Donnelly

Health Care in
New Communities

Norman H. Loewenthal
Raymond J. Burby, III

Ballinger Publishing Company • Cambridge, Massachusetts
A Subsidiary of J.B. Lippincott Company

NSF–RA–E '75–025

All of the material incorporated in this work was developed with the support of National Science Foundation grant number APR 72–03425. However, any opinions, findings, conclusions or recommendations expressed herein are those of the authors and do not necessarily reflect the views of the National Science Foundation.

International Standard Book Number: 0–88410–463–X

Library of Congress Catalog Card Number: 76–27978

Printed in the United States of America

Library of Congress Cataloging in Publication Data

Loewenthal, Norman H
  Health care in new communities.

  (New communities research series)
  Bibliography: p. 237
  Includes index.
  1. Community health services—United States. 2. New towns—United States. I. Burby, Raymond J., 1942– joint author. II. Title.
RA395.A3L63   362.1'0973   76–27978
ISBN 0–88410–463–X

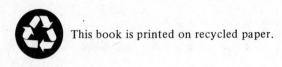

Contents

Chapter 5
Hospital Care and Ambulance Service

Chapter 6
Other Health and Social Services

Chapter 7
Health Insurance and Health Maintenance
Programs

Chapter 8
Health Care for Target Populations

List of Figures and Tables

Preface

This volume is one of a series of books that summarizes the results of a nationwide study and evaluation of new community development in the United States. The study was initiated in May 1972 under the direction of Dr. Shirley F. Weiss, principal investigator, and co-principal investigators Dr. Raymond J. Burby, III, Dr. Thomas G. Donnelly, Dr. Edward J. Kaiser and Dr. Robert B. Zehner, at the Center for Urban and Regional Studies of The University of North Carolina at Chapel Hill. Financial support for the project was provided by the Research Applied to National Needs Directorate of the National Science Foundation.

The New Communities Study grew out of our concern for the lack of information about the outcomes of new community development in this country. When the original prospectus for the study was prepared, new community development was attracting an increasing amount of attention from both the private and the public sectors. Beginning with a few pioneering new community projects started in the 1940s and 1950s, such as Park Forest and the Levittowns, the 1960s saw a significant expansion in community building. By the end of the decade, over 60 private new community ventures were reported to be under development in eighteen states. The prospect for further expansion in new community development was greatly enhanced by the passage of Title IV of the 1968 Housing and Urban Development Act and the Urban Growth and New Community Development Act of 1970, which provided federal loan guarantees and other forms of assistance for approved new community projects. In the early 1970s, officials of the Department of Housing and Urban

Development were confidently projecting that ten new communities per year would be started under the federal new communities program.

Increasing public involvement in community building was accompanied by heightened expectations about the public benefits that would result from new community development. The Urban Growth and New Community Development Act of 1970 indicated that the Congress expected new communities to improve the quality of life in the nation by: (1) increasing for all persons, particularly members of minority groups, the available choices of locations for living and working; (2) helping to create neighborhoods designed for easier access between the places where people live and the places where they work and find recreation; and (3) providing adequate public, community, and commercial facilities (including facilities needed for education, health and social services, recreation and transportation). Congressional expectations about the benefits from new community development, however, were not shared by all observers of the new communities movement.

On the basis of an in-depth study of new communities in California conducted in the mid-1960s, Edward P. Eichler and Marshall Kaplan (1967, p. 160) concluded that, ". . . community building, even with public aid or under public sponsorship, can do little to solve the serious problems confronting American society." Three years later William Alonso reviewed many of the potential benefits of new community development, but ended up by concluding that, "On the whole, a national policy of settling millions of people in new towns is not likely to succeed and would not significantly advance the national welfare if it could be done" (1970, p. 16). The Twentieth Century Fund Task Force on the Governance of New Towns, which reported its findings in 1971, felt that few large-scale developments in the United States were living up to the promise of the new community concept, and Clapp (1971, p. 287) concluded that existing public programs ". . . to date appear inadequate to further the satisfaction of the major objectives of the new town concept."

Obviously, whether the benefits from new community development are real or imagined is a matter of crucial importance in the formulation of national urban growth policies. Since passage of the 1968 and 1970 federal new communities legislation, seventeen new communities have been approved for assistance. Loan guarantee commitments by the federal government now total $361 million. When completed in about 20 years, these new communities are expected to house almost one million persons, with private investments running into the billions of dollars. Given the conflicting opinions about the benefits of new communities and the major public and private investments involved in their development, it seemed appropriate to propose, and for the National Science Foundation to support, a full-scale evaluation of new communities now under development in the United States.

The need for objective information about the performance of new communities has been further underscored by the devastating impacts of the national economic recession, which has produced severe financial problems for the projects participating in the federal new communities program. During 1974 no new loan guarantee commitments were made by the New Communities Administration in the Department of Housing and Urban Development, and on January 14, 1975 the Department suspended further processing of applications for assistance. Faced with mounting financial difficulties with assisted projects, attention within the federal government and the new communities industry has shifted away from the outputs of the program to more pressing concerns for the economic viability of assisted new community ventures. However, the outputs of the program cannot be ignored. If new communities are to receive continued and expanded federal support, they not only must survive as financially viable undertakings, they must also produce benefits that could not be as readily achieved through conventional urban growth.

THE NEW COMMUNITIES STUDY

The University of North Carolina New Communities Study was undertaken to provide federal, state and local officials, we well as public and private developers, with an improved information base to use in judging the merits of new community development as an urban growth alternative. To assure that new communities do, in fact, realize the "quality of life" objectives set forth by the Congress, the study also sought to determine the critical factors affecting the success or failure of new communities in attacting socially balanced populations and meeting the needs of all of their residents.

In pursuing these two goals, the new communities study was designed to provide answers to five major policy questions: (1) Are federally guaranteed new communities contributing more to residents' quality of life than non-guaranteed new communities and less planned environments? (2) Which characteristics of housing, neighborhood design, community facilities and governmental mechanisms contribute most to the quality of life of new community residents, including minorities, low-income families, the elderly and teenagers?

(3) Which factors in the developer decision process lead to new community characteristics that contribute most to the qualify of life of new community residents? (4) How has the federal new community development program influenced developer decisions regarding housing, neighborhood design, community facilities and governmental mechanisms? (5) How can the federal new community development program be applied most effectively to produce communities which promise to improve the quality of life of their residents?

The research design that was formulated to answer these questions is based on the belief that an evaluation of new community development must involve more than a study of new communities. To provide a sound basis for conclusions about new community performance, comparisons using the same measurement techniques must be made between new communities and alternative conventional forms of urban development. This research strategy led to the selection of a sample of seventeen communities to represent different types of new communities that are under development in the United States and nineteen conventional communities. The new community sample includes two communities that are participating in the federal new communities program, thirteen nonfederally assisted new communities that were initiated prior to the federal program and two retirement new communities designed specifically for older households. Fifteen of the conventional communities were selected by pairing each of the two federally assisted and thirteen nonfederally assisted new communities with a nearby community containing housing similar to that available in the new community in terms of age, type and price range. Because the paired conventional communities did not have sufficient black and low- and moderate-income populations for comparison with the new communities, four additional conventional communities were selected. These included two suburban communities with subsidized housing and two suburban communities with predominantly black residential areas.

Data collection in the sample new and conventional communities was begun during the spring of 1973 and continued through the summer of 1974. Four types of information were assembled to answer the research questions. First, data on people's attitudes and behavior were collected through 90-minute interviews with 5511 new and conventional community adult residents and self-administered questionnaires returned by 974 young adults (age 14 to 20) living in the sample communities. Second, data about community characteristics, including the number, accessibility and quality of facilities and services available and selected housing and neighborhood characteristics, were obtained from community inventories completed for all 36 sample communities and from interviews with professional personnel serving the communities. Third, professionals' observations about the communities, as well as factual information about community service systems, were collected through interviews with 577 professional personnel, including school district superintendents, school principals, health officials and practitioners, recreation administrators and community association leaders. Finally, the plans and activities of developers, governments, and other institutions involved in the development of the new and conventional communities were secured during preliminary reconnaissance interviews in each community, two waves of interviews with developer personnel, accounts published in newspapers and other secondary sources, discussions with local governmental officials and also from the professional personnel survey.

NEW COMMUNITIES U.S.A.

The major findings and conclusions emerging from the new communities study are summarized in *New Communities U.S.A.* (D.C. Heath and Co., Lexington Books, 1976). Capsuling three years of research, the summary report focuses on the strengths and weaknesses of new community development in the United States, key factors which account for variation in new community performance and public policy options.

In comparison with conventional modes of suburban growth and development, new communities were found to be superior in five major respects. *First*, better land use planning and community design resulted in the provision of a wider choice of housing types for purchase or rent, more neighborhood amenities and services, and safer access to them. *Second*, new community households tended to accumulate less annual automobile mileage, in part because of consistently better access to community facilities and services. *Third*, new communities were characterized by better recreational facilities and services, which resulted in somewhat higher participation in outdoor recreational activities and much higher levels of resident satisfaction with community recreational service systems. *Fourth*, new community residents tended to give higher ratings to the overall livability of their communities and were more likely than conventional community residents to recommend their communities as particularly good places to which to move. *Fifth*, new communities were found to provide more satisfying living environments for target populations—black households, low- and moderate-income residents of subsidized housing and older persons—than the comparison conventional communities.

Given these benefits and assuming that the costs of new community development are no greater than those incurred in conventional urban growth, the study findings provide ample justification for federal efforts to encourage the increased production of new communities in this country. In fact, federal participation in the new communities field appears to be necessary if new communities are to serve as one means of achieving the goals set forth by the Congress in the Urban Growth and New Community Development Act of 1970.

While producing substantial benefits, new community develpment in the United States has fallen short of achieving the full potential of the new community concept for solving urban problems and creating a better urban environment. Aspects of community development and life where few overall differences were found between the new and conventional communities studied included: evaluations of housing and neighborhood livability; residents' social perspectives, rates of participation in neighboring, community organizations and community politics and satisfaction with various life domains and with life as a whole; the provision of some community services; and the organization and operation of community governance. Clearly, in some cases planners have been overly optimistic about the influence of improvements in the physical environment on people's attitudes and behavior. However, in many cases, including the attainment of population balance and the provision of superior public services, the gap between concept and reality can be traced to a variety of factors subject to change through public policy.

In order to optimize the potential that new communities offer for a quantum improvement in the character of urban growth and development, some means must be found to overcome the private developer's limited ability to assume public sector responsibilities and local government's inability to cope with fragmented urban service responsibilities and the debilitating effects of insufficient financial resources. The need to assist developers and local governments in the provision of public and community services was recognized in the Urban Growth and New Community Development Act of 1970, but many of the provisions of the Act designed to achieve this purpose were never implemented.

With the federal new communities program at a standstill, two basic, though not mutually exclusive, policy options are available. First, given waning developer interest in larger scale new communities, the program could be reoriented toward smaller scale planned unit developments, villages and experimental new communities. At the same time that assistance is directed toward smaller scale development, the existing new communities legislation could be amended to recharge those new communities already participating in the federal program. This would require expanded support for low- and moderate-income housing in new communities and the design of new incentives for the provision of high quality and innovative community service systems. Additionally, eligibility for such assistance could be extended to new communities not now federally assisted, if they subscribe to the goals of the program.

Another option, not excluded by the first, would be to return to the basic purposes embraced in the 1970 Urban Growth and New Community Development Act and link the production of new communities to the implementation of a national urban growth policy. If new communities are to be an integral part of a national urban growth policy, stronger measures than exist in current legislation for private developer and state and local government participation in new community development must be provided. This would require full funding and implementation of the 1970 new communities legislation as a first step. Beyond this, federal incentives are needed to encourage state government participation in new community projects, including state oversight of land use and development regulations, state initiatives to establish new governmental structures for new communities and state financial assistance in meeting the public overhead and front-end costs of new community development projects.

NEW COMMUNITIES RESEARCH SERIES

The seven volumes in the *New Commuunities Research Series*, published by Ballinger Publishing Company, explore in depth key facets of new community development in the United States. The books in this series are designed to give community development professionals and researchers in architecture, design, education, health care, housing, planning, recreation, social services, transportation and allied professions a fuller and more detailed description and analysis of the new community experience than could be provided in a summary report. In addition to their utility to persons concerned with new community development, these books summarize the results of a pioneering social science research effort. They report the findings of one of the first, and probably the most comprehensive, attempts to trace through sequences of actions and consequences in the community development process—from the decisions which led to the provision of housing and the production of facilities and services through their effects on individual and household attitudes and behavior.

A central premise of the new community concept has been that through comprehensive planning better relationships can be attained among many of the key variables that influence travel behavior. In *Access, Travel, and Transportation in New Communities*, Robert B. Zehner examines the availability of transportation and other community facilities and services in new communities and how they influence travel behavior. Particular attention is given to alternatives to the automobile, including walking and community transit, the journey to work, automobile ownership rates and annual household automobile mileage. By analyzing relationships between demographic and community characteristics on the one hand, and residents' travel behavior on the other, Dr. Zehner shows how community design can result in reduced travel and potential energy savings.

Economic Integration in New Communities: An Evaluation of Factors Affecting Policies and Implementation by Helene V. Smookler describes the processes of income and racial integration (and nonintegration) in fifteen new communities. The communities are analyzed to determine what factors made integration possible and how they contributed to the effectiveness of the integration programs and strategies that were utilized. The early effects of federal involvement in new community development are described. Dr. Smookler also examines the correlates of residents' integration attitudes, showing that significant differences in attitudes characterize communities with varying amounts of income and racial integration. Finally, the benefits of integration are analyzed in terms of the actual attitudes and perceptions of low-income and black residents living in integrated new communities.

Planned new communities have been viewed as ideal settings in which to develop better ways of organizing and delivering health care services. As described in *Health Care in New Communities* by Norman H. Loewenthal and Raymond J. Burby, III, however, a number of factors have prevented many new communities from achieving this potential. In addition to describing the approaches to health care that have characterized community building in the United States, the authors examine the impacts of available health care resources on residents' satisfaction with and utilization of health care facilities and services. Health care resources that are analyzed in the study include the provision of physicians' services, hospital care and ambulance service, social service programs, nursing and convalescent care facilities, public health facilities and health maintenance programs. Objective characteristics of health care systems, residents' attitudes and behavior, and health professionals' evaluations are interrelated and used as a basis for the formulation of health care policies for the next generation of new communities to be built in this country.

During the past five years increasing interest has been expressed in the quality of life in the United States and how it can and should be measured. The strategy used to assess the quality of life of new and conventional community residents, reported in *Indicators of the Quality of Life in New Communities* by Robert B. Zehner, is eclectic, ranging from measures focused on specific functional community service areas to more global concepts, such as residents' overall life satisfaction. A unique aspect of the data presented in this book is the discussion of residents' individual perceptions of the factors that influence the quality of life as they have defined it for themselves. Dr. Zehner also explores residents' satisfactions with a number of life domains—standard of living, use of leisure time, health, family life, marriage and work, among others. He also shows how satisfaction with each domain relates to satisfaction with life as a whole. Differences in the quality of life among nineteen classifications of residents, including blacks, low- and moderate-income persons and the elderly, are highlighted, as well as observed differences in the quality of life between new and conventional communities.

Recreation and Leisure in New Communities by Raymond J. Burby, III provides a comprehensive description and analysis of this key community service system. A comparative evaluation of the experiences of fifteen new communities in developing recreational service systems is presented. Key agents and their roles in developing community recreational resources are identified. Dr. Burby also discusses the administration of recreational service systems, including their governance, approaches to recreational planning and methods of financing facilities and services. The effectiveness of alternative approaches to organizing the provision of recreational services is evaluated in terms of recreational resources produced and residents' use of and satisfaction with facilities and services. Particular attention is given to how the recreational needs of young adults, elderly persons, women, blacks and subsidized housing residents have been met. Recreational service system characteristics that influenced residents' participation in outdoor recreational activities, satisfaction with the facilities and services used most often and overall evaluations of community recreational resources are identified and used as a basis for suggestions about the best approaches to the design and development of community recreational facilities and services.

Who moves to new communities and why? Why are families considering moving from new communities? What factors attract black families and low- and moderate-income households to new and conventional suburban communities? How do residential mobility processes shape the population profiles of new communities? These and related questions are addressed in *Residential Mobility in New Communities: An Analysis of Recent In-movers and Prospective Out-movers* by Edward J. Kaiser. In this book, Dr. Kaiser examines the inflow of residents to new communities, paying particular attention to the characteristics of recent in-movers, their reasons for selecting a home in a new community and the improvements that were realized as a result of the move. Because the number and profile of out-movers influence the profile of residents left behind, Dr. Kaiser also examines the rate and type of household being lost to new communities through out-mobility. The characteristics of those households most likely to move are identified, together with the key reasons for their moving intentions. Separate chapters are devoted to the retrospective residential choices and prospective mobility of black households, subsidized housing residents and the residents of federally assisted new communities.

The last book in the series, *Schools in New Communities* by Raymond J. Burby, III and Thomas G. Donnelly, examines school development processes and outcomes in the sample of new and conventional communities. Five topics are covered in this study. First, the capacity of school districts to cope with large-scale community development projects is examined through an analysis of the experiences of 27 school districts in developing educational programs for and building new schools in nonfederally and federally assisted new communities. School districts' experiences in serving new communities are traced from each district's initial contacts with developers, through various phases of the school development process, to current issues in the operation of new community schools. Second, school development outcomes are evaluated in terms of both the objective characteristics of school plants and educational programs and the subjective attitudes of educators and parents. Third, links between characteristics of the schools and parents' evaluations of the schools attended by their children are identified. Fourth, the impact of school availability on the attractiveness of new communities to various population groups is reported, including the contribution of public schools to households' decisions to move to new communities and their satisfaction with the community as a place to live after they have occupied their homes. Finally, suggestions for increasing the effectiveness of school development processes are offered.

THE RESEARCH TEAM

The New Communities Study, summary report and monographs in the *New Communities Research Series* were made possible by the combined efforts of a large team of researchers and supporting staff assembled at the Center for Urban and Regional Studies of The University of North Carolina at Chapel Hill. The team members and their roles in the study were the following:

Dr. Shirley F. Weiss, principal investigator and project director, who had primary responsibility for management of the study and coordination of the research efforts of the team of co-principal investigators and research associates. Dr. Weiss's research focused on the overall new community development process, implementation, fiscal concerns and federal assistance, as well as shopping center and other commercial facilities.

Dr. Raymond J. Burby, III, co-principal investigator and deputy project director, who assumed primary responsibility for implementation of the research design and preparation of the project summary report. Dr. Burby's research focused on new community planning and governance, the recreation and leisure service system, schools and health care planning and delivery.

Dr. Thomas G. Donnelly, co-principal investigator, who assumed primary responsibility for the extensive data processing for the study. Dr. Donnelly's research focused on the development and utilization of efficient computation routines for the data analyses and on educational development processes in new communities.

Dr. Edward J. Kaiser, co-principal investigator, who helped formulate the original research design and research management strategy, and offered invaluable advice throughout the study. Dr. Kaiser's research focused on residential mobility processes in new communities.

Dr. Robert B. Zehner, co-principal investigator, who assumed primary responsibility for the design and conduct of the household survey. Dr. Zehner's research focused on transportation and travel in new communities, neighborhood and community satisfaction and the quality of life of new community residents.

David F. Lewis, research associate, who prepared a comparative analysis of the population characteristics of new communities, their host counties and host SMSAs, and contributed to the analysis of housing and neighborhood satisfaction in new communities.

Norman H. Loewenthal, research associate, who undertook a major portion of the professional personnel survey design and field work and assumed primary responsibility for the analysis of health care service systems in new communities.

Mary Ellen McCalla, research associate, who assumed responsibility for immediate supervision of the household survey sampling, field work and coding operations, supervision of the community inventory map measurement and professional personnel survey coding, and contributed to the analysis of the social life of new communities.

Dr. Helene V. Smookler, research associate, who assumed primary responsibility for the design and conduct of developer decision studies and the analysis of economic integration in new communities.

Invaluable assistance throughout the study was provided by Barbara G. Rodgers, who served as administrative aide, research assistant and publications manager.

The research work was supported by a staff of technical specialists, research assistants, interviewers, coders and office personnel too extensive for a complete listing. In particular, the efforts of the following persons should be recognized: research assistants Jerry L. Doctrow, Mary C. Edeburn, Leo E. Hendricks, Christopher G. Olney and Raymond E. Stanland, Jr.; and, secretaries Cathy A. Albert, Lisa D. McDaniel, Linda B. Johnson, Lucinda D. Peterson and Diana Pettaway.

THE NATIONAL SCIENCE FOUNDATION

The new communities study was made possible by research grant APR 72—03425 from the Research Applied to National Needs Directorate of the National Science Foundation. Throughout the course of the study, the research team benefited greatly from the continuing interest and constant encouragement of Dr. George W. Baker, the project's program manager. Dr. Baker worked with the research team to achieve scientific excellence in each phase of the study.

Of course, the findings, opinions, conclusions or recommendations arising out of this research grant are those of the authors and it should not be implied that they represent the views of the National Science Foundation.

SITE AND ADVISORY COMMITTEES

The process of refining the initial research design was aided by the expert advice of the Site Visit Committee and the panel of anonymous peer reviewers whose ideas were synthesized by Dr. George W. Baker.

An important source of guidance and consultation was made pos-

sible by the project's Advisory Committee, drawn from experts in
new community development, city planning, economics, political
science and sociology. Jonathan B. Howes, Director, Center for Urban and Regional Studies, The University of North Carolina at Chapel
Hill, ably served as chairman of the Advisory Committee which in-
cluded: Dr. George W. Baker, National Science Foundation; Profes-
sor F. Stuart Chapin, Jr., The University of North Carolina at Chapel
Hill; Dr. Amos H. Hawley, The University of North Carolina at
Chapel Hill; Morton Hoppenfeld, The Rouse Company (resigned
March 5, 1975); Dr. Richard M. Langendorf, University of Miami;
Floyd B. McKissick, McKissick Enterprises, Inc.; Dr. Frederick A.
McLaughlin, Jr., New Communities Administration, Department of
Housing and Urban Development (appointed in 1973); Dr. Peter H.
Rossi, University of Massachusetts; Dr. Joseph J. Spengler, Duke Uni-
versity; Dr. Lawrence Susskind, Massachusetts Institute of Technol-
ogy; Dr. Dorothy S. Williams, Department of Housing and Urban
Development (1972–73); and Dr. Deil S. Wright, The University of
North Carolina at Chapel Hill.

While their collective and individual contributions to the conduct
of the study are gratefully acknowledged, it goes without saying that
neither the Site Committee, the Advisory Committee, nor any individual members bear responsibility for the findings and interpretations in the *New Communities Research Series* and other publications of the project.

NEW COMMUNITIES POLICY
APPLICATIONS WORKSHOP

A New Communities Policy Applications Workshop was held in
Chapel Hill at The University of North Carolina from November 17
to 19, 1974. The workshop brought together invited representatives
of federal, state, local, private and academic user communities to
review the methodology and preliminary findings of the study. The
workshop was structured to assure that critical feedback to the research team would be secured from formal and informal discussion
sessions and to provide a forum for the consideration of broad issues
in new community development.

The Policy Applications Workshop was an invaluable part of the
research process. The following participants offered many astute
observations and critical comments which were helpful to the research team.

Representing the federal government: Dr. Harvey A. Averch, National Science Foundation; Dr. George W. Baker, National Science

Foundation; Bernard P. Bernsten, U.S. Postal Service; Larry W. Colaw, Tennessee Valley Authority; Dr. James D. Cowhig, National Science Foundation; Dr. Frederick J. Eggers, U.S. Department of Housing and Urban Development; Richard L. Fore, U.S. Department of Housing and Urban Development; James L. Gober, Tennessee Valley Authority; George Gross, House Budget Committee, U.S. House of Representatives; Charles A. Gueli, U.S. Department of Housing and Urban Development; Benjamin McKeever, Subcommittee on Housing of the Committee on Banking and Currency, U.S. House of Representatives; Dr. Frederick A. McLaughlin, Jr., U.S. Department of Housing and Urban Development; Paul W. Rasmussen, U.S. Department of Transportation; Dr. Salvatore Rinaldi, U.S. Office of Education; Ali F. Sevin, Federal Highway Administration; Dr. Frederick T. Sparrow, National Science Foundation; Otto G. Stolz, U.S. Department of Housing and Urban Development; Jack Underhill, U.S. Department of Housing and Urban Development; Margaret L. Wireman, U.S. Department of Housing and Urban Development; and Theodore W. Wirths, National Science Foundation.

Representing state, local and community government: D. David Brandon, New York State Urban Development Corporation; W.C. Dutton, Jr., The Maryland–National Capital Park and Planning Commission; Brendan K. Geraghty, Newfields New Community Authority; James L. Hindes, Office of Planning and Budget, State of Georgia; Mayor Gabrielle G. Pryor, City of Irvine, Calif.; Roger S. Ralph, Columbia Park and Recreation Association; Anne D. Stubbs, The Council of State Governments; and Gerald W. von Mayer, Office of Planning and Zoning, Howard County, Md.

Representing new community developers: James E. Bock, Gerald D. Hines Interests; Dwight Bunce, Harbison Development Corporation; David J. Burton, Harbison Development Corporation; Gordon R. Carey, Warren Regional Planning Corporation; David Scott Carlson, Riverton Properties, Inc.; Eva Clayton, Soul City Foundation; Mark H. Freeman, League of New Community Developers; Morton Hoppenfeld, DEVCO—The Greater Hartford Community Development Corporation; Joseph T. Howell, Seton Belt Village; Floyd B. McKissick, The Soul City Company; Richard A. Reese, The Irvine Company; Jeffrey B. Samet, Harbison Development Corporation; Elinor Schwartz, League of New Community Developers; Michael D. Spear, The Rouse Company; and Francis C. Steinbauer, Gulf-Reston, Inc.

Representing public interest groups and new community/urban affairs consultants: Mahlon Apgar, IV, McKinsey and Company;

Evans Clinchy, Educational Planning Associates; Ben H. Cunningham, The Hodne-Stageberg Partners; Harvey B. Gantt, Gantt/Huberman Associates; John E. Gaynus, National Urban League, Inc.; James J. Gildea, Barton-Aschman Associates; Nathaniel M. Griffin, Urban Land Institute; Guy W. Hager, Planning and Management Consultant; William H. Hoffman, National Corporation for Housing Partnerships; Jack Linville, Jr., American Institute of Planners; Hugh Mields, Jr., Academy for Contemporary Problems; William Nicoson, Urban Affairs Consultant; Dr. Carl Norcross, Advisor on New Communities; Robert M. O'Donnell, Harman, O'Donnell and Henninger Associates; Donald E. Priest, Urban Land Institute; Edward M. Risse, Richard P. Browne Associates; George M. Stephens, Jr., Stephens Associates; Eugene R. Streich, System Development Corporation; and Doris Wright, REP Associates.

Representing the academic community: Dr. Allen H. Barton, Columbia University; Professor David L. Bell, North Carolina State University; Professor Richard D. Berry, University of Southern California; Donald W. Bradley, Michigan State University; William A. Brandt, Jr., University of Chicago; David J. Brower, The University of North Carolina at Chapel Hill; Lynne C. Burkhart, University of Massachusetts; Professor F. Stuart Chapin, Jr., The University of North Carolina at Chapel Hill; Dr. Lewis Clopton, The University of North Carolina at Chapel Hill; Dr. Robert H. Erskine, The University of North Carolina at Chapel Hill; Dr. Sylvia F. Fava, Brooklyn College of The City University of New York; Dr. Nelson N. Foote, Hunter College of The City University of New York; Russell C. Ford, The University of North Carolina at Chapel Hill; Dr. Gorman Gilbert, The University of North Carolina at Chapel Hill; Dr. David R. Godschalk, The University of North Carolina at Chapel Hill; Dr. Gideon Golany, The Pennsylvania State University; Professor Philip P. Green, Jr., The University of North Carolina at Chapel Hill; Dr. George C. Hemmens, The University of North Carolina at Chapel Hill; Dean George R. Holcomb, The University of North Carolina at Chapel Hill; Jonathan B. Howes, The University of North Carolina at Chapel Hill; Frederick K. Ickes, The University of North Carolina at Chapel Hill; Dr. Suzanne Keller, Princeton University; Joseph E. Kilpatrick, The University of North Carolina at Chapel Hill; Professor Alan S. Kravitz, Ramapo College of New Jersey; Dr. Richard M. Langendorf, University of Miami; Dean Claude E. McKinney, North Carolina State University; Dr. Robert W. Marans, The University of Michigan; Susan L. Marker, Bryn Mawr College; Dr. Michael J. Minor, University of Chicago; Professor Roger Montgomery, University of California,

Berkeley; Daniel W. O' Connell, Harvard University; Dean Kermit C. Parsons, Cornell University; David R. Paulson, The University of North Carolina at Chapel Hill; Dr. Francine F. Rabinovitz, University of California,' Los Angeles; Dr. Peter H. Rossi, University of Massachusetts; Dr. Arthur B. Shostak, Drexel University; Dr. Michael A. Stegman, The University of North Carolina at Chapel Hill; Dr. Robert Sullivan, Jr., Duke University; Dr. Lawrence Susskind, Massachusetts Institute of Technology; Professor Maxine T. Wallace, Howard University; Dr. William A. Wallace, Carnegie-Mellon University; Kenneth Weeden, The University of North Carolina at Chapel Hill; Professor Warren J. Wicker, The University of North Carolina at Chapel Hill; Dr. Deil S. Wright, The University of North Carolina at Chapel Hill; and Dr. Mary Wylie, The University of Wisconsin—Madison.

Representing the press: Barry Casselman, *Appleseeds* and *Many Corners* newspapers; Thomas Lippman, *The Washington Post*; William B. Richards, *The Washington Post*; and Barry Zigas, *Housing and Development Reporter.*

Foreign observers: Åsel Floderus, The National Swedish Institute for Building Research; and Hans Floderus, Building and Town Planning Department, Avesta, Sweden.

To list all the people who contributed to this study is impossible. Among others, these would include 6485 residents who spent time responding to the household survey interview, the 577 professionals who shared their knowledge and opinions about the study communities and the 173 informed individuals who were interviewed in connection with the developer decision studies.

A final note of thanks is due the new community developers and their staffs who were generous in making available their time and expert knowledge to the research team. In reciprocation, this series is offered as an aid in their continuing efforts to realize better communities and a more livable environment.

Shirley F. Weiss and **Raymond J. Burby, III**

The University of North Carolina
at Chapel Hill
December 10, 1975

Authors' Note

The assembly of data and other material for this book was made possible by the cooperation and assistance of a number of persons and agencies. We would like to thank the new community developers and health care professionals in all parts of the nation who generously contributed their time and knowledge of health care in new communities. A special note of thanks is also due Dr. Conrad Seipp, Health Services Research Center, The University of North Carolina at Chapel Hill, and Dr. Robert Sullivan, Department of Community Health Sciences, Duke University, for their advice during the formulation of research questions and survey instruments.

We are indebted to our colleagues, Drs. Thomas G. Donnelly, Edward J. Kaiser, Shirley F. Weiss and Robert B. Zehner, for their substantive research contributions throughout this study.

Finally, we would like to acknowledge the contributions of present and former staff members of the Center for Urban and Regional Studies. Mary Ellen McCalla assisted in the preparation of the household survey instruments and conduct of the household survey fieldwork and supervised data coding operations. Jerry L. Doctrow, Leo E. Hendricks and David F. Lewis conducted portions of the health professional survey and community inventory fieldwork. Mary C. Edeburn provided assistance in all phases of data processing. Barbara G. Rodgers supervised the central office staff and the production of the final manuscript.

Norman H. Loewenthal
Raymond J. Burby, III

The University of North Carolina
at Chapel Hill
March 15, 1976

※ *Chapter 1*

Summary of Findings

New community development has often been regarded as an opportunity for both the public and private sectors to produce better cities. If this is so, the provision of health care facilities and services must be an integral aspect of the community building process. In this book the American experience in providing health care in new communities is examined. Approaches to health care that have characterized community building, their impacts on residents' utilization of and satisfaction with health care services and health professionals' evaluations are considered and related to the formulation of health care policies for the next generation of new communities to be built in this country.

This summary chapter describes the methods and limitations of the study together with highlights of the findings. Major subjects that are addressed include new community residents' orientations to health and health care, developers' activities in the health care field, availability of medical practitioners and residents' utilization of primary care services, hospital care, emergency ambulance service, social services, nursing and convalescent facilities, public health facilities and health insurance and prepaid health plans. The chapter concludes with residents' and professionals' overall evaluations of health care in new communities and suggestions for improving the planning and delivery of this essential community service.

METHODS OF THE STUDY

The new communities studied included thirteen communities developed by the private sector without federal assistance, two communities that are participating in the federal new communities program, and, to provide an additional basis for analyses of health care and the elderly, two retirement new communities designed specifically for older households.

Nineteen conventional communities were included in the study to provide a basis for evaluations of new communities in comparison with less planned traditional modes of urban development and to control for contextual factors, such as climate. Each of the nonfederally assisted and federally assisted new communities was paired with a significantly less planned conventional community that was similar to the new community in terms of the age, price range and type of housing available and location. Because the sample of paired conventional communities did not have sufficient black and low- and moderate-income populations for comparison with the new communities, information was gathered in four additional conventional communities. These included two suburban communities with subsidized housing and two with predominantly black residential areas.

Locations of the new and conventional communities are illustrated in Figure 1–1. The nonfederally assisted new communities are: Columbia, Md., Reston, Va. and North Palm Beach, Fla. on the East Coast; Forest Park, Oh., Elk Grove Village, Ill. and Park Forest, Ill. in the Midwest; Sharpstown, Tex. and Lake Havasu City, Ariz. in the Southwest; and in California, Foster City, outside San Francisco and Valencia, Westlake Village, Irvine and Laguna Niguel in the Los Angeles area.

The federally assisted new communities are Jonathan, Minn. and Park Forest South, Ill., two of the first three new communities to be approved for assistance. The retirement new communities are Rossmoor Leisure World, Laguna Hills, Calif. and Sun City Center, Fla.

Within each community, three types of data were collected. First, interviews with 144 professional health care personnel and the developers of ten new communities that began development during the 1960s were conducted during 1973 and 1974 to obtain information about the organization of health care service systems, objective data on health care resources and professionals' evaluations of the adequacy and quality of resources. Second, additional data on the characteristics of health care resources were collected during the spring of 1973 through a field inventory of facilities and services available in each community and through a series of map measure-

Figure 1–1. New Communities

• New Community
o Conventional Community

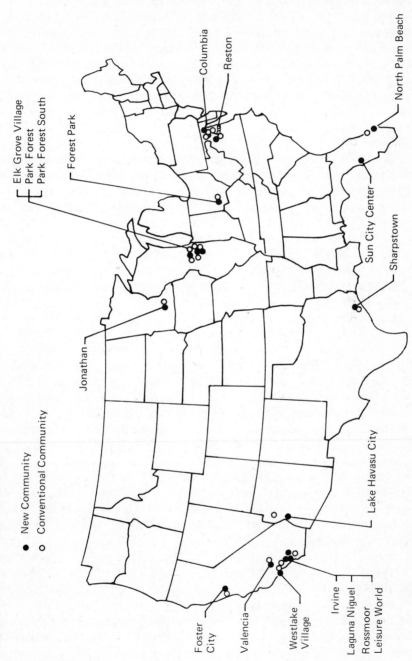

Elk Grove Village
Park Forest
Park Forest South

Forest Park

Columbia
Reston

North Palm Beach

Sun City Center
Sharpstown

Jonathan

Lake Havasu City

Foster City
Valencia
Westlake Village
Irvine
Laguna Niguel
Rossmoor
Leisure World

ments and calculations. Third, data on residents' awareness and utilization of health care resources and their satisfaction with health care facilities and services were collected through interviews conducted in the spring of 1973 with 5511 new and conventional community adult residents, and self-administered questionnaires returned by 974 young adults in the fourteen to twenty age bracket. A complete description of sampling and data collection procedures is provided in Appendix A. A series of brief vignettes that summarize selected characteristics of the new and conventional communities is provided in Chapter 2.

Before reviewing the findings of the study, several limitations of the research methods should be noted. The results of the study have been derived from cross-sectional data collected in new and conventional communities during 1973 and 1974. Although the results of earlier studies and subsequent changes were taken into account where data were available, longitudinal analysis and monitoring of new communities over time will be required for a dynamic view of health care in new communities.

It should also be stressed that the new and conventional communities studied were by no means completed communities. Some new communities had gone farther in the development process than others —Park Forest, for example, had achieved about 90 percent of its target population—but, on average, the new communities studied were only about one-fifth completed. Thus, this is a book about developing new communities rather than completed communities. Particular circumstances in individual new and conventional communities will change over time as their populations grow and the provision of more health care facilities and services becomes possible.

The two federally assisted new communities and their paired conventional communities were in the very initial stages of development. The findings for them provide an early empirical picture of the results of the federal new communities program and benchmarks for comparison with later studies of these two and other federally assisted communities. They should not, however, be used to judge the entire federal new communities program.

RESIDENTS' ORIENTATION TO HEALTH AND HEALTH CARE

A basic factor underlying new and conventional community residents' orientation to health and health care was their general satisfaction with their own health. On a seven-point scale, 88 percent of the nonfederally assisted new community respondents and 84 percent of the paired conventional community respondents rated their health in the top three categories (completely satisfied and satisfied). The high level of satisfaction with personal health explains, in part, why residents were usually unconcerned with the availability of health care facilities and services in their decisions to move to new communities or in their perceptions of the factors that made their communities good places in which to live. For example, only 2 percent of the new community respondents mentioned that the availability of health and medical services was a factor in their decision to move to a new community. Among various segments of the population, only elderly households indicated a greater than average interest in health and medical services in their decisions to move. However, even among this group of residents health and medical services were mentioned by only 9 percent and ranked thirteenth among the factors they regarded as important in their selection of a home in a new community.

Only 2 percent of the new community respondents mentioned health care facilities and services as a major contributor to the livability of their communities. Only 4 percent mentioned inadequacies in the health care system as an important issue or problem in their communities. That health care is at the periphery of most residents' interest is further indicated by the factors they mentioned as contributors to their overall quality of life. When asked to name the "main things your overall quality of life depend on," being in good health was mentioned by only 15 percent of the new community respondents. Of more importance to the respondents were economic security, family life, personal strengths (such as honesty, fortitude and intelligence), social relationships, the quality of the physical environment, contentment/well-being/happiness, job satisfaction and leisure activities.

NEW COMMUNITY DEVELOPERS AND HEALTH CARE

Health care was also on the periphery of most new community developers' interests. In a few new communities, including Park Forest, North Palm Beach and Sharpstown, developers left community health care entirely to the entrepreneurial instincts of doctors and surrounding health care institutions. A more common course of action, however, was to engage in one or two health care projects. For example, doctors were actively recruited by the developers of Forest Park and Lake Havasu City. In other new communities, such as Reston, Elk Grove Village, Foster City, Westlake Village, Irvine and Laguna

Niguel, developers built or cooperated in the construction of medical office buildings and clinics that provided space for fee-for-service medical practitioners. A number of developers also became actively involved in community hospital projects. The Centex Corporation donated ten acres of a 40-acre site for the Alexian Brothers Hospital in Elk Grove Village. The Newhall Land and Farming Company donated land and staff time to aid in the planning and construction of the Henry Mayo Newhall Memorial Hospital in Valencia. In Westlake Village, the American-Hawaiian Steamship Company helped a local group secure licensing approval for the proprietary Westlake Community Hospital. Robert P. McCulloch donated land for and attempted to resolve the conflicts among two competing groups that eventually built two hospitals in Lake Havasu City. The Irvine Company agreed to donate an eighteen-acre site for the proposed Western World Medical Foundation Hospital in Irvine. Gulf-Reston, Inc. supported a proposal by Beveraly Enterprises to build a community hospital in Reston.

In contrast with the *ad hoc* approaches to health care that characterized most new community development projects, Columbia's developer and the developers of the two federally assisted new communities, Jonathan and Park Forest South, pursued comprehensive approaches to community-based health care. Health planners were among the diverse group of professionals whose ideas helped give direction to Columbia's growth. At an early stage in the planning process a relationship was formed with the Johns Hopkins Medical Institutions of Baltimore which led to the development of the Columbia Medical Plan, a comprehensive prepaid group practice medical program that was organized and planned by The Johns Hopkins University, The Johns Hopkins Hospital and Connecticut General Life Insurance Company.

Jonathan's and Park Forest South's project agreements with the federal government spelled out an extensive range of developer obligations to insure that residents' health care needs were met. In Jonathan the specific obligations of the Jonathan Development Corporation included providing information to residents on existing health care resources, investigating the possibility of establishing a community-wide health plan, selling or leasing office space for clinic use and attracting appropriate medical facilities and supporting personnel. The plan for Jonathan's ultimate development envisioned a general hospital located in the town center and medical facilities in each of its village centers. The project agreement between the Park Forest South Development Company and the Department of Housing and

Urban Development committed the company to the development of a comprehensive system of care based on a new hospital, community health centers and a comprehensive insurance plan for residents. Among the specific responsibilities of the developer were the donation of land for hospital construction, building and leasing office space for medical practitioners and encouraging community participation in health care planning. The developer was also required to provide leadership in the planning of community health care programs (possibly including a prepaid insurance plan), in the use of cable television, and in the establishment of a centralized system of medical record keeping.

Health care professionals serving the new communities were asked whether they felt that adequate attention had been given to the provision of health care services, facilities and programs in new community planning. In five nonfederally assisted new communities—Elk Grove Village, Lake Havasu City, Park Forest, Valencia and Westlake Village—and both federally assisted communities a majority of the professionals thought that initial health care planning was adequate. In the remaining new communities, however, health professionals were more critical of developers' attention to planning. In most cases professionals acknowledged developers' efforts on specific health care projects, but felt that a comprehensive approach to health care, including the establishment of effective social services, had been mostly lacking.

Health care planning for new community development was often hindered by developers' lack of expertise in the health care field and by the lack of incentive in terms of consumers' market behavior to devote company staff time and funds to community health care. A more serious problem, however, was the highly decentralized, free-enterprise character of health care delivery in the areas where new communities were under development. Regional health planning councils, where they existed, were of little help to developers in assessing community health care needs and organizing a program of health care services. County public health agencies often lacked the inclination to engage in health care planning at the community level. Medical societies were mostly concerned with the placement of doctors and were not in a position to offer comprehensive advice about health services. Existing health care institutions, such as hospitals, more often than not were more concerned with protecting the integrity of their service areas than in encouraging the establishment of new, and possibly competing, health care facilities and services. When this situation was combined with developers' natural disinclination to become involved in a subject with which they were not familiar, the low level of attention to comprehensive community health care planning should not be surprising.

MEDICAL PRACTITIONERS

The ratio of primary care physicians to population commonly has been used to gauge the adequacy of health care available to a region or community. In contrast to the national average of 81.7 primary care physicians (including osteopaths) per 100,000 population, the thirteen nonfederally assisted new communities had an average of 68.2 per 100,000 population, while the paired conventional communities had 63.3 per 100,000 population. Only four new communities—Laguna Niguel, North Palm Beach, Sharpstown and Westlake Village—exceeded the national average of physician availability. Physician availability in Jonathan was similar to the average of the more mature nonfederally assisted new communities, but Park Forest South had no practicing physicians at the time of the field survey in the spring of 1973. As a whole, the conventional communities exceeded the national average of 47.3 dentists per 100,000 population, while the new communities were somewhat below the national average.

In terms of the location of primary care, new and conventional community residents both tended to live within short distances of the nearest primary care physician. Among the nonfederally assisted new communities, the median road distance from the homes of household survey respondents to the nearest general practitioner was just over a mile (6800 feet). The conventional community respondents had to travel only slightly farther (8800 feet).

In addition to primary care, information regarding the availability of fourteen medical specialists was gathered for each new and conventional community. Although the variety of medical and dental practitioners was somewhat greater in the new than in the conventional communities (averages of 6.5 vs. 4.8 of the fourteen types of practitioners surveyed), in neither type of community could the variety of medical specialists be described as extensive.

Statistical analyses of the data from the sample communities were used to determine which community characteristics, if any, accounted for differences in the availability of physicians. In planned new communities, larger ratios of physicians to population were associated with communities that were closer to a metropolitan central business district, older and that had hospitals. There was also a strong correlation between physicians per 100,000 population and professionals' ratings of medical office facilities. The variety of selected specialists was strongly correlated with the age of a community, the availability of a community hospital, population and the number of general practitioners in a community.

PRIMARY CARE UTILIZATION

New communities tended to have more physicians per capita than the paired conventional communities, but new community development did not result in greater than average use of physicians' services. Most of the new and conventional community respondents (83 percent and 86 percent) reported that they had a regular doctor or clinic. There were also few differences in the proportions of respondents who reported that they had had a regular check-up during the previous year (71 percent and 70 percent) or in the median number of visits made to see doctors during the previous year (2.0 and 2.1 visits).

Objective indicators of the adequacy of community health resources had no influence on the number of times respondents had been to see doctors during the previous year. Instead, the critical factor influencing use of a doctor or clinic was respondents' own assessments of the status of their health. People visited doctors more frequently if they felt that their health was poor. Also, women tended to make more visits than men, as did respondents who had a regular doctor or clinic. Because an interest in preventive care influenced respondents to seek physicians' services, an important question is whether increased availability of health care resources encouraged individuals to have check-ups or to arrange for regular sources of care. The evidence suggests that it did not. Having a regular source of care was not associated with the number of family physicians per 100,000 population or the distance to the nearest general practitioner. Similarly, the likelihood of having had a check-up during the previous year was also not influenced by the ratio of physicians to population or by the distance to the nearest general practitioner.

The distances traveled by residents to regular doctors or clinics were considerably greater than the distance to the nearest available general practitioner. For example, although the median distance to the nearest general practitioner's office was just over a mile, those new community respondents who had a regular source of care traveled a median distance of over five miles to obtain regular care. Conventional community respondents traveled even farther to their regular sources of care, a median distance of over seven miles. The only new and conventional communities in which a majority of the respondents had a regular source of care within the community were either isolated from concentrations of doctors or were large cities with an abundant supply of medical practitioners.

HOSPITAL CARE

As of the spring of 1973 only three of the fifteen nonfederally and federally assisted new communities had hospitals—Elk Grove Village and Westlake Village each had one community hospital and Sharpstown had two. Hospitals were in the planning or construction stage in a number of other new communities. Two community hospitals were under development in Lake Havasu City, both of which had begun operation by 1975. A hospital opened in Columbia in July of 1973 and one was scheduled for completion in Valencia in 1975. Two additional hospitals were planned for Sharpstown and hospital proposals were pending in Irvine, Park Forest South and Reston. Including hospitals in the surrounding region that health professionals viewed as serving the communities studied, the new communities were served by an average of 650 hospital beds per community, while the conventional communities were served by an average of 620 beds per community.

Overall, the accessibility of the nearest hospital facility was somewhat better in the new communities than in the paired conventional communities. The median nonfederally assisted new community respondent lived about a mile and a half closer to the nearest hospital (14,800 feet vs. 22,200 feet). However, comparisons of each new community with its paired conventional community indicate that for seven of the thirteen nonfederally assisted new communities and for both federally assisted communities, the paired conventional community residents were more likely to live closer to the nearest hospital. New and conventional community respondents were asked whether hospital care was available to the residents of their community. Similar proportions of respondents in each setting, 73 percent and 72 percent, thought that care was available.

New and conventional community respondents who were aware of a hospital serving their community were asked whether they would recommend the use of the hospital. In general, consumer confidence in hospitals was highest in those new and conventional communities with a hospital within or adjacent to the community and lowest in those communities where residents had to travel relatively long distances for hospital care.

A second approach used to evaluate hospital care was to ask health care professionals serving each community whether they felt that care was adequate. In four nonfederally assisted new communities and federally assisted Jonathan, each of the professionals interviewed said that hospital care was adequate to meet the needs of the community. In contrast, hospital care was unanimously judged to be adequate in eight of the paired conventional communities as well as the conventional community paired with Jonathan. Hospital care was unanimously viewed as inadequate in four new communities (including federally assisted Park Forest South) and two conventional communities. In the remainder of the communities professional opinion regarding the adequacy of care was mixed.

A number of health care professionals were concerned about hospital over-bedding and the unnecessary duplication of facilities. Controversies involving the provision of new and expanded hospital facilities had arisen in Columbia, Irvine, Lake Havasu City, Park Forest South, Reston and Westlake Village. The experiences of these communities illustrate a basic dilemma in the provision of hospital facilities in new communities. Hospital construction has been a favored means of involvement in health matters by new community developers and brings with it a number of health care services for the community. But the activities of developers in support of hospital projects may exacerbate the widespread problems of excessive hospital beds and duplication of services. Because most new communities are satellites of metropolitan areas, it is rarely necessary for them to have hospitals of their own if adequate emergency services are available to transport residents to existing health care institutions. Alternatives to hospital construction include emergency care stations, county-operated health care clinics, clinics operated in conjunction with health maintenance organizations and counseling centers for emotional problems.

AMBULANCE SERVICE

Many of the health care professionals serving new communities felt that one of the greatest health care needs was emergency treatment facilities. However, there were only four new communities—Irvine, Laguna Niguel, Lake Havasu City and Park Forest South—in which a majority of the health care professionals thought that existing emergency care were inadequate. Professionals' evaluations of emergency ambulance service was generally based on their perceptions of the nature of the organization providing the service and its cost, rather than the location (within or outside of the community) from which the service originated. They were more likely to view emergency service favorably if it was provided by public fire departments rather than by private companies or funeral homes. Since private service was more expensive, professionals' assessments were also linked to cost.

Although ambulance crews received some sort of emergency care training in virtually every community in the study, the lack of adequate training was a widespread deficiency noted by professionals. Another problem area noted by professionals was that of cooperation with hospitals. This was a potential difficulty in every new community, since none of the systems serving them was provided by a hospital.

SOCIAL SERVICES

On the whole, health professionals viewed social services less favorably than any other area of health care. In eight new communities, including Columbia, Elk Grove Village, Forest Park, Foster City, Lake Havasu City, Laguna Niguel, North Palm Beach and Valencia, and in both federally assisted communities half or more of the professionals interviewed said that social service programs were inadequate. The conventional communities fared no better—in eleven of the fifteen communities health professionals felt that improvements were needed.

Household survey respondents were asked whether each of six social services—help with a drinking problem, help with a drug problem, help with an emotional problem, family and marital counseling, family planning and public assistance and welfare—was available to the residents of their communities. Their responses indicated that in the minds of a substantial proportion of new and conventional community residents there are serious gaps in service coverage. For example, only two of the six services—help with a drug problem and help with an emotional problem—were perceived to be available by half or more of the new community respondents, even though health professionals indicated that most of the services were available in the immediate vicinity of each of the communities studied. New community residents were somewhat more likely to be aware of various social services than residents of the paired conventional communities. In addition, five new communities—Park Forest, Columbia, Foster City, Reston and Elk Grove Village—stood out in terms of the relatively high proportions of residents who reported that the services were available in their community or its vicinity.

Although some health and social service programs in the new and conventional communities were offered by public agencies or were supported by public funds, many others were run by church groups or voluntary associations. The variety of sources from which services were offered was viewed by health professionals as a potential problem. Nevertheless, sources of information about health and social services and referral mechanisms were available in most of the communities in the sample. In some of the communities, information about health and social services was provided by the developer, multi-unit complex builders or developer-controlled homes associations. In others, similar material was made available to local governments, as in Park Forest, or by organizations such as the Junior Chamber of Commerce, as in Elk Grove Village. Health fairs had been used in and near Park Forest South and Irvine for the same purpose. In Jonathan a two-way cable television system was developed, in part, to provide a "telemedicine" system which enabled doctors to communicate with both patients and other doctors.

NURSING AND CONVALESCENT CARE FACILITIES

Nursing and convalescent facilities were not generally located in the sample communities nor were they usually perceived as available by residents. Forty-four percent of the new community and 50 percent of the conventional community respondents reported that they knew of such a facility in their community or its vicinity. On the whole, health professionals did not see a great need for additional convalescent and nursing home facilities, however. Lake Havasu City, where about 20 percent of the household heads were retired, and Park Forest South were the only new communities in which health professionals were unanimous about the need for such facilities. In contrast, a majority of the professionals who were serving eight of the new communities and ten of the conventional communities felt that additional convalescent and nursing home facilities were not needed.

PUBLIC HEALTH FACILITIES

Facilities offering public health services were not only absent from most of the new and conventional communities studied, but were also quite distant from them. Among the new communities, the median distance to the nearest public health clinic was over seven miles, while the conventional community residents had to travel even farther for public health services, the median distance to the nearest facility being over nine miles.

Health professionals had divided opinions as to whether existing public health facilities were of any use to new community residents.

In eight new communities, including both federally assisted communities, half or more of the professionals interviewed thought that such facilities were of value to residents, particularly for certain types of services, such as immunizations and, less frequently, social services. In seven new communities, health professionals thought that public health facilities were not a useful source of care. Two explanations for this opinion predominated: (1) because public health services were geared to lower income people, residents of the new communities reputedly considered them inappropriate for their own use or believed that they were ineligible for public services; and (2) public health facilities were too far away or too difficult to reach. Other professionals were critical of the quality of the facilities, which were described as poorly equipped, or disapproved of their methods of dispensing care, observing that clinics "treat categories of diseases, not people."

HEALTH INSURANCE

Well over 90 percent of the new and conventional community respondents held some type of health insurance. Although the proportion of respondents who held health insurance did not vary widely among new communities or between new and conventional communities, it did vary among different groups of new community residents. As would be expected, income had a strong influence on insurance coverage. The proportion of respondents who had some type of insurance ranged from 83 percent of those with incomes under $5,000 per year to 94 percent of those with incomes of $25,000 or more. In addition, respondents who had not attended high school (88 percent), renters (90 percent), persons under 30 years old (92 percent) and persons who were separated (86 percent) or divorced (89 percent) were less likely than others to be covered by health insurance.

HEALTH MAINTENANCE ORGANIZATIONS:
THE COLUMBIA EXPERIENCE

Membership in prepaid health plans (9 percent of the new community respondents) was somewhat greater than in the nation as a whole, where less than 5 percent of the population is enrolled. Membership in prepaid plans was much higher, however, in two California new communities—Foster City (23 percent) and Valencia (18 percent)—where the Kaiser Foundation Health Plan, Inc. concentrates its activities and in Columbia (39 percent), the only new community with a community-based health maintenance organization (Columbia

Medical Plan). Because it is unique among new communities, particular attention was given to the membership characteristics and performance of the Columbia Medical Plan, which was formed in 1969 to make available quality medical care at reasonable cost and to insure the accessibility of and continuity of care 24 hours a day.

Membership in the Columbia Medical Plan did not vary by race. However, the plan attracted proportionately more members among the more affluent households in Columbia. Members of the plan were only about half as likely to have family incomes of less than $10,000 per year (9 percent) as Columbia residents who had not joined the plan (20 percent). On the other hand, members of the plan were much more likely than nonmembers to have annual incomes of $25,000 or more (32 percent vs. 19 percent). The Columbia Medical Plan also tended to attract proportionately more members among married households with older household heads and/or spouses. Eighty-two percent of the plan members living in Columbia were married versus 72 percent of the residents of Columbia who had not joined the plan. Twenty-nine percent of the plan members were under 30 years old versus 51 percent of the nonplan Columbia residents. While almost three-fourths of the members of the Columbia Medical Plan owned their own home, a majority (54 percent) of those who did not join the plan were renters. Finally, members of the Columbia Medical Plan tended to have lived in Columbia for a longer period of time than non-members, suggesting that while residents may retain their former physicians upon moving to Columbia, there is a tendency to join the plan after households become adjusted to their new surroundings.

In spite of nearly unanimous reports of having a regular doctor or clinic by members of the Columbia Medical Plan and the emphasis of the plan on preventive care, the proportion of plan members who had had a routine check-up in the previous year did not differ significantly from the proportion of nonplan members who had had a check-up (77 percent vs. 72 percent). However, analysis of the mean number of physician visits in a one-year period by Columbia residents indicated that members of the Columbia Medical Plan were less reluctant to visit doctors than were those who did not belong to the plan (means of 5.4 visits vs. 4.2 visits). While utilization of physicians' services was greater for members of the plan, obtaining those services was not accomplished without difficulty. Among the Columbia respondents with a regular doctor or clinic, more than twice as many members of the plan as nonmembers (29 percent vs. 12 percent) reported problems in arranging appointments. Also of great concern in terms of the operation of the plan was the fact that 21 percent of the respondents who belonged to it reported not seeing a doctor on at least one occasion when they wanted to during the previous year.

Columbia residents who belonged to the Columbia Medical Plan were more likely than nonplan members to be aware of and willing to recommend the use of a variety of health and social services in the community, including dental care, emergency medical care, family and marital counseling, family planning, health care for children, help with a drinking problem, help with an emotional problem and prenatal care. In addition, plan members gave much higher ratings to the quality of health care facilities and services in Columbia (37 percent vs. 11 percent rated facilities and services as excellent).

Based on the Columbia experience, new communities appear to be particularly appropriate settings in which to establish prepaid health plans. The community-based health maintenance organization is an attractive way to provide comprehensive health services in locations where few other sources of care are available. In addition, the absence of competing forms of care may increase the chances for successful operation of the prepaid plan. However, the real lesson of Columbia's experience is not that plans such as the Columbia Medical Plan should be the exclusive source of health care in the area, but that they should be designed to be available to all members of a balanced community who wish to join and use them. Much of the value of a prepaid plan is lost if it fails to serve all members when needed, as appeared to be the case in Columbia, or if, as was also the case, the cost of membership tends to exclude a significant proportion of the community.

OVERALL EVALUATIONS OF HEALTH CARE IN NEW COMMUNITIES

On an aggregate level, new community residents were somewhat more likely than residents of the paired conventional communities to rate health and medical services as better than those in the communities from which they had moved. Twenty-five percent of the new community respondents rated services as better versus 20 percent of the conventional community respondents, a difference that is small but statistically significant. However, almost as many new community respondents (24 percent) rated services as not as good as where they had lived before.

There were no new communities in which a majority of the respondents thought that health and medical services were better than in their former communities. Columbia, with 47 percent of the respondents rating services as better, ranked first, followed by Sharpstown (45 percent better) and Elk Grove Village (40 percent better). Each of these communities had a well-developed health care system. Columbia, as discussed above, was the only new community studied that had a community-based health maintenance organization. Sharpstown exceeded national standards for the number of primary care physicians per capita and had two community hospitals. Elk Grove Village had only an average number of physicians per capita, but had a large hospital and an active community mental health agency.

In almost half of the new communities—Irvine, Laguna Niguel, Lake Havasu City, Reston, Valencia and federally assisted Park Forest South—residents were more likely to have rated health and medical services as not as good as in their previous communities as to have rated them as better. Residents' dissatisfaction with services was greatest in Lake Havasu City (84 percent rated services as not as good as in their former communities) and Valencia (56 percent not as good). However, in both of these new communities hospital projects which, when completed, would improve households' ratings, were under way at the time of the household survey in the spring of 1973. Similarly, the improvements in emergency care, the opening of another medical building and completion of a proposed hospital in Irvine, extension of a proposed prepaid health plan to Reston and implementation of the proposed comprehensive health care system in Park Forest South should also result in better ratings from the residents of these communities.

In addition to ratings given by the general population of new community residents, ratings by various target populations were also examined. In the five new communities in which subsamples of subsidized housing residents were interviewed, subsidized housing residents were significantly more likely than either nonsubsidized housing residents of the same new communities (36 percent vs. 25 percent) or subsidized housing residents living in conventional communities (36 percent vs. 19 percent) to feel that health and medical services were better than those of their previous communities. Black residents of new communities (27 percent) were just as likely as nonblack residents living in the same communities (28 percent) and blacks living in conventional communities (24 percent) to feel that health and medical services were better than in their former communities. Elderly (65 years old and older) new community residents were significantly more likely than the elderly residents of conventional communities (23 percent vs. 13 percent) to rate health and medical services as better than those in the communities from which they had moved. Elderly persons in Sun City Center, the Florida retirement community, were no more likely than new community elderly residents (21 percent vs. 23 percent) to rate services as better than those of their former communities. On the other hand, more than two-thirds (72 percent) of the elderly residents living in the California retirement community, Rossmoor Leisure World, rated health and medical services there as better than those in their previous communities. In Rossmoor, the Leisure World Foundation's Office of Medical Administration provided an extensive array of services designed to meet the health care needs of older persons.

Additional insight into the quality of health care in new communities was sought through the survey of professional health care personnel. On an aggregate level, health care professionals gave higher ratings to community health care facilities and services than the household survey respondents. For example, while two-thirds of the household survey respondents rated new community health care facilities and services as excellent or good, three-fourths of the professionals rated facilities and services that highly. However, whereas the new community household survey respondents were more likely than the conventional community respondents to rate facilities and services highly (66 percent vs. 54 percent gave excellent or good ratings), the conventional communities received a somewhat higher proportion of excellent or good ratings from health professionals (77 percent vs. 75 percent).

Analyses of health care professionals' evaluations of community health care facilities indicated that their ratings were associated with both objective characteristics of the health care system and their subjective evaluations of various attributes of community health care. Professionals tended to give higher ratings to communities with hospitals, more primary care physicians per 100,000 population, a greater variety of medical specialists and a larger number of special facilities in hospitals serving a new community. Health care professionals' ratings were also associated with their views about the adequacy of hospital care and with their ratings of doctors' office facilities. However, there were negative associations between professionals' overall ratings of community health care and their ratings of the adequacy of health care planning and of developer initiative in this field. These associations were due to instances in which planning and developer initiative, though well regarded, had yet to result in better than average health care facilities and services, as in Park Forest South, and to cases where excellent facilities and services were not viewed as the result of a particularly laudable planning process, as in Sharpstown.

CONCLUSIONS

Depending on how one chooses to read them, the findings discussed in this book can lead either to complacency or concern with regard to the status of health care in planned new communities. The residents of new communities tended to be satisfied with their own health. Both residents and health care professionals rated health care facilities and services highly and new communities compared well with less planned conventional communities. Residents' use of regular sources of care and the practice of having annual check-ups were common and the level of utilization of physicians' services was comparable to national figures. Subsidized housing residents, blacks and the elderly tended to be as satisfied with health care facilities and services as the general population of new communities. In many cases they were more satisfied than similar population groups living in conventional suburban communities.

On the other hand, the availability of health care resources and residents' satisfaction with care were by no means high in all areas. In a number of locations, many residents settled for health and medical care services that they regarded as inferior to those that were available to them before they moved to a new community. Although utilization of health care services was not influenced by the availability of health care resources, satisfaction with care was affected. Where the level of health care resources was low, residents tended to be unhappy about health care in their communities. New community residents, moreover, were alarmingly unaware of the social service programs that were available to them, even where the need was strong. Although health care professionals noted that emotional difficulties were among the major health problems facing the residents of new communities, only about half of the new community residents interviewed were familiar with sources of assistance in this area. Perceptions of numerous other services were low as well, even where health professionals indicated that the resources in question were close at hand. In addition to problems relating to the availability of care and to perceptions of services, there was abundant evidence of problems in quality, delivery or appropriateness of services offered in such areas as hospital care, ambulance service and public health facilities.

Planning for health care in new communities was not, on the whole, highly regarded by health care professionals. With some notable exceptions, developers made few significant contributions toward improving health care resources. Although there was little evidence that developer involvement in the health field had a major impact on the level of health resources, this could be attributed to the fact that few developers were involved in comprehensive approaches to community health care. The emphasis on hospital building in a number of communities contributed to the irrational and wasteful process by which these facilities were planned and developed and failed to meet the more immediate needs of residents. In some locations where developers acknowledged extensive responsibilities in health care, implementation was lacking.

Deficiencies in planning for health care in new communities and inadequacies in the resources available suggest that there is an important role in health care planning that can be played by new community developers. Although it would be a mistake to assume that all problems in a field as complex as health care can be solved on a community level or that developers should bear full responsibility for solving them, the developer, as the single entity in control of a tract of land large enough to be called a community, is in a unique position to coordinate the efforts of health care institutions and to facilitate the implementation of health care projects. On the other hand, while new community developers have an appropriate role to play in health care planning and delivery, their focus cannot be restricted solely to the community. The information presented in this book indicates that planners and developers should tie their communities into the regions in which they are located rather than attempt to build all needed facilities in their community. In addition, there is a clear need for greatly improved programs of information and referral which would, in effect, bring health care resources "closer" to community residents.

While resisting the temptation to plan for the community as an isolated unit that is separate from its surroundings, new community planners and developers do need to consider locating certain types of resources within a new community. Areas of particular need revealed in this book include more primary care physicians, more public health facilities, a greater range of social services, more health and social programs designed—in terms of costs, training of personnel and problems emphasized—with lower income residents, the elderly and teenagers in mind. The development of health maintenance organizations and of community-based clinics to support them also appears to be a promising way of providing care to new community residents. Although an eventual goal of health planning should be the provision of readily accessible comprehensive health services, it must be recognized that a first step should be to assure that basic care is available when needed. In order to link a new community with resources in the surrounding area and to provide care that is close to home, increased emphasis should be placed on developing efficient, well-equipped ambulance services operated by thoroughly trained personnel. Less urgent facilities may also be developed at an early stage of new community growth, but the highest priority should be placed on steps which establish a new community as a safe place in which to live.

✷ *Chapter 2*

New Communities
in America

Widespread criticism of the character of population distribution and metropolitan expansion has produced a continuing search for better ways to accommodate growth and to manage the urban environment. One reaction to the problems of metropolitan growth and development has been the attempt to achieve orderly, planned urbanization patterns through the construction of large-scale new communities.

Although a single widely accepted definition of a new community has yet to be developed, there is general agreement about the ideal characteristics of new community projects. For example, many of the potential benefits from new community development are attributed to comprehensive planning of the new community development site. Accordingly, a master plan that establishes categories of land use and circulation and allocates them to various sections of the site is critical in distinguishing new communities from conventional forms of urban development. To facilitate comprehensive planning a new community development site must be large. Few land development projects of less than 2000 acres are called new communities. In addition, to insure that the plan is implemented over the entire site, a new community project must be held in some form of single ownership or control during the development process.

Other attributes expected of new community projects respond to various problems associated with conventional modes of urban expansion. In order to reduce travel and to increase community identity, new communities are expected to be as self-sufficient as possible. Self-sufficiency is achieved by setting aside land for, and actively recruiting, industrial, commercial, public, recreational and institutional facilities and services that are appropriate to the expected population. The idea of a complete community embodied in the notion of self-sufficiency also implies that provision is made for a variety of life styles and for social diversity. To achieve these goals new communities are expected to offer different types of housing—single family detached, townhouses and apartments—and to provide housing in a full spectrum of price ranges. The availability of a range of housing types and prices together with a lack of established social stratification patterns is viewed as one means of facilitating the diminution of urban ghettos and the elimination of social and racial segregation patterns which characterize established communities.

New community planning is expected not only to meet the technical requirements of comprehensive preplanning, but also to reflect the application of modern planning and urban design concepts. These concepts include grouping commercial activities in attractively designed centers; increasing pedestrian and traffic safety through the use of curvilinear and cul-de-sac streets; establishing a hierrarchical form of residential areas—from dwelling units to neighborhoods to villages—to provide logical service areas and to increase interaction among residents; and developing landmarks and other visual symbols to identify facilities and to increase community awareness.

Finally, to reduce vehicular trips and to increase interaction among the residents, facilities and services in new communities are expected to be placed so that they are in close proximity to each other and convenient to all residents. To further reduce dependence on the automobile, the new community concept also calls for the provision of a variety of modes of local travel, including walking paths connecting homes with facilities and some form of community transit.

THE COMMUNITY BUILDING MOVEMENT

The elements of the new community concept are an ideal construct.[a] They have emerged from a growing public awareness of the problems of metropolitan growth and increasing acceptance of new communities as one means of mitigating such problems in new urban development. However, unlike the new communities movement in other parts of the world, where new community development has been an integral aspect of national growth policies, community building in

---

[a]This section is based on Chapters 2 and 3 of Raymond J. Burby, III and Shirley F. Weiss, et al. (1976). Also, see John W. Reps (1965); Clarence S. Stein (1957); Paul Conklin (1959); Edward P. Eichler and Marshall Kaplan (1967); Advisory Commission on Intergovernmental Relations (1968); James A. Clapp (1971); and Hugh Mields, Jr. (1973).

the United States has been largely a product of the private sector. As a result, the accretion of public objectives to be achieved through new community development has been a gradual process (see Nicoson, 1976).

In a sense, the new communities movement in the United States is not at all new. Many colonial communities—Annapolis, Williamsburg, Savannah and the villages of New England among others—were built according to carefully drawn plans. The westward expansion of the United States brought with it a host of planned communities, although many were laid out on the basis of a simple gridiron pattern by land speculators and the railroad companies. During the Nineteenth and early Twentieth Centuries, some 52 company towns— including Gary, Indiana; Pullman, Illinois; and Kingsport, Tennessee —were established. Utopian and religious movements also contributed to the development of new communities, producing Salt Lake City in Utah, the Salem of Winston-Salem, North Carolina, Oneida in New York, and the Harmony Society towns in Pennsylvania and Indiana.

During the first two decades of this century, a number of privately sponsored, large-scale communities were developed in suburban areas to offer residents an escape from the undesirable aspects of industrialized cities. The best examples of these developments are the Country Club District in Kansas City, Forest Hills Gardens on Long Island and Palos Verdes Estates near Los Angeles. During the 1920s, the English garden cities movement initiated by Ebenezer Howard in 1898 and the prototype towns of Letchworth and Welwyn Garden City influenced American entrepreneurs and planners to design and develop suburban communities based on garden city principles. Many current urban design ideas, including superblocks and pedestrian-vehicular separation, were incorporated in the design of Radburn, New Jersey, begun by Clarence Stein and Henry Wright in 1928. Because of the depression, most of the American attempts to replicate the English garden city idea could not be completed. However, the 1930s saw the first large-scale federal involvement in community building. Three new communities—Greenbelt, Maryland, Greenhills, Ohio; and Greendale, Wisconsin—were started by the federal Resettlement Administration. Other federal enterprises during the 1930s and 1940s also spawned new communities. Large power projects led to the construction of Boulder City, Nevada and Norris, Tennessee. Using these communities as examples, the Atomic Energy Commission built Los Alamos, New Mexico, Oak Ridge, Tennessee, and Hanford (now Richland), Washington, to house workers and their families who were employed at isolated AEC plants.

Large-scale community development projects started after World War II capitalized on the pent-up housing demand created by the war and related housing shortages, easy financing offered by the Veterans Administration and the Federal Housing Administration and highway construction which opened up peripheral areas for residential settlement. New communities initiated during the late 1940s through the 1950s—including Levittown, New Jersey; Elk Grove Village, Illinois; Forest Park, Ohio; North Palm Beach, Florida; Park Forest, Illinois; and Sharpstown, Texas—were characterized by two major departures from conventional postwar patterns of suburban development. First, in contrast to the small scale of most suburban subdivisions, community builders assembled land for projects that encompassed thousands of acres. Second, in contrast to the notable lack of land use planning in many suburban areas and resultant suburban sprawl, community builders began development of their projects with carefully drawn master plans that reserved land for a variety of urban functions and included provisions for a variety of housing types. On the other hand, the first community builders of the modern era paid relatively little attention to site planning, architectural excellence and community amenities that have since become a hallmark of new community development in the United States.

The new communities of the 1940s and 1950s were built and merchandized by developers who had their roots in the home building and real estate industries. Their major concerns were providing land and building housing for the broad middle- and lower-middle income segments of the housing market who were moving to suburban areas in increasing numbers and capturing returns from the commercial development attracted by the market they had created. The innovative planning principles, such as superblocks, cluster development and neighborhood greenways, that were pioneered in the 1930s by Radburn, the greenbelt communities and the British garden cities were not continued. In some cases developers relied on traditional land use planning concepts because of financial considerations; in others developers used planning engineers who did not embrace the advanced planning concepts; and in others local governmental land use regulations inhibited innovative community design.

During the 1960s, community building—principally in California and in the Washington-Baltimore area—moved closer to the current concept of a new community. California new communities, such as Foster City, Irvine, Laguna Niguel, Valencia and Westlake Village, represent a sharp departure in community building technique from the new communities initiated during the previous decade. California community builders were among the first to recognize the market for communities that featured a variety of recreational amenities. Earlier new community developers were steeped in the lore of homebuilding. They marketed the home first and the community second. Land was reserved for recreational facilities and other neighborhood and community amenities, but their actual development was left to the initiative of the residents and local government. In contrast, the California community builders took an alternative approach. They sought reputable builders who were able to market their own housing products and concentrated on producing and marketing their community's image.

California new community developers paid much closer attention to landscaping and architectural style than was common in the older new communities. Community facilities—particularly recreational facilities that contributed to community image—were provided earlier in the development process. Neighborhood site planning was emphasized, with homes often clustered and related to adjacent open space networks and path systems. The major tradeoff the California community builders made was in housing prices. While new communities initiated during the previous decade provided homes within the means of a broad segment of the population, the California community builders stuck largely to the middle- and upper-middle income markets that could afford elaborate community amenity packages.

Two new communities in the Washington-Baltimore region, Reston, Virginia and Columbia, Maryland have been widely cited as models of the modern new community concept. Reston and Columbia, which are described in greater detail later in this chapter, match the California new communities' concern for environmental design and amenities, but add a concern for population balance and diversity which is missing from the western communities. Both communities have attracted sizable black and low- and moderate-income populations. In addition, they have experimented with a variety of innovative approaches to the development of community institutions and the provision of community facilities and services.

Throughout the 1960s the accelerating pace of new community development in the private sector was matched by mounting public interest in new communities as a means of organizing metropolitan growth and providing a better urban environment. New community development began to occupy a prominent place in metropolitan growth plans; state legislation to foster new community development began to be enacted; and a national movement calling for federal support of new communities gathered strength. The drive for an expanded federal role in new community development was capped by hearings before the House of Representatives Ad Hoc Subcommittee on Urban Growth (Ashley Committee) in 1970. The committee's report, *The Quality of Urban Life*, made a strong case for a variety of types of federal assistance to new communities and led directly to the enactment of the Urban Growth and New Community Development Act of 1970 (Title VII of the Housing and Urban Development Act of 1970) which provides the legislative basis for the current federal new communities program.

The Urban Growth and New Community Development Act of 1970 also represented the culmination of a long effort within the federal government to enact new communities legislation. The first new communities bill of the modern era was drafted by the Housing and Home Finance Agency in 1964 and presented to Congress as Title II of the Housing Act of that year. Title II authorized up to $50 million in mortgage insurance for land acquisition and development for large-scale new community projects, but died in committee when it failed to receive support from new community proponents and was actively opposed by the National Association of Home Builders and National Association of Real Estate Boards. In addition, the bill was cooly received by central city mayors, who opposed increased federal support of suburban development and feared the effects of new communities on the competitive position of central cities.

In 1965 virtually the same bill was introduced again as Title X of the Housing and Urban Development Act, but the maximum mortgage guarantee was reduced to $10 million. The same doubts about the bill as appeared in 1964 were voiced again and, though it passed, assistance was limited to smaller scale subdivision projects. In 1966, however, the administration secured favorable testimony from a number of new community developers and diluted opposition from various groups by calling for an experimental new community program. It was successful in mustering sufficient support to amend Title X to provide mortgage insurance of up to $25 million for new community land acquisition and site improvements. Title X resolved many of the legislative obstacles to a more effective federal role in new community development. Thus, although the provisions of the act were not sufficiently attractive to the development industry, and no new community projects were ever supported under Title X, when an expanded new community assistance program was introduced as Title IV of the 1968 Housing and Urban Development Act, it passed with much less difficulty.

Title IV provided a number of inducements for developer involvement in the program which were missing from the earlier Title X legislation. Where Title X provided mortgage insurance guarantees on loans to developers, Title IV authorized the secretary of Housing and

Urban Development to guarantee the bonds, debentures, notes and other obligations issued by new community developers for land acquisition and development. Title IV pledged the full faith and credit of the United States Government to pay the guaranteed obligations in the event that developers could not meet the scheduled payments. In addition, the act authorized supplemental grants of up to 20 percent of the required local costs of federal grants-in-aid for water, sewer and open space. In return for more attractive federal aid, Title IV stiffened eligibility requirements, with much greater emphasis on the planning and land use characteristics of assisted projects, and tied the supplemental grants to an assisted project's provision of a substantial number of housing units for low- and moderate-income persons.

The mortgage insurance and loan guarantees offered by Title X and Title IV were designed to overcome one of the major obstacles to expanded new community development in the United States—the difficulty in obtaining money over a long period at interest rates that were sufficiently low to make the development project economically feasible. The 1970 new communities legislation (Title VII) was designed to overcome many of the financial difficulties experienced by new community developers, while at the same time achieving a much broader array of federal goals for new urban growth.[b]

Both the Democratic and Republican party platforms of 1968 spoke of the need for new communities as one response to the "crisis of the cities." In 1969, the National Committee on Urban Growth Policy (sponsored by the National Association of Counties, National League of Cities, United States Conference of Mayors and Urban

[b]Title VII was designed to achieve ten objectives: (1) Encourage the orderly development of well-planned, diversified, and economically sound new communities, including major additions to existing communities, and to do so in a manner that will rely to the maximum extent on private enterprise; (2) Strengthen the capacity of state and local governments to deal with local problems; (3) Preserve and enhance both the natural and urban environment; (4) Increase for all persons, particularly members of minority groups, the available choices of locations for living and working; (5) Encourage the fullest utilization of the economic potential of older central cities, smaller towns and rural communities; (6) Assist in the efficient production of a steady supply of residential, commercial, and industrial building sites at reasonable cost; (7) Increase the capability of all segments of the homebuilding industry, including both small and large producers, to utilize improved technology in producing the large volume of well-designed, inexpensive housing needed to accommodate population growth; (8) Help create neighborhoods designed for easier access between the places where people live and the places where they work and find recreation; (9) Encourage desirable innovation in meeting domestic problems whether physical, economic or social; and (10) Improve the organizational capacity of the federal government to carry out programs of assistance for the development of new communities and the revitalization of the nation's urban areas. See U.S. Department of Housing and Urban Development, Office of the Secretary (1971).

America, Inc.) recommended that federal assistance be extended to create 100 new communities averaging 100,000 population each and ten new communities of at least one million each by the year 2000 (National Committee on Urban Growth Policy 1969). The following year, in his State of the Union Message, President Nixon noted that, "the federal government must be in a position to assist in the building of new cities and the rebuilding of old ones." In April 1970, the Department of Housing and Urban Development presented the President with a series of options for an expanded new communities program and recommended that federal assistance be extended to ten new communities each year. However, because of the inflationary state of the economy, the President felt that the program should not be implemented.

In spite of the President's resistance to an expanded new communities program, the Congress moved ahead. In the House of Representatives, Congressman Thomas L. Ashley and twelve other members sponsored HR 16647, while Senators Sparkman and Muskie introduced the same bill on the Senate side, S 3640. According to Hugh Mields Jr. (1973, p. 26), "The Bill's basic political thrust was to make certain that all communities—big, medium, and small—could benefit from its provisions. Hence, new towns of any form—freestanding, satellite, or intown—were to be related to some of the hard problems facing the inner cities. Also, Congress wanted to make it possible for small towns in predominantly rural areas to develop plans for accelerated growth and support that growth...." The Department of Housing and Urban Development did not publicly support the bill, but agreed to go along with the legislation if certain changes were made. The administration's position led to a series of compromises, mostly notably the deletion of direct loans to developers for land acquisition, infrastructure and industrial development, and the bill finally passed Congress in December 1970 (see Mields 1971).

The major mechanism that was established to achieve the objectives of the Urban Growth and New Community Development Act of 1970 was the loan guarantee. Eligible new community developers may receive a federal loan guarantee of up to $50 million to cover up to 80 percent of the value of real property before development and 90 percent of the land development costs. Public developers, such as cities, counties or public development corporations, can receive a federal guarantee covering 100 percent of the value of real property and 100 percent of land development costs. The aggregate of outstanding obligations that can be incurred through loan guarantees is $500 million. In addition, a number of other types of assistance were authorized. The 20 percent supplemental grants initially authorized by Title IV were extended to thirteen federal grants-in-aid programs. The secretary of Housing and Urban Development was authorized to loan developers up to $20 million for a period of fifteen years after the start of development so that they could make interest payments on their debts. Public service grants to enable local governments to provide educational, health, safety and other services during the first three years of development were authorized. Up to two-thirds of the cost of special planning studies was authorized so that developers could plan programs that were fully responsive to social and environmental problems and that supported the use of new and advanced technology.

By March 1975 the Department of Housing and Urban Development had guaranteed debentures totaling $275 million for thirteen privately sponsored new community projects. Two other projects sponsored by the New York State Urban Development Corporation which did not seek guarantee assistance had been certified as eligible for other assistance under the program. These fifteen new community development projects, located in ten states, were originally projected to have a total population of about 818,000 and to provide 218,000 jobs upon completion of 20- to 30-year planned development periods (see Melvin Margolies 1975).

In spite of a promising beginning, the federal new communities program has experienced a number of difficulties. From the start the new communities program lacked political support within the Executive Branch. The Office of New Communities Development (which later became the New Communities Administration) was understaffed during the first years of the program, and a number of provisions of the legislation were never implemented, including interest loans to developers, public service grants and the provision of technical assistance. Another set of difficulties arose from the newness of the program, its complexity and the need for both the Office of New Communities Development and participating private developers to learn the new community business. Developers complained about the lack of consistency and coordination within the government (see U.S. Congress, House of Representatives, Committee on Banking and Currency 1973), while federal officials found that developers' initial projections of start-up costs were too low and projections of the pace of development to be achieved were too high (see Trevino 1974).

The problems of the new communities program were first evidenced by a drop in private developers' interest in applying for assistance. The number of preapplications received by the Office of New Communities Development dropped from 23 preapplications in 1972, to five in 1973, to only one in the first six months of 1974. Second, new communities that had already received loan guarantee assistance began to experience severe financial problems. Jonathan, the first federally assisted new community under Title IV, failed to make a $468,000 interest payment, which HUD was forced to cover, when it found that it had a two and one-half years inventory of lots and homes for sale. Park Forest South was placed in default on its loan guarantee when HUD had to make a $1.05 million interest payment. By the spring of 1976 HUD found itself making interest payments on the debt of seven of the thirteen new communities that had received loan guarantee assistance.

In response to the serious financial problems of its assisted new community projects, the Department of Housing and Urban Development suspended further processing of applications for assistance on January 14, 1975. The federal new communities program is now being reevaluated by the Congress and the administration. Until a future policy is determined, HUD is concentrating on maintaining the financial viability and functioning of the thirteen projects that have received loan guarantee assistance.

After more than two centuries of new community development, the new communities movement in the United States is now at a standstill. Some observers have proposed that rather than large-scale new communities, public policy should encourage the development of planned neighborhood "growth units" of from 500 to 3000 residential units (see American Institute of Architects 1972). Others, feeling that a full-scale new community production program may be impossible to achieve with present economic and governmental conditions, have argued for an experimental approach to new community development that focuses on new ideas, concepts and techniques that can best be applied and tested in new community settings (see Trevino 1974). To still others, the problem has been a lack of administration support of the federal new communities program. If such support is forthcoming, then it is felt that new community development in the United States may be regenerated, so that "the new communities program will be the vital community development tool envisioned by its authors in the Congress and by public and private officials who support the program" (Freeman 1974).

Although the future course of new community development cannot be accurately predicted, at last count 175 private and federally assisted new communities were planned or under development in 32 states, the District of Columbia and Puerto Rico ("New Community Chekclist Update" 1974). These communities provide a unique opportunity to examine more closely the benefits and problems of community-scale development and a chance to insure that future public policy is based on a full understanding of this innovative approach to urban growth and development.

SELECTION OF NEW COMMUNITIES
FOR THE STUDY

In order to select a representative sample of new communities for intensive study, a multi-stage sampling procedure was utilized. The first step in the process was to identify new communities that were being developed in the United States. When the sample new communities were being selected in early 1972, the most reliable compilation of new communities in existence was a list of post World War II new communities and large-scale developments prepared by the New Communities Division of the Department of Housing and Urban Development (1969). The communities on the HUD list were screened against two sets of criteria. First, the communities were evaluated in terms of their conformance to five criteria which are basic to the new community concept:

1. *Unified ownership*—community development under the direction of a single entrepreneur or development company to insure unified and coordinated management of the development process.
2. *Planning*—development programmed in accordance with an overall master plan.
3. *Size*—2000 or more acres planned for an eventual population of 20,000 or more people to allow for social diversity and to support a variety of urban functions.
4. *Self-sufficiency*—provision for a variety of urban functions through the reservation of land for residential, commercial, industrial, public and institutional uses.
5. *Housing choice*—provision of a variety of housing choices, including, at a minimum, opportunities for owning and renting and for single-family and apartment life styles.

The application of these criteria to the communities on the HUD list significantly narrowed the number of projects that were eligible for inclusion in the study. Large-scale land development projects that were excluded from further consideration included special purpose communities, such as resort and retirement projects; suburban planned unit developments, which could not meet the size and self-sufficiency criteria; and new towns-in town, which could not meet the size criterion.

Three additional criteria were applied to meet the specific needs of the overall new communities study. These included:

6. *Location*—new communities located outside of the contiguous 48 states were eliminated in order to limit data collection costs.
7. *Age*—new communities that ceased all active development prior to 1960 were eliminated in order to simplify recall problems in case studies of development decisions.
8. *Population*—new communities with less than 5000 residents on January 1, 1972 were eliminated to insure that communities had enough homes, facilities and services in place to provide an adequate basis for evaluation.

The two screening processes eliminated over half of the communities on the HUD list.

From the remaining new communities, thirteen privately developed communities were selected for the study. Five new communities were selected because they contained unique features of particular interest to the research team:

1. Columbia, Maryland—100 percent sample of stratum: communities with 10 percent or more nonwhite population on January 1, 1972.
2. Irvine, California—100 percent sample of stratum: regional cities with projected populations over 150,000.
3. Lake Havasu City, Arizona—100 percent sample of stratum: freestanding new communities.
4. Park Forest, Illinois—100 percent sample of stratum: recognized outstanding completed post World War II new community.
5. Reston, Virginia—100 percent sample of stratum: recognized outstanding design.

A simple random sample of eight additional communities was then selected from the communities remaining in the sample frame. These included:

6. Elk Grove Village, Illinois
7. Forest Park, Ohio
8. Foster City, California
9. Laguna Niguel, California
10. North Palm Beach, Florida
11. Sharpstown, Texas
12. Valencia, California
13. Westlake Village, California

The privately developed new communities selected for study allowed adequate coverage of the range of variation in the characteristics of new communities under private development in the United States. There is no evidence that the inclusion of a greater number of new communities would have yielded greater variation in community characteristics.

Finally, although both Jonathan, Minnesota and Park Forest South, Illinois had fewer than 5000 residents as of January 1, 1972, these two communities were selected to insure the inclusion in the study of new communities that were participating in the federal new communities program. At the time the sample was drawn, the universe of federally assisted new communities included: Flower Mound, Texas; Jonathan, Minnesota; Maumelle, Arkansas; Park Forest South, Illinois; Riverton, New York; and St. Charles Communities, Maryland. Most of these were in the very initial stages of development. Only Jonathan and Park Forest South had enough occupied housing for a baseline evaluation. Because at least two federally assisted new communities were required to avoid the problem of generalizing from a unique case, both were included in the sample.

SELECTION OF PAIRED CONVENTIONAL COMMUNITIES

For each of the sample new communities, a less planned conventionally developed area was delineated to serve as a control and basis of comparison. The new communities and paired conventional communities were otherwise matched in terms of the age of housing, range of housing costs and location within the metropolitan area. In some cases it was necessary to delineate a set of contiguous subdivisions as a comparison area in order to match more nearly the range of housing costs in the paired new community. An effort was also made to match on mix of housing types; however, this could not be done consistently because the range of housing types available in new communities was not found regularly in other suburban settings.[c]

The paired conventional communities were chosen during site visits to the market areas of the sample new communities on the basis of consultations with county and municipal planning agencies

[c]Where older, established communities were listed as comparison communities, only the tracts or neighborhoods within these communities that matched the new community as to age and price range of housing were included in the universe from which the household sample was selected (see Appendix A). Respondents in such areas were asked about the whole community rather than only the subselected tracts in which they lived in questions referring to the community.

Table 2–1. **Distance from Central Business District, Estimated Population, and Target Acreage for Sample New Communities and Their Paired Conventional Communities at Beginning of Study**

New Communities/Paired Conventional Communities	New Community	Conventional Community
	New Communities and Conventional Communities	
	Number of Miles from Metropolitan Central Business District[a]	
Nonfederally Assisted New Communities/Paired Conventional Communities		
Average for nonfederally assisted new/paired conventional communities	21.5	22.5
Columbia/Norbeck-Wheaton, Md.	19	15
Elk Grove Village/Schaumburg, Ill.	26	30
Forest Park/Sharonville, Oh.	15	15
Foster City/San Mateo, Calif.	25	30
Irvine/Fountain Valley, Calif.	8	11
Laguna Niguel/Dana Point, Calif.	23	27
Lake Havasu City/Kingman, Ariz.	b	b
North Palm Beach/Tequesta, Fla.	7	17
Park Forest/Lansing, Ill.	29	27
Reston/West Springfield, Va.	18	13
Sharpstown/Southwest Houston, Tex.	10	12
Valencia/Bouquet Canyon, Calif.	32	38
Westlake Village/Agoura/Malibu Junction, Calif.	40	35
Federally Assisted New Communities/Paired Conventional Communities		
Jonathan/Chanhassen, Minn.	25	20
Park Forest South/Richton Park, Ill.	32	30

[a] Road distance from central business district of central city of Standard Metropolitan Statistical Area (as defined for the 1970 United States Census) in which community is located.

[b] Freestanding community (i.e. not in a Standard Metropolitan Statistical Area).

[c] Data from 1970 United States Census.

and local real estate firms, analyses of census tract data and visual comparisons of all areas that met the matching criteria. Table 2–1 summarizes information on the location, population and acreage of the sample new communities at the start of the study, together with comparable data on the location and population of the paired conventional communities.

Table 2—1. continued

New Communities and
Conventional Communities

Estimated Population		New Communities Only		
New Community	*Conventional Community*	*Percent of Target Population*	*Target Population*	*Target Acreage*
17,900	21,800	38.5	71,346	11,646
24,000	20,000	22	110,000	18,000
23,000	25,200	39	58,500	5,760
17,000	11,000[c]	49	35,000	3,725
15,000	79,000[c]	42	36,000	2,600
20,000	49,900	6	338,000	64,000
8,500	6,600	21	40,000	7,936
8,500	7,300[c]	14	60,000	16,630
12,500	2,600[c]	42	30,000	3,362
30,600	25,800[c]	87	35,000	3,182
20,000	35,000	27	75,000	7,400
34,000	10,000	97	35,000	4,100
7,000	6,000	28	25,000	4,000
13,000	5,000	26	50,000	11,709
1,500	5,100	3	50,000	8,194
3,200	4,800	3	110,000	8,291

Six additional communities were selected to serve as controls and as another base of comparison with the responses of new community elderly residents, black residents and low- and moderate-income residents of subsidized housing. Two of the communities were retirement new communities designed specifically for the elderly. Rossmoor Leisure World is located in the Laguna Hills section of Orange County, California. Sun City Center is located in Hillsborough County, south of the city of Tampa, Florida. Two conventional communities, the Seat Pleasant area, Maryland, outside of Washington, D.C., and Markham, Illinois, in the Chicago area, contained predominantly black single-family detached subdivisions that provided housing similar to that available to black families in new communities. In two other communities, Laurel, Maryland, in the Washington area, and Richton Park, Illinois, south of Chicago, federally subsidized housing projects were utilized as sampling frames to select low- and moderate-income households that could be compared to similar groups living in new communities.

The primary criterion used in the selection of these special comparison communities was that they be located in the vicinity of the sample new communities. This was done in order to limit regional variation and to facilitate comparisons among the communities. The special comparison communities are similar to the other sample communities in terms of the age and price range of housing available. They were selected in much the same manner as the paired conventional communities—on the basis of site visits and consultations with local planning agencies and realtors.

THE NEW AND CONVENTIONAL COMMUNITIES

The new communities selected for this study all meet the basic criteria for new community status. They are large. Their development has been guided by comprehensive master plans and directed by unified development organizations. Each community contains a mixture of land uses and housing types. At the same time, the communities selected differ in a number of important ways. These include the motivation and social consciousness of their developers, regional contexts of development, stage and pace of growth, governmental structure and population characteristics. The diversity among new communities in America is highlighted by the following vignettes, which describe the development status and selected characteristics of each of the new communities studied and, for comparative purposes, their paired conventional communities.

Columbia, Maryland
Columbia is being developed on 18,000 acres in rural Howard County, Maryland, midway between the beltways surrounding Washington, D.C. and Baltimore. The idea for this new community was conceived by Baltimore mortgage banker and shopping center developer James Rouse in mid-1962, when he began secretly acquiring more than 140 parcels assembled for Columbia's development. On October 29, 1963 Rouse announced that he had acquired a tenth of

the land in Howard County and proposed the building of an entirely new city. In mid-1965 the plans for Columbia were approved by Howard County and the development site was rezoned in accordance with a recently completed new-town section of the county zoning ordinance. Construction began in June 1966 and the first homes in Columbia were occupied the following year.

Columbia's land use plan starts with a neighborhood of 2000 to 5000 people built around a neighborhood center consisting of an elementary school, park and playground, swimming pool, community center building and, in some cases, a convenience store. Two to four neighborhoods are then combined to form a village of from 10,000 to 15,000 people. Village centers provide supermarkets and other convenience shopping facilities, community meeting facilities, land for middle and high schools and major community recreational facilities. Nine villages surround a town center complex that will include a regional mall, office buildings, a hotel-motel, restaurants, theaters and a 40-acre town center park and music pavilion. More than 20 percent of Columbia's development acreage will be set aside for open space, with another 20 percent reserved for business and industry.

When study of Columbia began in 1972, the population had grown to 24,000 of a projected 110,000 residents at full development. As shown in Table 2-2, Columbia provided a relatively high proportion of rental housing (43 percent) and a variety of housing types, with over a third of the housing stock composed of apartments and townhouses. Twenty percent of the population was nonwhite, but Columbia residents, both white and nonwhite, tended to be middle class and affluent.

By 1972 Columbia's residents had access to a wide variety of community facilities and services. These included an assortment of recreational facilities—an indoor ice rink, two lakes for boating, an indoor swimming pool and eight outdoor neighborhood pools, two golf courses, an indoor tennis club and numerous outdoor courts, an athletic club, miniature golf, a professional dinner theater, an outdoor concert pavilion, several restaurants and lounges and hundreds of acres of parks and open spaces. Shopping facilities included the Columbia Mall, a regional center with two department stores and three village centers with supermarkets, banks, drug stores, gas stations and assorted specialty shops. The Howard County Public Library operated a branch in Columbia, and four college-level institutions were present in the community. These included the two-year Howard Community College, the new four-year Dag Hammarskjold

Table 2–2.   Housing and Population Characteristics, Spring 1973

↑   continued below   ↑

| New and Paired Conventional Communities | Tenure (%) | | Housing Characteristics[a] | | | Median Home Value |
	Own	Rent	Single Family	Townhouse	Apartment	
Columbia, Md. (NC)	57	43	57	14	29	$44,100
Norbeck-Wheaton, Md. (CC)	53	47	69	7	24	52,200
Elk Grove Village, Ill. (NC)	83	17	79	2	19	38,400
Schaumburg, Ill. (CC)	83	17	72	9	19	36,300
Forest Park, Oh. (NC)	88	12	85	6	9	27,300
Sharonville, Oh. (CC)	85	15	84	4	13	26,100
Foster City, Calif. (NC)	71	29	53	16	31	46,100
West San Mateo, Calif. (CC)	74	26	69	0	31	61,400
Irvine, Calif. (NC)	80	20	56	28	16	42,800
Fountain Valley, Calif. (CC)	84	16	59	24	17	36,200
Jonathan, Minn. (NC)	52	48	45	16	39	33,500
Chanhassen, Minn. (CC)	59	41	59	0	41	40,600
Laguna Niguel, Calif. (NC)	96	4	80	0	20	40,300
Dana Point, Calif. (CC)	95	5	100	0	0	36,100
Lake Havasu City, Ariz. (NC)	68	32	65	0	35	31,800
Kingman, Ariz. (CC)	74	26	70	0	30	20,900
North Palm Beach, Fla. (NC)	88	12	50	0	50	35,500
Tequesta, Fla. (CC)	98	2	50	0	50	40,300
Park Forest, Ill. (NC)	78	22	63	35	2	24,800
Lansing, Ill. (CC)	80	20	79	0	21	30,300
Park Forest South, Ill. (NC)	68	32	48	12	40	30,600
Richton Park, Ill. (CC)	66	34	47	16	37	25,300

Table 2-2. continued

New and Paired Conventional Communities	Population Characteristics			
	Race[b] White (%)	Education[c] Some College + (%)	Occupation[c] White Collar (%)	Median Income
Columbia, Md. (NC)	80	83	89	$17,300
Norbeck-Wheaton, Md. (CC)	98	79	87	17,800
Elk Grove Village, Ill. (NC)	99	56	65	17,600
Schaumburg, Ill. (CC)	99	55	68	15,400
Forest Park, Oh. (NC)	91	60	58	16,400
Sharonville, Oh. (CC)	100	41	61	15,100
Foster City, Calif. (NC)	93	76	81	20,200
West San Mateo, Calif. (CC)	92	71	89	20,300
Irvine, Calif. (NC)	95	80	87	19,000
Fountain Valley, Calif. (CC)	97	75	76	17,500
Jonathan, Minn. (NC)	97	62	75	11,800
Chanhassen, Minn. (CC)	100	69	81	15,000
Laguna Niguel, Calif. (NC)	99	79	77	17,500
Dana Point, Calif. (CC)	99	73	70	15,300
Lake Havasu City, Ariz. (NC)	100	42	48	12,100
Kingman, Ariz. (CC)	98	40	46	12,800
North Palm Beach, Fla. (NC)	99	65	82	16,900
Tequesta, Fla. (CC)	99	61	83	17,500
Park Forest, Ill. (NC)	91	67	75	16,100
Lansing, Ill. (CC)*	100	50	63	12,800
Park Forest South, Ill. (NC)	90	74	73	16,800
Richton Park, Ill. (CC)	99	54	57	12,700

(Table 2-2. continued overleaf . . .)

Table 2–2. continued

↑ *continued below* ↑

| New and Paired Conventional Communities | Tenure (%) | | Housing Characteristics[a] | | | Median Home Value |
| | Own | Rent | Single Family | Townhouse | Apartment | |
			Housing Type (%)			
Reston, Va. (NC)	52	48	25	25	50	58,000
West Springfield, Va. (CC)	37	63	30	31	39	50,800
Sharpstown, Tex. (NC)	62	38	52	11	37	31,200
Southwest Houston, Tex. (CC)	74	26	56	4	40	30,800
Valencia, Calif. (NC)	82	18	80	0	20	37,500
Bouquet Canyon, Calif. (CC)	95	5	100	0	0	30,400
Westlake Village, Calif. (NC)	81	19	56	13	31	47,500
Agoura/Malibu Junction, Calif. (CC)	99	1	80	0	20	35,400

Table 2–2. continued

New and Paired Conventional Communities	Population Characteristics			
	Race^b White (%)	Education^c Some College + (%)	Occupation^c White Collar (%)	Median Income
Reston, Va. (NC)	95	85	90	19,900
West Springfield, Va. (CC)	97	82	87	20,100
Sharpstown, Tex. (NC)	95	85	85	15,900
Southwest Houston, Tex. (CC)	100	79	90	17,600
Valencia, Calif. (NC)	97	79	81	19,000
Bouquet Canyon, Calif. (CC)	96	71	68	15,300
Westlake Village, Calif. (NC)	97	81	87	21,600
Agoura/Malibu Junction, Calif. (CC)	95	69	85	17,500

NC = New Community
CC = Conventional Community

[a] Housing characteristic data are based on household surveys in each of the study communities. Because respondents in the conventional communities were sampled to match the housing distribution in the paired new communities, housing characteristic data do not necessarily reflect housing characteristics of an entire conventional community.

[b] Refers to race of household survey respondents.

[c] Data refer to characteristics of household heads.

College, a branch of Antioch College and Loyola College of Baltimore. Over 65 firms had located in the Columbia industrial parks. Total employment in the community was more than 15,000.

Columbia's growth and development had also been marked by a number of institutional innovations. Recreational facilities, early childhood educational programs, and a community transit system were operated by the Columbia Park and Recreation Association, a unique automatic membership homes association that was incorporated in 1965. The Protestant Columbia Cooperative Ministry was formed in 1966 to seek out new opportunities for mission and service. Catholics, Jews and Protestants shared common religious facilities in The Interfaith Center located in Wilde Lake Village. The Columbia Medical Plan, a prepaid group practice health care program provided by the Columbia Hospital and Clinics Foundation in affiliation with the Johns Hopkins Medical Institutions, was formed to meet community health care needs. Innovation in the schools, including operation of a model high school in Wilde Lake Village, had drawn national attention.

Norbeck-Wheaton. Columbia was paired with the conventional community of Norbeck-Wheaton, located on the urban fringe of Montgomery County fifteen miles northeast of downtown Washington. Major facilities serving the community's 20,000 residents included the Aspen Hill and Rock Creek Village neighborhood shopping centers, Manor Country Club, four neighborhood parks, sections of the North Branch and Rock Creek (regional stream valley) parks, ten schools and a public library. There were no hospital or medical facilities in Norbeck-Wheaton and only one major employment facility, Vitro Laboratories, which employed about 3600 persons. Although Norbeck-Wheaton did not have as large a minority population as Columbia, other characteristics of the population, including education, occupation and income were similar (see Table 2-2).

Elk Grove Village, Illinois

Elk Grove Village is being developed by the Centex Construction Company on a 5760-acre site located 26 miles northwest of Chicago's Loop. The original plan for Elk Grove Village, prepared by the Dallas firm of Phillips, Proctor, Bowers and Associates, envisioned a community of neighborhood schools and parks surrounded by single-family subdivisions and apartments. Shopping needs were to be accommodated by a series of small community shopping centers within easy access of residential neighborhoods. With room for over 450 establishments, the Centex Industrial Park in Elk Grove Village was designed to provide a major source of employment opportunities for community residents, as well as to assure an adequate tax base.

In order to free itself of Cook County zoning and subdivision controls and also to meet the need for municipal services, Centex incorporated Elk Grove Village in 1956, fully thirteen months before the first homes in the community were occupied. By 1972 the population stood at 22,900 and over 27,000 persons were employed in the industrial park. A relatively high proportion (41 percent) of Elk Grove Village's residents had migrated from Chicago. They were predominantly middle class and overwhelmingly white.

Major facilities in Elk Grove Village included the Alexian Brothers Hospital, a community high school and ten elementary and junior high schools, four neighborhood and community shopping centers and a municipal center. The Elk Grove Village Park District, formed in 1966, operated recreational programs at nineteen park sites, including a large community recreational center and swimming pool complex. Village residents also had access to the adjacent 3800-acre Ned Brown Forest Preserve, which is owned and operated by the Cook County Forest Preserve District.

Schaumburg, Illinois. Paired with Elk Grove Village, the village of Schaumburg lies just to the west, some 30 miles from the Loop. Schaumburg also incorporated in 1956 and by 1970 had a population of 18,830 persons housed in a series of residential subdivisions, apartments and condominium complexes. Schaumburg is the location of one of the largest regional shopping centers in the nation, the Woodfield Mall, which opened in 1971 with three levels, 215 shops, three department stores and over two million square feet in its initial phase. Other facilities found in Schaumburg included a number of strip commercial shopping centers, five industrial parks, ten neighborhood and community parks and a commuter bus service. Schaumburg residents also benefited from Cook County Forest Preserve District lands which surrounded the community on three sides and provided some 10,000 acres for recreational use.

Forest Park, Ohio

Forest Park is located in Hamilton County, fifteen miles northwest of the city of Cincinnati. The development site was once a part of a 6000-acre parcel acquired by the federal government in the early 1930s for the Greenbelt Program. In addition to building the town of Greenhills, the federal government used part of the land for a flood control project and gave some 2000 acres to Hamilton County for a regional park. In 1952 the remaining acreage was declared surplus and the government began looking for a buyer.

In order to prevent the land from being developed in a piecemeal fashion, a group of Cincinnati leaders formed the Cincinnati Community Development Corporation to acquire 3400 acres from the federal government for a planned new community. In 1954 the Warner-Kanter Corporation acquired the site and retained the firm of Victor Gruen and Associates to prepare a master plan which, according to the terms of its land sales agreement, the Community Development Corporation reviewed and approved. Gruen's plan featured a series of residential neighborhoods surrounding neighborhood elementary schools. Land was also reserved for industrial uses and for a community center.

The first residents moved to Forest Park in 1956. In 1961 the residents voted to incorporate, in part to ward off an annexation attempt by neighboring Greenhills. By 1972, the population of Forest Park had grown to 17,000, almost half of its target population of 35,000. Compared with most of the other new communities in the sample, Forest Park had attracted a larger black population (9 percent), and had a lower proportion of household heads who had attended college (60 percent) and who were employed in white collar occupations (58 percent). However, as is also shown in Table 2–2, Forest Park was solidly middle class, with the median family income standing at $16,400. In addition, Forest Park had the highest proportion of residents (85 percent) among the communities studied who were living in single-family detached homes.

The major facilities found in Forest Park included a growing industrial park which in 1972 had attracted twelve manufacturing firms, the corporate headquarters and home office of the Union Central Life Insurance Company and a neighborhood shopping center. Educational needs were accommodated at a community high school located adjacent to a municipal center and central park and at three elementary schools and a junior high school. Recreational facilities included a nonprofit community swimming pool and the Winton Woods regional park, which was operated by the Hamilton County Park District.

Sharonville, Ohio.   Forest Park was matched with the conventional town of Sharonville, located several miles to the east and twelve miles north of Cincinnati. Although the town was originally platted in 1818, it had barely 1000 residents in 1950, when it began a period of steady growth. Sharonville was in the path of major industrial growth out the Mill Creek Valley from Cincinnati. By the early 1970s over 30 manufacturing plants with over 7000 employees had located in the community. This strong industrial base enabled the city of

Sharonville to establish a park and open space system that included two community swimming pools and adjacent recreational centers. An additional amenity is the Sharon Woods regional park operated by the Hamilton County Park District. Compared with the residents of Forest Park, those living in Sharonville had similar socioeconomic characteristics. Sharonville, however, had no black residents.

Foster City, California

Foster City is being developed on the west shore of San Francisco Bay. The 2600-acre development site was acquired by T. Jack Foster and his three sons in 1959. Known as Brewer's Island, the land had been used as pasture by a dairyman early in the century and was later partially converted to evaporating ponds by Leslie Salt Company. A unique feature of Foster City's development was the creation of the Estero Municipal Improvement District in 1960 to finance reclamation of the low-lying development site and to provide a vehicle for the provision of various urban services. During the first years of development the district was controlled by the Fosters and caused considerable controversy in Foster City because of its high bonded indebtedness ($63.86 million in 1970) over which the residents had no control.

Foster City's General Plan was prepared in 1961 by the firm of Wilsey, Ham and Blair. The plan laid out a series of nine residential neighborhoods, a town center, satellite shopping centers and an industrial park. Each neighborhood was to be served by small parks and schools. A key feature of the plan was a lagoon system that was designed to provide a major recreational amenity and to serve as the key to successful marketing of the project.

By 1972 Foster City had grown to a community of 15,000 people living in six of the projected nine residential neighborhoods. Three shopping centers were in operation and a professional theater made its home in the community. However, the location of a nearby regional shopping center had slowed growth of Foster City's town center and school construction was far behind schedule. In order to gain more control over the development process, the residents of Foster City voted to incorporate in April 1971. With incorporation, the Estero Municipal Improvement District was made a subsidiary of the new city government.

The residents of Foster City tended to be affluent (the median income was $20,200) and high proportions of the residents had attended college (76 percent of the household heads) and were working in white collar occupations (81 percent of the employed household heads). The community was racially integrated (3 percent black) and had attracted a number of families of Asian descent (4 percent).

West San Mateo, California. Foster City was paired with two residential subdivisions and adjacent apartment complexes located 30 miles south of San Francisco, at the western edge of the city of San Mateo, which borders Foster City. San Mateo had experienced its most rapid growth during the 1950s. While Foster City was developing during the 1960s on bayfill to the east, much of the remaining undeveloped land in San Mateo developed in the hills to the west.

San Mateo is an established city of 79,000 persons. In 1972 it had a well-developed downtown, a major regional shopping center and an extensive municipal park system. Other amenities and facilities included the Bay Meadows Race Track, Peninsula Golf and Country Club, College of San Mateo and the San Mateo County Hospital. Most of these facilities, however, were as accessible to Foster City residents as to the conventional subdivisions in West San Mateo. Although median home values were considerably higher in West San Mateo than in Foster City ($61,400 vs. $46,100), in most other respects the residents of these two communities were very similar (see Table 2-2).

Irvine, California

The 88,000-acre Irvine Ranch is strategically located in the path of Southern California population growth, 40 miles south of Los Angeles in Orange County. Extending 22 miles inland from the Pacific Ocean, the Irvine Ranch will be the site of the nation's largest new community. A population of 430,000 is expected by 1990.

Planning for a new community at Irvine began in 1959 when 1000 acres were donated to the University of California for a new campus. William L. Pereira was retained by the University to plan the campus. Seeing the need for a supporting community, he was commissioned by The Irvine Company to prepare the plans for a 10,000-acre university-oriented community in the central portion of the Irvine Ranch. Pereira's plan was subsequently incorporated into the South Irvine Ranch General Plan which was approved by the Orange County Board of Supervisors in February 1964. This plan was then superceded by the 1970 Irvine General Plan which proposed that a new city of 53,000 acres be developed in the central portion of the ranch. Incorporated in 1971 as the City of Irvine, this portion of the Irvine Ranch was selected for the study.

Originally encompassing 18,300 acres and a population of about

20,000 persons, the city of Irvine has since annexed over 7000 additional acres, and has extended its long-range planning over an area of 64,000 acres comprising its approved sphere of influence. The city has adopted a plan that includes three growth options. Option 1 follows Irvine Company plans for a series of villages and environmental corridors, two large industrial complexes and a new regional commercial center at the juncture of the Santa Ana and San Diego freeways. A midrange population of 337,800 is projected. Option 2 assumes maximum urbanization and projects a midrange population of 453,000. Option 3 is based on minimum urbanization assumptions, including reservation of a 10,000-acre section of coastal hills as open space, and projects a midrange population of 194,000.

When Irvine was selected for study in 1972, work was underway on five villages within the city limits: Walnut, Valleyview, New Culver, University Park and Turtle Rock. The villages were composed of individual neighborhoods with neighborhood recreational facilities operated by homes associations. A neighborhood shopping center was operating adjacent to University Park and another was ready for construction next to Walnut Village. The University of California at Irvine was in full operation and a small town center building was open adjacent to the university. A public golf course had been constructed by The Irvine Company. Over 16,000 employees were working in the highly successful Irvine Industrial Complex, the first of the two industrial areas to be developed. As shown in Table 2–2, Irvine residents were affluent (median income of $19,000) and overwhelmingly tended to be employed in white collar occupations. Eighty percent of the residents owned their own homes. The median home value was $42,800. Ninety-five percent of the residents were white.

Fountain Valley, California. Fountain Valley is located along the San Diego Freeway four miles north of Irvine. Although the community incorporated in 1957, residential tract development did not begin until January 1962 when the first 100 acres were approved for residential use. During the next ten years, approximately 2500 acres were zoned or developed for single-family homes and apartments. Population growth was equally spectacular, increasing from 597 persons when the community incorporated to 31,826 in 1970 and an estimated 49,000 in 1972. Fountain Valley contained a number of neighborhood shopping centers, a large industrial area, a county park with a golf course and a community civic center. Ninety-seven percent of the population was white, with three-fourths of the sampled household heads having attended college and about the same proportion (see Table 2–2) employed in white collar occupations. The median income of the Fountain Valley households included in the study was $17,500.

Jonathan, Minnesota

Jonathan was the first new community to be approved for assistance under the provisions of Title IV of the 1968 Housing and Urban Development Act. It is located in rural Carver County, 25 miles southwest of downtown Minneapolis within the Twin Cities Metropolitan Area. The planning area for the community encompassed 8166 acres of rolling hills interspersed with wooded areas along a ravine system that runs through the property. Jonathan is located a short distance north of and has been annexed by the farm-center town of Chaska, which had over 5000 residents when the study began in 1972.

The development of Jonathan was initiated in 1966 when the Ace Development Corporation (subsequently to become the Jonathan Development Corporation) was formed to manage the development process and the Carver Company was organized to spearhead land acquisition for a new community envisioned by the late Henry T. McKnight, a former Minnesota State Senator with interests in downtown real estate, land development and cattle ranching. Between 1965 and 1970, when a project agreement with the Department of Housing and Urban Development was signed, the concept for Jonathan evolved through three distinct phases. As originally planned, the community was to be developed on about 3000 acres in two upper- and middle-income residential villages. However, on the basis of a financial analysis and development program prepared by the firm of Robert Gladstone and Associates in 1966, the scope of the project was expanded to encompass 4800 acres with a target population of 41,300 persons after a 20-year development period. Finally, the project was further expanded when Jonathan completed its application for a federal loan guarantee under Title IV. The project area was expanded to 6000 acres (and subsequently to over 8000 acres), projected population was increased to approximately 50,000, industrial acreage was expanded from 500 to 1989 acres and a commitment was made to provide over 6500 housing units for low- and moderate-income families.

The design concept for Jonathan is shaped by the existing road system and a 1700-acre open space grid (21 percent of the site) following the natural ravines and drainage courses through the property. Within the matrix of existing highways and proposed open space, five villages, each to house approximately 7000 residents in a variety of housing types, were proposed. Village centers were to provide basic facilities for daily living, including shopping, post offices, municipal services and elementary schools. A town center was to serve as a regional multifunctional center with major retail, medical, office and entertainment facilities.

In 1972, when Jonathan was selected for the study, the population of the community stood at 1500 persons housed in 420 dwelling units, 148 of which were constructed under the FHA Section 235 and Section 236 subsidized housing programs. The initial phase of the first village center was in operation and provided some convenience shopping facilities and a medical clinic. A man-made lake had been constructed adjacent to the village center, with an accompanying recreational pavillion. Walking paths connected homes to the village center, the lake and a neighborhood park with a baseball diamond and tennis court. Although schools had yet to be constructed in Jonathan, the industrial park was growing, with 45 firms providing 1080 jobs by the end of 1973.

Reflecting the character of the Twin Cities area, Jonathan's population was predominantly (97 percent) white. However, because of the high proportion of subsidized housing, the median income of the Jonathan households, $11,800, was the lowest of any of the new communities studied. Almost two-thirds of the household heads had attended college and three-fourths were employed in white collar jobs.

Chanhassen, Minnesota. Jonathan was paired with the nearby village of Chanhassen, which was located adjacent to Jonathan's northeast and eastern planning boundaries. Encompassing 24 square miles, Chanhassen's population was estimated at 5100 in 1972. The community had a small downtown with a nationally known dinner theater, 60-acre village park, elementary school and a high school. Housing included a series of scattered single-family detached subdivisions and a number of apartment houses located near the downtown. The residents sampled in Chanhassen were somewhat more affluent than those in Jonathan (median income of $15,000 vs. $11,800), but were similar in terms of educational attainment and occupation.

Laguna Niguel, California

Laguna Niguel is being developed within and on the hills overlooking a valley extending seven miles from the Pacific Ocean to the San Diego Freeway in southern Orange County. The 7936-acre development site, once part of the Moulton Ranch, was acquired in 1960 by the Boston firm of Cabot, Cabot & Forbes. Victor Gruen and

Associates prepared the community master plan, which included a parkway running from the Pacific Coast Highway to the San Diego Freeway to serve as the spine of the community, with a series of residential neighborhoods located on either side. Nineteen schools and six neighborhood shopping centers were envisioned for an ultimate population of 80,000. A major civic and town center was planned in the heart of the community. An industrial area was to be located adjacent to the freeway and a resort complex adjacent to the Pacific beaches.

Because of slow sales throughout the 1960s, Laguna Niguel was sold to the Avco Corporation in 1971, after some 2300 homes had been completed. Since that time, Avco has invested heavily to speed the pace of development. However, concern for the fragile environment of the southern California coastal hills and the increasing cost of developing hillside land has led to a sharp reduction in the projected population—to 43,000 residents by 1983.

In 1972, when Laguna Niguel was selected for the study, the community had 8500 residents. Most of them, 96 percent, owned their own homes and 80 percent of the households occupied single-family detached dwellings. Like most of the other new communities studied, Laguna Niguel had attracted a middle class population. Median family income was $17,500, almost 80 percent of the household heads had attended college and 77 percent were employed in white collar occupations. Laguna Niguel had also attracted a higher than average proportion of retired households (21 percent).

In spite of its slow development pace, Laguna Niguel residents had a variety of community facilities available for their use. These included three shopping centers, a medical office building, a golf course, a tennis club and a beach club. Orange County had completed its South Coast Regional Civic Center in Laguna Niguel, located adjacent to the town center; Niguel Regional Park, which occupies a 167-acre site surrounding Niguel Lake; and a county beach park. Fifty-five firms had located in the Laguna Niguel Industrial Park and North American Rockwell had completed construction of a 1,000,000-square foot building designed to house 7000 employees, which has since been acquired by the U.S. General Services Administration.

Dana Point/Capistrano Valley, California. This conventional community, located just to the south of Laguna Niguel, consists of several subdivisions of single-family detached homes and a small shopping area located next to the Pacific Coast Highway. Major amenities in the area include the Dana Point Harbor and Marina, Doheny State

Park and Beach and a neighborhood park operated by the Capistrano Bay Park and Recreation District. The community is in an unincorporated portion of Orange County. In 1972 its population was estimated to be 6600. The Dana Point residents were somewhat less affluent than those living in Laguna Niguel. Median home value was $36,100 (vs. $40,300 in Laguna Niguel) and the median family income was $15,300 (vs. $17,500 in Laguna Niguel). Both Dana Point and Laguna Niguel were overwhelmingly white (99 percent).

Lake Havasu City, Arizona

Located 150 air miles northwest of Phoenix and 235 miles east of Los Angeles, Lake Havasu City was the only freestanding new community selected for the study. The idea of building an entirely new city in the Arizona desert originated with Los Angeles oilman and manufacturer Robert P. McCulloch. In 1959 McCulloch acquired 3500 acres adjacent to Lake Havasu for an outboard motor testing site. Two years late, when he was unable to expand his outboard motor plant in Los Angeles, McCulloch turned to the Lake Havasu site as the location for a new plant and a new city. With C.V. Wood, the former general manager of Disneyland, McCulloch went about acquiring an additional 12,990 acres of desert in a complex series of transactions that required release of the federally owned land to the state of Arizona and its subsequent sale at a public auction. McCulloch was the only bidder, paying approximately $73 an acre.

The general plan for Lake Havasu City was drawn up by Wood. Some 22 miles of lakefront were set aside for community use and are being developed as part of Lake Havasu State Park. The rest of the land was divided into some 40,000 residential, commercial and industrial building sites. In addition, 36 lots were set aside for neighborhood parks. Land sales have been conducted on a nationwide basis, with a private airline used to transport prospective lot purchasers to the community.

By 1972 Lake Havasu City had an estimated 8500 residents and most of the elements of a complete community. To bolster the economic base, McCulloch transferred his chain saw manufacturing operation (which has since been sold) to Lake Havasu City and bought the historic London Bridge and reassembled it in Lake Havasu City to bolster the tourist industry. Schools were provided by organizing an elementary school district from scratch (two elementary schools and a junior high school have been built) and by persuading the Mohave County Union High School District to build a community high school. Private investors have helped to build a thriving downtown, including a movie theater and bowling alley which were originally built by McCulloch and later sold to private operators. Two developer-owned golf courses are in operation. Lake Havasu City is also served by a weekly newspaper and a local radio station.

Lake Havasu City is the only one of the new communities studied with less than a majority (42 percent) of the household heads with at least some college education and with less than a majority (48 percent) employed in white collar jobs. The median income of Lake Havasu City households was $12,100, well below the average ($17,500) of the thirteen nonfederally assisted new communities studied. Because it is a freestanding community, Lake Havasu City has had to provide housing for the workers employed in its manufacturing and service jobs. In addition, it has attracted a relatively high proportion of retired households (23 percent vs. 10 percent for the entire sample of thirteen nonfederally assisted new communities).

Kingman, Arizona. Located 56 miles across the Arizona desert from Lake Havasu City, Kingman is the closest comparably sized community on the Arizona side of the Colorado River. Kingman was founded in the early 1880s, but was not incorporated as a city until 1952. With a population of 7312 in 1970, Kingman had a small downtown clustered near the Mohave County Courthouse, a long strip commercial section running along U.S. Highway 66 and a series of residential neighborhoods which follow a grid pattern of development. The economy centers on government, transportation and commercial services, with a small manufacturing sector. A golf course, three city parks and a municipal pool provided recreational amenities for Kingman's residents. As shown in Table 2-2, the socioeconomic characteristics of the residents interviewed in Kingman were similar to those of the Lake Havasu City respondents, though the median home value in Kingman was lower ($20,900 vs. $31,800).

North Palm Beach, Florida

North Palm Beach is a 2362-acre waterfront community located along the intercoastal waterway, seven and one-half miles north of West Palm Beach. The development site was acquired by North Palm Beach Properties in 1955. Early land development operations included the dredging of a series of canals and the bulkheading of all waterfront properties. The overall planning of the community was honored by the National Association of Home Builders for its design, layout, restrictions and facilities.

North Palm Beach Properties incorporated the community shortly after the development site was acquired and some months before the first homes were sold. The village government originally restricted its activities to public safety and housekeeping, but has gradually increased its functions. In addition to the North Palm Beach Country Club, which was purchased from the developer in 1961, the village operates a public marina, library, art center, and a small park system.

In recent years Palm Beach County has been one of the best housing markets in the country and the village of North Palm Beach has the highest growth rate in the county. During the past five years condominium apartment construction has soared. Commercial development is located in a series of shopping centers along U.S. Highway 1, the major north-south artery through the town. A small area is zoned for industrial use, but has not been occupied.

In 1972, the population was estimated to be 12,500, 42 percent of the 30,000 population projected at full development. Approximately half of the residents lived in apartments, though a high proportion (88 percent) owned their own dwelling units. North Palm Beach households tended to be white and middle class. The median family income was $16,900. A relatively high proportion of the household heads (27 percent) were retired.

Tequesta, Florida. North Palm Beach was paired with the small incorporated village of Tequesta, located nine miles to the north on the Loxahatchee River at Jupiter Inlet. This conventional community consisted of a patchwork of small subdivisions and condominiums. Community amenities include the Tequesta Country Club, the Community Public Library and a small art institution, the Lighthouse Gallery. In 1970 the population of Tequesta was 2576, with 4323 persons living in adjacent unincorporated areas. As shown in Table 2-2, Tequesta's residents were similar to those living in North Palm Beach in terms of socioeconomic characteristics. However, a higher proportion of the household heads (53 percent) were retired.

Park Forest, Illinois

Park Forest is the oldest new community included in the study. The community was begun in 1947 on some 2200 acres of Illinois prairie in southeast Cook County by American Community Builders, Inc., a partnership consisting of Nathan Manilow, Phillip M. Klutznick and Jerrold Loebl. Land planning was under the direction of Elbert Peets, who had earlier designed the town of Glendale for the United States Housing Authority.

Because of the vast housing market created by returning war veterans and the availability of financing for rental housing for veterans, initial residential building consisted of 3010 rental townhouses grouped in courts near the center of Park Forest. Several years later

these courts received national publicity as the home of William
Whyte's "organization man." Families who occupied the rental housing units and the single-family subdivisions that were subsequently
built provided customers for a large shopping center located at the
geographical and population center of Park Forest. The shopping
center was one of the first open malls in the country.

Park Forest incorporated as a village in 1949 and the village government assumed responsibility for various urban services in the
community. The village established an aggressive park development
program on land donated by the development company. In 1973 the
village recreation and parks department maintained 275 acres of
parks, operated a nine-hole golf course and supervised and staffed
some 80 recreational programs, ranging from preschool through adult
activities. A nonprofit community swimming pool corporation built
and operated an "aquatic center" open to all Park Forest residents.

Although industrial land was set aside in Park Forest, poor highway access limited its appeal to prospective firms. However, the community's location at the end of the Illinois Central's commuter rail
line to the Loop meant that the developer did not have to rely on
local employment as a source of housing demand. In fact, most of
the community's early residents worked 29 miles away in downtown
Chicago.

By 1960 Park Forest had a population of 30,000, just short of
current numbers. American Community Builders, Inc. disbanded in
1959. Since that time development has been limited. Park Forest had
the lowest median home value ($24,800) of any of the new commu-
nities studied. Nevertheless, two-thirds of the household heads had
attended college and three-fourths were working in white collar
occupations. The median family income of $16,100 was not too
much lower than the median of $17,500 for all thirteen nonfederally
assisted new communities studied. Nine percent of the households in
Park Forest were nonwhite.

Lansing, Illinois.   Park Forest was paired with the village of Lansing, located adjacent to the Indiana state line in southeastern Cook
County, 26 miles from Chicago's Loop. Although Lansing was incorporated as a village in 1893 (with a population of 200), major residential growth did not occur until after World War II. In 1950 both
Lansing and Park Forest had populations between 8000 and 9000
residents. Both communities more than doubled in population during
the 1950s. Lansing, however, had somewhat greater success than Park
Forest in attracting industrial development. In 1970 there were 30

manufacturing establishments and a total of 1000 manufacturing employees in the community. Major amenities in Lansing include a community park and swimming pool operated by the Lan-Oak Park District, a number of small neighborhood parks and a section of the Cook County Forest Preserve adjacent to the community's southwest boundary. The population of Lansing was 25,218 in 1970.

Park Forest South, Illinois

Park Forest South, the second federally assisted new community selected for the study, is located in Will County, 32 miles south of the Chicago Loop and immediately south of Park Forest. The idea for the community originated with the late Nathan Manilow, who was one of the principal partners involved in the building of Park Forest. When Park Forest's development company, American Community Builders, Inc., disbanded in 1959, Manilow retained control of the Park Forest Plaza shopping center through his solely-owned company, Park Forest Properties. In the mid-1960s Nathan Manilow and his son Lewis saw the potential for the expansion of Park Forest to a community of some 60,000 residents and began to assemble the necessary acreage to the south in Will County.

In June 1967 the Manilows persuaded the residents of a small bankrupt subdivision surrounded by Manilow land holdings to incorporate as the Village of Park Forest South. The Manilows then retained the firm of Carl L. Gardner and Associates to develop a comprehensive plan for the village and to prepare zoning and subdivision regulations. When these were completed, the Manilows requested annexation of 1200 acres of adjoining land which had been pre-zoned for a large planned unit development. This was accomplished on January 26, 1968 in exchange for a promise by the Manilows to support village fire protection and police services.

In order to secure development capital and financing the Manilows then proceeded on two fronts. First, additional equity participation in the venture was achieved in 1968 when Mid-American Improvement Corporation (owned by Illinois Central Industries, Inc.) became a partner in the new community and in 1969, when United States Gypsum Urban Development Corporation (owned by The United States Gypsum Company) was recruited. Each company took a 25 percent interest in the Park Forest South Development Company, with the Manilow Organization, Inc. acting as managing partner. Second, to generate the long-term capital required to develop a full-scale new community, assistance was sought from the Department of Housing and Urban Development under Title IV of the 1968 Housing and Urban Development Act. Park Forest South's participation in the federal new communities program was formally accomplished on March 17, 1971 when a project agreement was HUD was signed.

The Park Forest South planning area encompassed 8291 acres which were to be developed over a fifteen-year period for a target population of 110,000. Highlights of the development plan included the 753-acre campus of Governors State University, Governors Gateway Industrial Park and a multifunctional town center. These three elements were to be connected by the "Main Drag"—a three-mile linear strip development containing major commercial, recreational and municipal facilities served by a rapid transit system. Other commercial and institutional facilities were to be provided in a number of neighborhood centers designed to serve day-to-day needs. Rapid transit service to Chicago was to be initiated through an extension of the Illinois Central Gulf commuter rail line when 3000 dwelling units were occupied. A major hospital and medical complex with close connections with the university were planned. Almost 900 acres of major open space were to be provided, together with a more intimate open space network and path system running through individual neighborhoods. Finally, Park Forest South was expected to provide an estimated 4500 housing units to be constructed with assistance from federal low- and moderate-income housing subsidy programs and an employment base of over 28,000 jobs.

When Park Forest South was selected for the study in 1972, the community had a population of 3200 residents living in 1310 dwelling units. Recreational facilities were provided at two neighborhood swimming and recreational centers which were operated by private automatic membership associations. An elementary school had been completed, as well as a small convenience shopping center and a commercial ice skating rink. Development was well under way in the industrial park, which had 34 firms employing 925 persons by the end of 1973.

Because subsidized housing had yet to be occupied in Park Forest South at the time of the household survey in the spring of 1973, the median family income in the community ($16,800) was considerably higher than that of Jonathan ($11,800). However, Park Forest South had attracted a number of nonwhite families (10 percent of the population).

Richton Park, Illinois. Richton Park is located directly north of Park Forest South and adjacent to the western boundary of Park Forest. In 1972 the community had an estimated 4800 residents and was undergoing rapid residential growth. Recently developed projects included a large subdivision of single-family detached homes marketed under the FHA Section 235 subsidized home ownership program, as well as conventional single-family subdivisions, townhouses and apartments. Major community facilities included an elementary school and a high school, strip commercial shopping centers, a golf course and a neighborhood park and playground. In contrast to Park Forest South, Richton Park's population was almost entirely white. However, the median income of residents was lower ($12,700), and lower proportions of the household heads had attended college (54 percent) and were working in white collar occupations (57 percent).

Reston, Virginia

Reston is being developed on 6750 acres located in Fairfax County, eighteen miles northwest of Washington, D.C. The development site was acquired in March 1961 by Robert E. Simon, Jr. after he and his family had sold Carnegie Hall in New York City. The Reston master plan was prepared by the New York architectural firm of Whittlesey and Conklin and was approved by the Fairfax County Board of Supervisors in June 1962. The plan assigned about 23 percent of the site for recreational areas, provided for a 970-acre industrial park, and for a variety of housing types and commercial areas. These land uses were organized in a series of seven villages, each with a projected population of 10,000 to 12,000 people. A town center was designated to serve Reston's projected 75,000 residents and some 50,000 people in the surrounding region.

Throughout its early years Reston was plagued by a slow development pace and financial difficulties. These problems came to a head in September 1967 when the Gulf Oil Corporation, which had made a major loan to Simon for Reston's development, took over full financial and operational responsibility and formed Gulf-Reston, Inc. to manage the development process. Gulf increased its investment in Reston and by 1972 was able to report a positive cash flow.

In 1972 Reston had an estimated 20,000 residents living in two villages, Lake Anne and Hunters Woods. Over 50 tenants occupied the Lake Anne Village Center, which had attracted national attention because of its urbane design and mixture of shops and apartments. Two golf courses were operating, as well as a series of neighborhood swimming and tennis facilities and a riding stable. Medical and day care centers were functioning. Over 2000 persons were employed in Reston and construction was underway on a $54 million headquarters building for the United States Geological Survey.

Reston had one of the most educated and affluent populations of any of the new communities selected for the study. Eighty-five percent of the household heads had attended college, 90 percent were employed in white collar occupations and the median income was $19,900. The median home value was $58,000. Reston was racially integrated (5 percent of the population was nonwhite) and economically integrated (11 percent of the housing stock consisted of subsidized units).

West Springfield, Virginia. This conventional community in Fairfax County is located eighteen miles southeast of Reston and thirteen miles southwest of downtown Washington. With almost 35,000 residents in 1972, the West Springfield community was served by four neighborhood and community shopping centers but made no provision for industrial development. Recreational facilities were provided at Lake Accotink, Cardinal Forest and West Springfield Golf and Country Club and at facilities provided by individual tract and apartment developers. As shown in Table 2-2, the socioeconomic characteristics of the West Springfield residents were very similar to those of the Reston residents, although a significantly higher proportion rented their homes (63 percent vs. 48 percent).

Sharpstown, Texas

Sharpstown, which began development in 1953 on a 4100-acre site, is located ten miles southeast of downtown Houston. The community master plan followed traditional patterns, with single-family subdivisions surrounding neighborhood elementary schools and small parks. Although little emphasis was placed on architectural merit, homes were built and marketed within the means of a broad spectrum of consumers.

In 1972 Sharpstown had over 11,000 homes and apartments. The Sharpstown Center, a regional shopping center occupying a 77-acre site in the heart of the community, had opened in 1960. Other projects completed in the 1960s included a boy's preparatory school operated by the Society of Jesus, Houston Baptist College, which occupied a 196-acre campus in Sharpstown, a branch of the Houston Public Library, the Memorial Baptist Hospital's Southwest Branch and the Sharpstown General Hospital. Recreational and entertainment facilities included several neighborhood parks, the Sharpstown Country Club, a drive-in theater, 2100-seat movie theater and 3000-seat professional theater. Employment opportunities were provided at the many commercial establishments in Sharpstown and by firms located in the 755-acre Sharpstown Industrial Park.

Sharpstown is a middle class community. Eighty-five percent of the household heads had attended college and 85 percent were employed in white collar occupations. The median family income was $15,900. Five percent of the population was nonwhite.

Southwest Houston, Texas. This conventional community consists of three large subdivisions located southwest of Sharpstown at the edge of the Houston city limits. The subdivisions were developed gradually over a period of years and were tied together by a major thoroughfare and series of strip-commercial shopping centers. Major amenities and recreational facilities included the Braeburn Country Club, Southwest Branch of the Houston YMCA and the City of Houston's Southwest Tennis Center. Although the median income of households was higher than in Sharpstown ($17,600 vs. $15,900), educational and occupational characteristics of the household heads were similar, as was the median home value.

Valencia, California
Valencia is located 32 miles northeast of downtown Los Angeles in an unincorporated section of Los Angeles County. The community is being developed by the Newhall Land and Farming Company on a 4000-acre section of the 44,000-acre Newhall Ranch. The land was originally purchased by Henry Mayo Newhall in the 1870s.

The stimulus for the development of a new community on the Newhall Ranch was provided by approaching urbanization in the San Fernando Valley, seven miles to the south, and the Palmdale International Airport, which was proposed for nearby Antelope Valley. The general plan for Valencia was prepared by Thomas L. Sutton and Victor Gruen and Associates and was adopted by the Los Angeles County Regional Planning Commission in October 1965. The Valencia plan combines individual neighborhoods with schools and parks into a series of villages each with its own shopping and recreational centers, high schools, library and church. Paseos (pathways) connect superblocks of homes with neighborhood schools and parks. An open space system separates the villages. A major regional shopping and civic center is planned in the heart of the community, with employment opportunities to be provided at the 1000-acre Valencia Industrial Center.

By 1972 Valencia had an estimated 7000 residents living in over 2000 homes and garden apartments. The first village shopping center was in operation. Two educational institutions, California Institue of the Arts, a four-year art and music school conceived by Walt Disney, and College of the Canyons, a community college, had begun operations. In order to attract potential residents to Valencia, the Newhall Land and Farming Company had invested heavily in regional recreational and entertainment facilities. These included three golf courses, a $30 million family ride park called Magic Mountain, a public riding stable, a travel trailer park and a dune buggy/motorcycle park. Some fifteen companies had located in the Valencia Industrial Center, thus creating an employment base approaching 3000 jobs.

The median income of Valencia residents was $19,000. Seventy-nine percent of the household heads had attended college and 81 percent were employed in white collar occupations. Ninety-seven percent of the residents were white.

Bouquet Canyon, California.   The hills and valleys northeast of Valencia began to develop several years before Valencia's master plan was approved. The Bouquet Canyon community consists of a series of single-family detached residential subdivisions on the canyon floor. Shopping facilities were available at two centers located near the mouth of Bouquet Canyon and its junction with San Francisquito Canyon. The community was also served by a small park operated by the Los Angeles County Park and Recreation Department. As shown in Table 2-2, the Bouquet Canyon residents tended to be less affluent than those living in Valencia. The median family income was $15,300, $3,700 less than in Valencia.

Westlake Village, California

Westlake Village is surrounded by mountains in the picturesque Conejo Valley, 40 miles northwest of the Los Angeles Civic Center. The community is being developed on the 11,709-acre Albertson Ranch, which was acquired by shipping magnate Daniel K. Ludwig in 1964 after one year of litigation over title to the property. During 1964 and 1965 the Bechtel Corporation conducted master plan studies for Ludwig's American-Hawaiian Steamship Company, which was to manage the development process. Earthmoving began in 1966 and the first homes were occupied in 1967.

The Westlake Village master plan is based on interrelating a series of neighborhood clusters composed of homes, schools, parks, recreational facilities and small neighborhood shopping centers. A major regional shopping center was planned along the Ventura Freeway which bisects the community, and approximately 500 acres along the freeway were set aside for industrial use. Unique among American new communities, the Westlake Village plan also reserved a 170-acre parcel at the community's southern boundary for a cemetery. The theme for Westlake Village was established by a 150-acre artificial lake, which cost $2 million to construct.

In 1972 Westlake Village had an estimated 13,000 residents. Major community facilities and amenities included a community shopping center and two satellite centers, a motel-restaurant complex, an eighteen-hole, night-lighted golf course and tennis club, individual neighborhood swimming pools and recreational centers, two riding stables, a marina at Lake Westlake and a community hospital. A number of nationally-known firms had located in the industrial parks. Employment in Westlake Village was estimated to be 4500. Nevertheless, Westlake Village was in financial difficulty. In 1969 the Prudential Insurance Company converted a $30 million land loan into an equity investment in Westlake Village's development. By late 1972 disagreements between Prudential and the American-Hawaiian Steamship Company led to dissolution of the partnership, with Prudential keeping the undeveloped acreage in the community and American-Hawaiian the income property. Prudential has completed a second golf course and is proceeding with development.

Westlake Village had the highest median family income of the new communities studied ($21,600) and the second highest median home value ($47,500). Eighty-one percent of the household heads had attended college and 87 percent were employed in white collar occupations. Ninety-seven percent of the residents were white.

Agoura/Malibu Junction, California. The Malibu hills and canyons between Westlake Village and the new community of Calabassas Park, several miles to the south along the Ventura Freeway, have been steadily developing since the late 1960s. This conventional community of some 5000 residents consisted of a series of unrelated and widely separated subdivisions located on either side of the freeway. Shopping facilities were provided at a small convenience center located just off the freeway. A twelve-acre park site is owned by the Simi Valley Recreation and Park District and several subdivisions had neighborhood recreational facilities operated by homes associations. The residents were affluent (median income of $17,500) and high proportions of the household heads had attended college (69 percent) and were employed in white collar occupations (85 percent). Ninety-five percent of the residents were white.

SUMMARY

New community development has been proposed as a promising solution to a number of critical problems that accompany urban expanstion and metropolitan growth. After a long history of community building in the private sector, the federal government enacted legislation to foster the increased production of new communities. Although the federal new communities program is now at a standstill, much can be learned from a closer examination of new community projects that are under development.

The review of the community building experience in the United States presented in this chapter has highlighted the diversity that exists among new communities in this country and the gradual expansion of public objectives to be achieved through community-scale development projects. New communities initiated during the 1940s and 1950s were characterized by a larger scale of development than was typical of new suburban development and by their comprehensive land use planning. The California new communities of the 1960s added another ingredient of the new community concept—close attention to the quality of the built environment. Two new communities in the East—Columbia and Reston—then emerged as models of new community development by combining high quality environmental and urban design with a concern for population balance and diversity and the formulation of innovative approaches to the provision of community facilities and services. Their examples stimulated federal interest in new community development and the subsequent passage of federal new communities legislation.

The representative cross-section of communities selected for this study exemplifies the variation in development approaches and new community characteristics that now exists in the United States. Five new communities—Elk Grove Village, Forest Park, North Palm Beach, Park Forest and Sharpstown—were begun during the late 1940s through the mid-1950s. These communities, together with freestanding Lake Havasu City, paid less attention to many of the amenities and features—open space corridors, path systems, pedestrian-vehicular separation, neighborhood centers and recreational facilities—that are common in later new communities. However, they have provided more lower priced housing and have attracted a more balanced population than is characteristic of the amenity-conscious new communities developed during the following decade. In the five California new communities in the sample—Foster City, Irvine, Laguna Niguel, Valencia and Westlake Village—each offers an attractive residential environment that has attracted predominantly white, middle- and upper-middle income populations. Finally, Columbia, Reston and the two federally assisted new communities—Jonathan and Park Forest South—epitomize the modern new community concept. Their development has been marked by the attainment of racial and economic integration, environmental preservation and conservation, careful attention to high quality urban design and planning for a broad range of community facilities and services.

Chapter 3

New Communities, Health, and Health Care

Planned new communities have been regarded as ideal settings in which to develop better ways of solving human problems, including the provision of health care. Some definitions of the term new community are based on the extent of services offered. According to Robert Weaver (1964, p. 368), "the new community differs from the usual subdivision by reason of the fact that it is planned so as to provide within its limits more of the amenities and services required for daily living." To the extent that self-sufficiency is an objective of new community development, planning must include provisions for medical and health care facilities.

In 1967 Harold Herman and Michael I. Joroff emphasized the opportunities offered by new communities to integrate medical facilities with other community services as a means of encouraging their use. Planners involved in the Minnesota Experimental City Project (1969) have described extensive possibilities for innovations in health care in a planned community. A local government viewpoint has been expressed by Gabrielle Pryor, former mayor of the new community of Irvine, who noted, "If we as a city are really planning a 'New Town' then health care has to be a significant part of that effort" (*Irvine World News*, June 21, 1973).

Other writers, however, have expressed more limited expectations for health care in new communities. William Alonso (1969) dismissed as romantic the notion of self-contained new communities which supply all basic services to their residents. Edward P. Eichler and Bernard Norwitch (1970) pointed out that new communities in America are a means of developing the outskirts of metropolitan areas and have little potential for bringing about new solutions for old problems. According to Randall W. Scott (1971, p. 17), "a new town cannot be expected to provide all possible services for its populace, but rather, only those which are appropriate to its size and economic character." Thus, Marshall Kaplan (1973, p. 134), in describing the assumptions upon which the new community of Flower Mound, Texas would be planned, indicated that its young and affluent residents could be expected to be healthy, covered by insurance, and "willing to travel reasonably lengthy distances to find a doctor or dentist they like."

Among existing new communities, there have been relatively few published reports of activity in the field of health care, either in the United States or abroad. An exception is Greenbelt, Maryland which in the 1940s offered public health services, a small local hospital and a health association which sponsored a prepaid health program (see Clarence S. Stein 1957). Greenbelt's prepaid program foreshadowed the medical plan in Columbia, Maryland; but, as discussed later in this book, Columbia's extensive involvement in health care is an exception among modern new communities. Also, although federally assisted new communities have made extensive commitments for comprehensive health planning,[a] Mields (1973, p. 87) has noted that, "developers' most visible role in health services so far has been the reservation of land and space for facilities." Even in Britain and Scandinavia, with their well-established new communities programs, health and social services are not provided through new community planning, but through national programs of welfare and health care. As a result, health services are generally unavailable in the early stages of new community development (see Neil C. Sandberg 1973, p. 71).

In spite of this picture of varied expectations and unfulfilled promise, there appear to be a number of benefits that can be realized from a comprehensive approach to health care in new communities. For example, the Task Force on Organization of Community Health Services (1967, p. 15) called for the development of local mechanisms to assess health needs and determine objectives, "because it is in the local community that the citizen both encounters the threats to his health and seeks the protection and services he requires." The Na-

---

[a]Applicants for assistance under the federal new communities program have been required to provide ". . . a description of actions taken or to be taken to make maximum use of local, State and Federal assistance in establishing a health care system, including preventive medicine and health maintenance organizations; description of actions taken or proposed to be taken to meet special needs of low and moderate income residents and the elderly; description of innovations to be undertaken to improve health care and reduce cost" (U.S. Department of Housing and Urban Development 1972, p. 18).

tional Commission on Community Health Services (1966, p. 210) recommended legislation "to require all programs related to physical city planning . . . to provide for healthful distribution of population, protection from hazardous, noisy and unaesthetic environments [and for] the availability and accessibility of comprehensive health and welfare services." Paul Meadows (1970) has argued that a guiding principle for public health must be the assignment of power to the smallest unit consistent with a problem.

In 1948 the American Public Health Association developed standards for neighborhood planning which suggested that physicians, dentists and decentralized public health services be located within residential neighborhoods. Emphasis on the placement of health resources in the community or neighborhood reflects the desirability of readily available sources of care. What people want, according to Robert M. Heyssel (1971c, p. 137) is "guaranteed accessibility to medical care in time of need." However, planning for health care on a local level is not limited to questions of accessibility. The community approach may also contribute solutions to many health care problems, including adequacy of care, efficiency of delivery, comprehensiveness of services, consumer participation in health care planning and the development of health maintenance organizations.

The extent to which the benefits of community-based health care actually have been realized in new community development is examined in the following chapters which focus on physicians' services (Chapter 4), hospital care and ambulance service (Chapter 5), social services and public health facilities (Chapter 6), health insurance and health maintenance programs (Chapter 7), health care for target populations (Chapter 8) and residents' and professionals' overall evaluations of new community health care facilities and services (Chapter 9). As an introduction to these subjects, the remainder of this chapter offers three perspectives on health care in new communities. The first is health professionals' perceptions of health and health care problems in American new communities. Next, new community residents' orientations to health and the health care system are examined. The chapter concludes by describing new community developers' approaches to health care and health professionals' evaluations of the adequacy of developer activities in the health care field.

THE HEALTH CARE PROBLEMS
OF NEW COMMUNITIES

Health professionals serving each of the fifteen new communities studied were asked what they felt were the most important health or health-related problems facing the community. The question was stated in as broad a manner as possible in order not to limit the respondents to any particular type of concern. Five types of responses were elicited: (1) personal health and social difficulties; (2) unfavorable environmental conditions; (3) characteristics of the community population that produced problems; (4) inadequacies in facilities and services; and (5) problems of planning for health care. Many of the issues brought out in response to this question will be discussed in greater detail in the following chapters. The purpose of the present discussion is to provide an overview of the kinds of problems professionals regarded as most pressing.

Among the personal health and social difficulties mentioned were chronic disorders, venereal disease, lack of physical exercise and divorce. But by far the most common problems discussed were alcoholism, drug abuse and feelings of stress or anxiety. These problems were mentioned in numerous communities, both new and conventional, and were noted most often by county health officials. The problems, stated the officials, are related to one another and can be characterized in terms of a suburban malaise. For example, Elk Grove Village was seen as suffering from an "upper striving syndrome," which resulted from the fact that "people see magic in the suburbs, but to maintain their life style the men have to get extra jobs, [and] women work, making themselves less available to their families and thereby producing family stresses."[b] A health official in Palm Beach County believed that these problems are typical of upper middle class communities such as North Palm Beach.

While problems of stress and anxiety appear to be characteristic of suburbs generally, two Columbia health professionals indicated that there are special difficulties in a new community setting. Columbia was said to face greater than usual needs for primary psychiatric care as "a result of the special anxieties involved in pulling up roots and moving to an entirely new place." Columbia was seen to have too many "people searching for a task," and to have attracted too many people who have had difficulties adjusting elsewhere. In addition, it was felt that problems were compounded because the whole community experienced the stresses of moving at virtually the same time.

Environmental problems, mentioned almost exclusively in the California new and conventional communities, included air, water and noise pollution and the high incidence of traffic and other accidents.

[b]To preserve anonymity guaranteed respondents, quotations and paraphrases of health professionals' comments are not cited in this book. Interviews are on file at the Center for Urban and Regional Studies, The University of North Carolina at Chapel Hill.

A wide range of characteristics of community residents was cited as the basis for health care problems. The presence of children, elderly people and low- or moderate-income persons created special needs for doctors and special services in various communities. Several health professionals felt that an educated population with high expectations for the community may make excessive demands for care. However, others lamented that people lacked knowledge either of available health services or of their own health needs. The transient nature of the population was said to make it difficult to provide services. Problems of racial and economic integration were cited as sources of stress in one new community. In others, health professionals felt that the population was growing too rapidly for services to keep up with residents' health care needs.

A large majority of the comments of professionals were related to inadequacies in health care facilities, services and personnel. A number of their observations were of a general nature: available services were inadequate; residents were experiencing too much difficulty in obtaining care, especially primary health care; or services were too fragmented. To several professionals, the problem was the lack of an organized system of care. For example, according to one Columbia professional, the health care system should consist of "good, accessible primary health care with adequate delivery and reasonable cost, including physicians, supportive personnel and facilities."

However, most professionals' comments had to do with specific problems, and often a series of needs was enumerated. Reston's needs, for example, were said to include a hospital, nursing home beds, the development of a health delivery system not based on the hospital and a comprehensive health needs study for the county. Among the specific facilities mentioned, the greatest needs were for hospitals, emergency care facilities and nursing home and convalescent care facilities. Recommendations for these facilities came from all types of health professionals in both the new and conventional communities. Comments about hospitals included references to specific types of facilities, including inpatient, ambulatory care, intensive care, obstetrics wards and pediatrics wards. It was also felt in some cases that hospitals in the area were of the wrong kind (as in Laguna Niguel, where a large central facility was regarded as preferable to numerous smaller ones); or were poorly distributed (as in Cincinnati, leaving Forest Park on the excluded fringe of the service area); or that there were too many hospitals or hospital beds in the area (as in Sharpstown).

Other comments about the absence of facilities included physicians' office space (Columbia, Elk Grove Village), a mental health facility (Columbia) and public health facilities (Reston and North Palm Beach). Reference was also made to the effect on health care of the absence of certain nonhealth facilities, particularly those for public transportation. References either to problems in obtaining care or to increasing feelings of isolation were recorded in Park Forest, Elk Grove Village and Valencia.

Five types of health care service needs were mentioned frequently: (1) home health care; (2) mental health and psychiatric care; (3) preventive medicine; (4) emergency services; and (5) services and financial arrangements for low- and moderate-income people. Health professionals in several communities also commented on the need for expanded health department activities and for programs for the elderly. County health officials noted problems in coordination among agencies in several communities, and visiting nurses alluded to inadequate mechanisms for information and referral. "The main problem facing the whole area has to do with the lack of referral, lack of coordination and lack of effective delivery rather than lack of facilities," stated a visiting nurse official in Fairfax County (which contains Reston).

Numerous comments were made about the need for additional health personnel and almost all of them referred to general practitioners or internists. The problem was not limited to the lack of physicians, but included the "unnecessary difficulty in seeing a doctor at the time and place desired." Occasional references were also made in these interviews to the need for additional dentists, pediatricians, otolaryngologists, psychiatrists and supportive personnel for hospitals.

In spite of the preponderance of mentions regarding services and facilities, there was relatively little concern voiced over the cost of these services and facilities. Possibly this was due to the fact that the high cost of care is not limited to new communities. The lack of mention of cost may also reflect the feeling that most people living in new communities can pay their own way. Such a view is not inconsistent with the feelings expressed about services and financial arrangements for lower income people, who cannot pay their own way.

There was also surprisingly little concern expressed about problems in health care planning, in view of the fact that many of the sample communities are planned new communities with, according to many health professionals, too few health resources. Most of the comments relating to planning referred to problems of communiication and coordination among various agencies with planning responsibilities. Some feeling was expressed for more areawide planning as, for example, by professionals who were serving Forest Park and North Palm Beach, but there was also a lack of agreement as to the proper functions of regional planning. For example, a Laguna Niguel health professional criticized a comprehensive health planning council as being too permissive, thereby allowing hospital overbedding, while a professional in Reston faulted the county hospital authority as being too traditional and omnipresent, thereby stifling experimentation.

Overall, professionals seemed most concerned about basic health resources, such as primary care physicians, emergency services and hospitals rather than about problems of the overall health care system or issues such as referral, coordination, methods of delivery or planning. Health care professionals were interested primarily in immediate needs close to home. In outlying newly developed communities, whether planned or unplanned, these concerns are particularly acute.

RESIDENTS' ATTITUDES TOWARD HEALTH AND HEALTH CARE

Professionals' concerns for community-based health care contrasted sharply with new community residents' general lack of interest in health care matters. Residents' orientations to health and health care were examined from four perspectives. These included: (1) residents' assessments of the state of their own health; (2) the importance they attached to the availability of health and medical services in their decisions to move to new and conventional communities; (3) perceptions of health care facilities and services as an aspect of overall community livability and, conversely, as a community problem; and (4) residents' views on the importance of personal health as an aspect of their quality of life.

A basic factor underlying new and conventional community residents' orientations to health and health care was their general satisfaction with their own health. Residents were asked to rate their satisfaction with the status of their health on a seven-point scale ranging from "completely satisfied" to "completely dissatisfied." As shown in Table 3-1, 88 percent of the nonfederally assisted new community and 84 percent of the paired conventional community respondents rated their health in the top three categories (completely satisfied and satisfied). These results are similar to those reported by Angus Campbell, Phillip E. Coverse and Willard L. Rodgers (1976, p. 63), who found that 81 percent of a 1971 national cross-section sample of respondents were satisfied with their health.

Table 3–1.   Residents' Perspectives on Health and Health Care *(percentage distribution of respondents)*

Residents' Perspectives	Nonfederally Assisted New and Conventional Communities		Federally Assisted New and Conventional Communities			
	Thirteen New Communities	Thirteen Conventional Communities	Jonathan	Chanhassen	Park Forest South	Richton Park
Evaluation of Personal Health Status[a]						
Completely satisfied (1)	50[f]	45	52	49	49	53
Satisfied (2–3)	38	39	42	44	39	35
Neutral or dissatisfied (4–7)	12	15	6	7	12	12
Moved to Community Because of Health and Medical Services[b]						
Yes	2	1	1	0	0	0
No	98	99	99	100	100	100
Mentioned Health Care Facilities and Services as a Reason for Rating Community Livability Highly[c]						
Yes	2	1	3	2	1	0
No	98	99	97	98	99	100
Mentioned Health Care Facilities and Services as a Community Problem[d]						
Yes	4	5	0	3	5	4
No	96	95	100	97	95	96

Mentioned Personal Health Status as a Component of the Quality of Life[e]

Yes	15	14	9	12	15	17
No	85	86	91	88	85	83
Sample size	2838	1321	207	100	200	101

[a]*Question:* Now we have some questions about your health and health care. Of course, most people get sick now and then, but overall, how satisfied are you with your own health? Here is a card I'd like you to use to answer this question. Completely Satisfied 1 2 3 4 5 6 7 Completely Dissatisfied. Responses of "1" were classified as completely satisfied; responses of "2" or "3" as satisfied; and responses of "4" through "7" as neutral or dissatisfied.

[b]*Question:* Here is a list of things that people often consider when they move. Thinking of what attracted you to this place, could you tell me which *three* of these factors were most important in your (family's) decision to move to this community (originally)? Health and medical services was among a list of nineteen factors respondents were asked to select from.

[c]*Question:* I'd like to ask you how you feel now about this area as a place to live—I mean the area outlined on the map. From your own personal point of view, would you rate this area as an excellent place to live, good, average, below average, or poor?

[d]*Question:* In your opinion, what are the most important issues or problems facing the *community as a whole* at the present time? Anything else?

[e]*Question:* There's quite a bit of talk these days about the overall "quality" of people's lives. What does the phrase "quality of life" mean to you—that is, what would you say are the main things the overall "quality" of your own life depends on? Anything else?

[f]Statistically significant difference between new and conventional communities at the 0.05 level of confidence.

Although individuals' self-reports of their health status in response to a single question is simplistic, particularly when compared with the detailed lists of specific symptoms that are commonly used in epidemiological research, the major demographic variations in responses corresponded to those reported from more intensive studies. For example, the proportion of new community residents who were satisfied (responses of one, two or three on the seven-point scale) with their health was very high among respondents who were under 50 years of age (89 percent), but dropped steadily thereafter and was less than 80 percent among those 65 years of age or older. Ninety percent of the respondents with annual family incomes of $15,000 or more were satisfied with their health versus 86 percent of those with incomes between $10,000 and $15,000 and only 79 percent of those with incomes of less than $10,000. These age and income patterns are similar to those reported by the Health Interview Survey of the United States Public Health Service.[c]

Given the generally high levels of satisfaction with personal health among new and conventional community residents, it may well be that health and health care are taken for granted by a considerable majority of the population. For example, very few residents reported that the availability of health and medical services was an important factor in their decision to move to a new or conventional community (see Table 3-1). Even in Sharpstown, which had an extensive array of health care facilities and services, only 5 percent of the respondents mentioned them as an important factor in their selection of a home in the community. Among various segments of the population, only elderly households indicated greater than average interest in health and medical services in their decision to move to a new community. However, even among this group of residents health and medical services were mentioned by only 9 percent and ranked thirteenth among the factors they said were important in their selection of a home in a new community.

New and conventional community residents were asked to rate the overall livability of their communities. Ninety percent of the new community respondents and 86 percent of those living in the conventional communities said that their community was an excellent or good place to live. When they were asked their reasons for rating community livability highly, however, very few respondents (2 per-

---

[c]In contrast with the Health Interview Survey data, new community women were less satisfied with their health than were men (84 percent vs. 91 percent). However, other surveys, including Campbell, Converse and Rodgers (1976, p. 354) and Belloc, Reslaw and Hochstim (1971), have also found that women report more problems with their health than men.

cent and 1 percent) mentioned the availability of health care facilities and services. Later in the interview, respondents were asked to name the most important issues or problems facing their communities. In contrast with the grave concerns expressed by health professionals, inadequacies in health care facilities and services were mentioned by only 4 percent of the new community respondents and 5 percent of those living in the paired conventional communities.[d] In addition, only 3 percent of the new community respondents indicated that the provision of more health care facilities and services would be a major factor in making their communities better places in which to live.

New community residents' tendency to take health and health care for granted is further indicated by the factors they mentioned as contributors to their quality of life. At the start of the interview, respondents were asked: "There's quite a bit of talk these days about the overall 'quality' of people's lives. What does the phrase 'quality of life' mean to you—that is, what would you say are the main things the overall 'quality' of your own life depend on?" The most frequently mentioned contributor to the quality of life was economic security. Beyond that, family life, personal strengths (such as honesty, fortitude and intelligence), and friendships were mentioned by over 20 percent of the respondents. Surprisingly, being in good health was mentioned by only 15 percent of the new community respondents and ranked ninth among the factors that were cited as contributors to the quality of life.[e]

Two indirect approaches were used to provide additional perspectives on the relationship between health, health care and residents' perceptions of their quality of life. First, residents were asked whether the move to a new community had improved the quality of their lives, made it worse or hadn't made much difference. Residents were also asked whether various attributes of their communities, including health and medical services, were better, about the same, or not as good as in the communities from which they had moved. The

[d]Isolated Lake Havasu City was the only new community in which more than 10 percent of the respondents cited health care facilities and services as an important issue or problem. The lack of health care resources was the most frequently mentioned problem (34 percent of the respondents), but it was probably alleviated by the subsequent construction of two hospitals in the community.

[e]The proportion of nonfederally assisted new community respondents who mentioned various factors as contributors to their quality of life were: economic security (34 percent); family life (27 percent); personal strengths (23 percent); social relationships (20 percent); physical environment (18 percent); contentment/well-being/happiness (17 percent); job satisfaction (16 percent); leisure activities (16 percent); personal health (15 percent); religious values (11 percent); being a good parent (10 percent); quality and accessibility of community facilities (8 percent); and housing (8 percent).

statistical association between these two indicators provides an indirect measure of the contribution of health care services to residents' quality of life. Although a perceived improvement in health and medical care services was positively associated with perceived improvement in the quality of life ($r = .11$), the strength of the relationship was not strong, ranking eleventh in a univariate analysis and tied for ninth in a multivariate analysis of factors contributing to perceived improvements in the quality of life after moving. Community attributes that explained more of the variance in perceived improvements in the quality of life included perceived improvements in the type of people living in the neighborhood, recreational facilities, neighborhood appearance, layout and space of dwelling and lot, opportunities for participation in community life, proximity to the natural environment, convenience to work and the quality of home construction.

The second indirect approach focused on a global assessment of respondents' personal well-being at the time they were interviewed. New community residents were asked: "We have talked about various parts of your life; now I want to ask you about your life as a whole. How satisfied are you with your life as a whole these days?" Responses were measured on a seven-point scale, from completely satisfied to completely dissatisfied. In addition to this global measure, respondents were asked about their satisfaction with a series of life domains, including the status of their own health (see above). The statistical association between satisfaction with health and satisfaction with life as a whole provides another indirect indication of the role of health in subjective perceptions of the quality of life. As expected, there was a positive correlation ($r = .28$) between new community respondents' satisfaction with the status of their health and satisfaction with their life as a whole. However, in comparison with their satisfaction with other life domains, respondents' satisfaction with health explained relatively little of the variance in overall life satisfaction. Among ten life domains, satisfaction with health ranked seventh in the strength of its univariate association with respondents' overall life satisfaction and sixth in terms of its beta coefficient in a multiple regression analysis. More strongly associated with overall life satisfaction in the multivariate analysis were respondents' satisfaction with their standard of living, use of leisure time, marriage, job and family life. Life domains that were less important than health included respondents' evaluations of their dwelling units, neighborhoods and communities and their satisfaction with housework.[f]

[f]The Campbell, Converse and Rodgers (1976, p. 76) study of the quality of American life reported similar results. Based on a 1971 national cross-section

The preceding analysis was carried out on the total sample of non-federally assisted new community residents. As noted above, new community residents tended to be highly satisfied with their health and to be relatively unconcerned with health care matters. Nevertheless, various groups of residents, particularly the elderly and lower income persons, were more likely than others to indicate health problems and to be concerned about the availability of health and medical care services. This raises the question of whether health was also more important to some residents' satisfaction with their lives than to others. To check out this possibility, a total of fourteen demographic subgroups were examined with separate correlation and regression analyses. For most groups, including those based on sex, race, marital status and education, health continued to be only moderately associated with overall life satisfaction. Again, however, health was more important to elderly and lower income residents. The correlation between satisfaction with health and satisfaction with life as a whole was $r = .42$ for persons age 65 and older and $r = .35$ for persons with annual family incomes of less than $10,000. In the multiple regression equations developed to explain residents' overall satisfaction with their lives, health ranked third for the elderly behind satisfaction with the use of their leisure time and family life. In the case of lower income residents, it ranked fourth behind satisfaction with family life, the job and the dwelling unit.

DEVELOPER APPROACHES TO HEALTH CARE

New community developers' approaches to community-based health care have been shaped by several major considerations. As the builders of balanced and, to some extent, self-contained residential settlements, developers usually have been expected to attend to the health care needs of their residents.[g] Working against developer involvement, however, has been the residents' general lack of interest in health care matters. As discussed above, households rarely moved to new communities because of health and medical care facilities and

---

sample of respondents, satisfaction with personal health ranked fourteenth among seventeen variables in explaining the variance in an index of well-being. The most important life domains in explaining respondents' assessments of their well-being were nonworking activities, family life, standard of living, work, marriage, savings and investments, friendships, housing and place of residence.

[g]The most explicit statement of this expectation is the regulations governing the federal new communities assistance program. As noted earlier in this chapter, developers participating in the program are required to describe proposed actions to establish a health care system and to give particular attention to the needs of low- and moderate-income residents and the elderly.

services, even when they were readily available. Health care was a relatively insignificant aspect of either their quality of life or the factors residents felt were important in making their communities good places to live. What is more, few residents cited health care as a major community problem. Thus, there has been little consumer demand for major developer involvement in the health care field. In addition, as real estate entrepreneurs, new community developers are not necessarily the most appropriate agents to engage in the planning and provision of community health care facilities and services. Health care is not their area of expertise and there has been little incentive in terms of consumers' market behavior to devote company staff time and funds to community health care.

Given these conflicting forces, it is not surprising that new community developers varied in their approaches to health care. In a few new communities, including Park Forest, North Palm Beach and Sharpstown, developers left community health care entirely to the entrepreneurial instincts of doctors and surrounding institutions. Because the developers had assembled lucrative markets, health care providers were responsive to the need for health care in North Palm Beach and Sharpstown. These communities ranked first and second in terms of the number of general practitioners per capita (see Chapter 4). Developer indifference, however, was not always counterbalanced by the initiative of doctors and other health care providers. Although Park Forest was the oldest new community studied and had ample time to attract fee-for-service practitioners, it ranked well below both state and regional averages of physicians per capita.

Since private initiative could not always be counted upon to meet a new community's needs for health care services, a number of developers took positive actions to encourage doctors to locate in their communities. For example, doctors were actively recruited by the developers of Forest Park and Lake Havasu City; in the latter case, the developer subsidized the community's first doctor until his practice was well established. In other new communities, such as Reston, Elk Grove Village, Foster City, Westlake Village, Irvine and Laguna Niguel, developers built or cooperated in the construction of medical office buildings and clinics that provided attractive space for fee-for-service medical practitioners.

A number of developers also became actively involved in community hospital projects, although their efforts were sometimes not successful. The Centex Corporation donated ten acres (of a 40-acre site) for the Alexian Brothers Hospital in Elk Grove Village. The Newhall Land and Farming Company donated land and staff time to aid in the planning and construction of the $6.5 million Henry Mayo

Newhall Memorial Hospital in Valencia. This nonprofit institution provides 100 beds and an adjacent medical services complex. In Westlake Village, the American-Hawaiian Steamship Company helped a local group secure licensing approval for a proprietary community hospital in the face of strong opposition from surrounding hospitals. Robert P. McCulloch donated land for two community hospitals in Lake Havasu City and attempted to resolve conflicts between competing groups which led to the eventual construction of both hospitals.

At Irvine the developer has worked for a number of years to plan and secure approval of a 133-acre hospital and medical center complex to be operated by the Western World Medical Foundation of Newport Beach. To facilitate the lowest possible cost for medical care, The Irvine Company agreed to donate an eighteen-acre site for a 162-bed hospital and to sell the remainder of the acreage for the $400 million medical complex at residential land price levels (one-fifth of the price of the proposed site in alternative industrial land uses). Profits from the medical complex were to be used by the foundation to increase hospital services and reduce its operating costs. However, this ambitious undertaking has been stalled by a series of controversies involving nearby hospitals and the medical school at the University of California at Irvine.

Gulf-Reston, Inc. also actively supported an ill-fated community hospital proposal. In this case, a 125-bed general hospital to be built and operated by a proprietary corporation, Beverly Enterprises, was denied state certification when it was opposed by the Reston Community Association, Fairfax County Hospital Association and a nearby county. The issues involved in this and other new community hospital proposals are discussed in Chapter 5.

In contrast with the *ad hoc* approaches to health care that characterized most new community development projects, Columbia's developer and the developers of the two federally assisted new communities, Jonathan and Park Forest South, pursued comprehensive approaches to community-based health care.

Health planners were among the diverse group of professionals whose ideas helped give direction to Columbia's growth, and at an early stage of the planning process a relationship was formed with the Johns Hopkins Medical Institutions of Baltimore. That relationship led to the development of the Columbia Medical Plan, a comprehensive prepaid group practice medical program organized and planned by The Johns Hopkins University, The Johns Hopkins Hospital and Connecticut General Life Insurance Company. The purpose of the program, which commenced operation less than two years afters Columbia's opening, is to make available quality medical care at reasonable cost and to insure the accessibility of and continuity of care 24 hours a day.[h]

The Rouse Company not only gave enthusiastic support to the plan—by providing space for its clinic, donating land for the Howard County General Hospital (formerly the Columbia Medical Center) and providing assistance in problems of zoning—but initially also discouraged competing forms of medical practice in the community by not providing office space designed for fee-for-service physicians. However, this policy changed, in part because less than half of Columbia's population enrolled in the group practice medical plan. Office space was made available in the village centers for private physicians, and The Rouse Company took an interest in projects outside the medical plan, such as community mental health and the location of a county health office and a nursing home in Columbia.

Jonathan's and Park Forest South's project agreements with the federal government spelled out an extensive range of developer obligations to insure that residents' health care needs be met. The Project Agreement between the Jonathan Development Corporation and the Department of Housing and Urban Development (1970) required that the developer "provide a framework for facilities for preventive and remedial medical services with easy access for all residents to physicians' offices for regular medical attention." The specific obligations of the developer included providing information to residents on existing health care resources, investigating the possibility of establishing a community-wide health plan, selling or leasing office space for clinic use and attracting appropriate medical facilities and supporting personnel. The plan for Jonathan's ultimate development envisioned a general hospital located in the town center and medical facilities in each of its village centers.

The Park Forest South Development Company's Project Agreement with the Department of Housing and Urban Development (1971) committed the company to the development of a comprehensive system of care based on a new hospital, community health cen-

[h]Further information on the operation of the Columbia Medical Plan is provided in Chapter 7. Prepaid group practice medical plans were active in two other communities, but in each case their availability was not a result of developer initiatives. Over 20 percent of the Foster City respondents were members of the Kaiser Foundation Health Plan, which had a clinic and hospital in nearby Redwood City. Beginning in the spring of 1974, Reston residents could participate in the Georgetown University Community Health Plan through membership in the Reston Community Association. The University operated the Reston-Georgetown Medical Center out of offices located in Reston's Hunters Woods Village Center.

ters and a comprehensive insurance plan for residents. Among the specific responsibilities of the developer were the donation of land for hospital construction, building and leasing of office space and the encouragement of community participation in health planning. The developer was also required to provide leadership in the planning of community health programs (possibly including a prepaid insurance plan), in the use of cable television and in the establishment of a centralized system of medical record keeping. When necessary, the developer was to "reserve land" and use his "best efforts" to locate in the community various health care resources, such as convalescent homes or extended care facilities.

Although their project agreements required extensive commitments to health care, the developers of Jonathan and Park Forest South had to contend with a number of problems in organizing health care systems. One of the most basic difficulties was the lack of adequate supporting populations for a number of health care services. The problem of acquiring health care services before an adequate population was present was resolved in Jonathan by renting space in the first village center for the establishment of a satellite branch of the Lakeview Clinic (group practice), which had its headquarters in the nearby city of Waconia. Future difficulties could be expected, however, when Jonathan attempted to implement its proposal for a community hospital. The administrators of the two hospitals that were serving Jonathan—St. Francis Hospital in Shakopee and Ridgeview Hospital in Waconia—indicated that their facilities would adequately serve Jonathan and that they would strongly oppose a new hospital. In addition, as of 1973 detailed attention had not been given to other forms of health care that might be needed in the community. Although Jonathan's project agreement spoke of a community-wide plan for health services and preventive medicine, such planning was not expected to get under way for a couple of years.

In contrast to Jonathan's pragmatic approach to health care, but lack of detailed planning, health care planning occupied a central role in the development of Park Forest South. A key feature of Park Forest South's proposed health care system was to be a 180-bed, short-term general hospital with related mental health and ambulatory care facilities and services. After a number of years of discussion with potential hospital sponsors, Lewis Manilow secured a commitment from Rush-Presbyterian-St. Lukes Medical Center of Chicago to own and operate a branch hospital in Park Forest South and to extend the Center's prepaid comprehensive health plan to the community. In July 1972 plans for the construction of the proposed hospital and medical center in Park Forest South were announced to the public and target completion dates of 1975 for the first phase medical center and early 1976 for the entire hospital complex were established.

Although the developer donated 40 acres of the proposed hospital site and Rush-Presbyterian-St. Lukes Medical Center agreed to underwrite approximately $8 million in construction costs, Hill-Burton funds were needed to finance the remaining portion of the $10,470,000 cost of the hospital. To be eligible for the federal funds, approval of the Park Forest South hospital had to be obtained from the Will-Grundy-Kankakee Comprehensive Health Planning Council located in Joliet, the county seat of Will County. An application was submitted in October 1972 and eleven months later, in September 1973, the proposed hospital was rejected by the Health Planning Council on the grounds that a hospital was not needed in Park Forest South. Since Medicare, Medicaid and Blue Cross–Blue Shield coverage would not be extended to the hospital without the approval of the regional health planning council, the decision effectively removed the kingpin of Park Forest South's health plan. As an interim solution to the new community's health care needs, Rush-Presbyterian-St. Lukes proposed to open a limited medical service center on the first floor of an apartment building in Park Forest South, while it continued to fight for approval of the proposed hospital project.

Health care professionals serving the new communities were asked whether they felt adequate attention had been given to the provision of health care services, facilities and programs in new community planning. In five nonfederally assisted new communities—Elk Grove Village, Lake Havasu City, Park Forest, Valencia and Westlake Village—and both federally assisted communities a majority of the professionals thought initial health care planning was sufficient.

In eight other new communities, however, health professionals were more critical of the developers' attention to planning. In many cases, including Forest Park, Laguna Niguel, North Palm Beach and Sharpstown, professionals felt consideration of health care had been mostly lacking in initial community plans, though this was not always viewed as a problem. In the Sharpstown area some professionals felt health care should be left to private initiative and the working of the free enterprise system. In the case of Forest Park, it was argued that planning was a regional concern and the community was too small an area to address citizens' health care needs.

In a number of cases health care professionals acknowledged specific developer efforts to secure some health care resources, but felt that planning for a wide range of community health care needs had been ignored. For example, a private physicians' group in Columbia thought that The Rouse Company had been too zealous in promoting the Columbia Medical Plan, to the detriment of other forms of care. Columbia's developer was censured by other professionals for not devoting enough resources to establishing an effective social service structure and for giving only lip service to community mental health needs. Gulf-Reston, Inc. was said to have taken a "passive reactionary" stance toward health care; that is, the developer was said to react to outside proposals for meeting various community health care needs, but not to initiate such proposals. The Irvine Company's efforts to provide medical office space and its support of the Western World Medical Foundation hospital proposal were acknowledged. Nevertheless, some professional respondents were critical of the timing of health resources provision, while others expressed concern over the proposed hospital's effect on the chronic overbedding problem which was mounting in Orange County.

Although health care professionals were sometimes critical of developers' efforts in the health care field, the problems of new community health care planning cannot be attributed solely to developers' shortcomings. The highly decentralized, free-enterprise character of health care delivery in the United States discourages preplanning at the community level. Regional health planning councils, where they existed, were of little help to developers in assessing community health care needs and organizing a program of health care services. County public health agencies lacked the funds, and often the inclination, to engage in health care planning at the community level. Medical societies were mostly concerned with the placement of doctors and were not in a position to offer comprehensive advice about health services. Existing health care institutions, such as hospitals, were sometimes interested in establishing branches in new communities, but more often than not their chief concern was in protecting the integrity of their service areas by discouraging the provision of additional and competing hospital facilities. In sum, institutions that could promote health care planning at the community level were almost completely absent in the vicinity of many of the new communities studied. When this situation was combined with developers' natural disinclination to become deeply involved in subjects with which they were not familiar, the low level of attention to comprehesive community health care planning should not be surprising.

 *Chapter 4*

Physicians' Services

Most new community residents' basic point of contact with the health care delivery system comes when they seek the services of a physician or a dentist. The availability of doctors in a community is one indicator of the adequacy of primary care. Another is residents' actual health care seeking behavior—the distances they traveled to secure primary care, the number of times they thought they needed care but did not seek help and their rate of use of and satisfaction with their personal doctors. This chapter examines physicians' services in the new and conventional communities, including factors that influenced the availability of services, professionals' perceptions of the need for more primary care, and accessibility and other factors that influenced residents' utilization of medical services.

AVAILABILITY OF MEDICAL PRACTITIONERS

The ratio of primary-care physicians to population has commonly been used to gauge the adequacy of health care available to a region or community. According to H.K. Schonfield, J.F. Heston and I.S. Falk (1972), for example, there is a need for 133 primary care physicians (general practitioners, internists and pediatricians) per 100,000 population. This is far above the national average of physician availability, which in 1970 stood at 81.7 primary care physicians (includ-

ing osteopaths) per 100,000 population (see National Center for
Health Statistics 1971, pp. 147—155).[a]

As shown in Table 4—1, most new communities met neither of
these standards. The thirteen nonfederally assisted new communities had an average of 68.2 primary care physicians per 100,000
population, while the paired conventional communities had 63.3 per
100,000 population. Only North Palm Beach and Sharpstown had
more than 133 primary care physicians per 100,000 population.
These two new communities, together with Westlake Village and
Laguna Niguel, exceeded the national average of primary care physician availability. In contrast, four nonfederally assisted new communities—Irvine, Valencia, Foster City and Forest Park—had fewer than
one-fourth the national average of physicians per 100,000 population. Physician availability in Jonathan was similar to the average of
the more mature nonfederally assisted communities, but Park Forest
South had no practicing physicians at the time of the field survey in
the spring of 1973. The conventional communities had also had difficulty attracting primary care physicians. Only four of these communities exceeded the national average, although six had more primary
care physicians per capita than their paired new communities. As a
whole, the conventional communities exceeded the national average
of 47.3 dentists per 100,000 population, while the new communities
were somewhat below the national average (see National Center for
Health Statistics 1971, p. 75).

In terms of the location of primary care, new and conventional
community residents both tended to live within short distances of
the nearest primary care physician. Among the nonfederally assisted
new communities, the median road distance from the homes of
household survey respondents to the nearest general practitioner was
just over a mile (6800 feet). The conventional community respondents had to travel only slightly farther (8800 feet). Table 4—2 com-
pares the accessibility of physicians in each new community with its
paired conventional community. For seven of the thirteen paired
comparisons (nonfederally assisted new communities), the new community residents tended to live closer to a general practitioner. Also,
new community residents were significantly more likely to have a

---

[a]Although physician to population ratios often have been used to gauge one
aspect of the "health care crisis," some critics dispute their value. Boris Senior
and Beverly A. Smith (1972), for example, have pointed out that most studies
using physicians per population ratios have failed to show relationships between
such ratios and delivery of care. There is no clear relationship, for example, between these ratios and mortality rates. The present study used physician-popula-
tion ratios as a gross measure of the availability of a basic health resource, but
the use of the measure is not meant to suggest that this ratio is wholly indicative
of the overall adequacy of care.

Table 4–1. Primary Care Physicians and Dentists Practicing in New and Conventional Communities, Spring 1973

	Per 100,000 Population	
New and Conventional Communities	*Physicians[a]*	*Dentists*
Nonfederally Assisted New and Paired Conventional Communities		
Thirteen New Communities	68.2	45.3
Thirteen Conventional Communities	63.3	58.0
New and Paired Conventional Communities		
Columbia (NC)	66.3	103.6
Norbeck-Wheaton (CC)	40.0	0.0
Elk Grove Village (NC)	65.6	30.6
Schaumburg (CC)	75.5	75.5
Forest Park (NC)	17.6	11.8
Sharonville (CC)	45.5	27.3
Foster City (NC)	13.3	53.3
West San Mateo (CC)	106.3	124.1
Irvine (NC)	15.0	20.0
Fountain Valley (CC)	38.1	10.0
Laguna Niguel (NC)	94.1	47.1
Dana Point (CC)	30.3	0.0
Lake Havasu City (NC)	58.8	124.1
Kingman (CC)	136.8	23.5
North Palm Beach (NC)	232.9	104.4
Tequesta (CC)	232.9	77.6
Park Forest (NC)	49.0	32.6
Lansing (CC)	19.4	50.4
Reston (NC)	60.0	25.0
West Springfield (CC)	37.5	17.3
Sharpstown (NC)	137.5	41.7
Southwest Houston (CC)	20.0	60.0
Valencia (NC)	0.0	0.0
Bouquet Canyon (CC)	0.0	0.0
Westlake Village (NC)	84.6	84.6
Agoura–Malibu Junction (CC)	120.0	0.0
Federally Assisted New and Paired Conventional Communities		
Jonathan (NC)	66.1	198.3
Chanhassen (CC)	0.0	19.8
Park Forest South (NC)	0.0	0.0
Richton Park (CC)	62.6	271.6

NC = New Community   CC = Conventional Community
[a]Includes general practitioners, internists, osteopaths, pediatricians and obstetrician-gynecologists.

Table 4–2.   Accessibility of Physicians' Services, Spring 1973

New and Conventional Communities	Median Road Distance (feet) to Nearest General Practitioner/ Internist[a]	Percent of Households with General Practitioner/ Internist within One-half Mile of Home[b]
Nonfederally Assisted New and Paired Conventional Communities		
Thirteen new communities	6,800	12[c]
Thirteen conventional communities	8,800	8
New and Paired Conventional Communities		
Columbia (NC)	11,600	0
Norbeck-Wheaton (CC)	3,100	6
Elk Grove Village (NC)	7,200	4
Schaumburg (CC)	6,700	14[c]
Forest Park (NC)	5,400	12
Sharonville (CC)	6,400	10
Foster City (NC)	9,800	0
West San Mateo (CC)	14,900	0
Irvine (NC)	5,300	19
Fountain Valley (CC)	5,400	12
Laguna Niguel (NC)	6,900	15[c]
Dana Point (CC)	7,900	5
Lake Havasu City (NC)	13,200	5
Kingman (CC)	8,000	0
North Palm Beach (NC)	6,600	18
Tequesta (CC)	3,700	44[c]

Park Forest (NC)	5,200	19[c]
Lansing (CC)	5,100	3
Reston (NC)	5,400	16[c]
West Springfield (CC)	5,000	4
Sharpstown (NC)	9,000	8[c]
Southwest Houston (CC)	15,400	0
Valencia (NC)	3,900	13[c]
Bouquet Canyon (CC)	20,000	0
Westlake Village (NC)	5,800	21[c]
Agoura–Malibu Junction (CC)	8,400	0
Federally Assisted New and Paired Conventional Communities		
Jonathan (NC)	3,700	29[c]
Chanhassen (CC)	23,000	0
Park Forest South (NC)	12,100	0
Richton Park (CC)	3,800	9[c]

NC = New Community   CC = Conventional Community

[a] Rounded to nearest 100 feet.

[b] Road distance to nearest general practitioner/internist from household survey respondents' dwellings.

[c] Statistically significant difference between new community(ies) and paired conventional community(ies) at 0.05 level of confidence (percent only).

general practitioner within their neighborhoods—the area within one-half mile of their homes.

In addition to primary care, information regarding the availability of fourteen medical specialists was gathered for each new and conventional community.[b] The variety of medical and dental practitioners was somewhat greater in the nonfederally assisted new communities than in the paired conventional communities (averages of 6.5 vs. 4.8 of the fourteen types of practitioners surveyed), but in neither type of community could the variety of medical specialists be described as extensive. Specialists that were practicing in more than half of the thirteen nonfederally assisted new communities included pediatricians (eleven communities), obstetricians/gynecologists (ten communities), psychiatrists (eight communities), opthalmologists (seven communities), orthopedists (seven communities) and otolaryngologists (seven communities).

Physicians' Services in Relation to Community Needs

More important than the relative availability of care in new and conventional communities is the question of how well available resources were meeting community needs. A large number of health professionals indicated that the major health-related problem facing their communities was an insufficient number of physicians, or, in some cases, the absence of certain types of specialists. At a later point in the interview, the health professionals were asked their views on each community's present and future needs for physicians. Again, a large number of professionals, from almost every community in the sample, expressed the need for additional practitioners, particularly as the communities grew over the next five years. Elk Grove Village illustrates this situation. Increased use of the emergency room at the Alexian Brothers Hospital in Elk Grove Village was attributed to the shortage of physicians (as well as to increases in population and in the number of automobile accidents). A study of health needs undertaken in Schaumburg, Elk Grove Village's paired conventional community, reported a scarcity of physicians as one of its major findings (see Ernst and Ernst 1972, p. 4). Reston, a wealthy community with relatively few doctors, was described as a "Golden Ghetto."

The health care professionals also mentioned the need for a wide range of specialists in the new communities studied. Two types were

[b]These were pediatricians, obstetricians/gynecologists, child psychologists, chiropractors, dermatologists, ophthalmologists, optometrists, orthodontists, orthopedists, osteopaths, otolaryngologists, podiatrists, psychiatrists and urologists.

mentioned with particular frequency: pediatricians and specialists in the field of mental health, including psychiatrists, psychologists and child psychologists. A shortage of obstetrician-gynecologists was also noted in a number of communities.

The availability of physicians was not described in universally bleak terms, however, with respect either to general practitioners or to specialists. North Palm Beach, because of the wealth of the area and the community's favorable location, was described as a natural magnet for private practitioners. In Columbia there was a rapid increase in the number of psychiatrists and related specialists, which was attributed to newly available office space and an increase in awareness of the need for care. Lake Havasu City Community Hospital had surprisingly little trouble attracting physicians and other personnel from elsewhere in the region; the attractiveness of the area was credited with helping to draw a noted neurologist to the community.

Nor was the problem entirely one of the number of practitioners. There was a need for doctors to be available at all hours of the day (Reston, Laguna Niguel and its paired conventional community, Dana Point); for doctors more willing to make house calls (Park Forest); and for their offices to be better distributed (Norbeck-Wheaton, paired with Columbia). A number of professionals also felt that residents experienced too much difficulty in locating sources of primary care and in making arrangements to obtain it.

Sources of Problems and Suggested Solutions

There were indications in several communities as to why problems may have existed. In Columbia, the predominance of the Columbia Medical Plan and the issue of eligibility at Columbia's hospital for doctors outside the plan were said to discourage private practice, to the disappointment of several health professionals. One result was that Columbia was reputedly the home of a large number of physicians who did not practice in the community. In Reston, the developer's office was faulted for not cooperating with the Reston Community Association in attracting physicians; the residents' group, according to one health professional, was interested in achieving a balance of services, while Gulf-Reston, Inc. sought mainly to fill office space.

Several solutions to the problem of availability were suggested by health professionals serving the sample new and conventional communities. A hospital official who served Irvine believed that there was a need for "front line" physicians to screen patients and refer them to appropriate types of practitioners. Reston attracted national attention with a "Patients and Partners" program sponsored by Georgetown University in which residents were trained to provide much of their own basic care. Reports of the health care needs of two new communities, Elk Grove Village and Park Forest, called on their muncipalities to take steps to attract physicians. Health professionals in Columbia, Reston, North Palm Beach and two conventional communities, Schaumburg and Tequesta, suggested that constructing hospitals or extending hospital privileges would help attract doctors. In the same vein, Westlake Community Hospital was built in part to encourage doctors to come to Westlake Village.

Statistical analyses of the data from the sample communities were also used to determine which community characteristics, if any, accounted for differences in the availability of physicians. The dependent variables in these analyses were the number of primary care physicians per 100,000 population and the variety of specialists among the fourteen types surveyed.

In planned new communities, larger ratios of physicians were associated with communities that were closer to the central business districts of metropolitan areas ($r = .30$), older ($r = .39$) and that had hospitals ($r = .36$). There was also a strong correlation between physicians per 100,000 population and professionals' ratings of office facilities ($r = .36$). Among both new and conventional communities the most important factor was the availability of a hospital in the community ($r = .31$).

The variety of selected medical specialists was strongly correlated with the age of the community ($r = .49$). Among conventional communities as well as planned new communities there were strong correlations with the number of hospitals ($r = .42$ in new communities and $r = .61$ for both new and conventional communities), the population of the community ($r = .48$ and $r = .66$, respectively) and the number of family doctors per capita ($r = .55$ and $r = .54$, respectively). These findings show that doctors, not surprisingly, are drawn to communities by the presence of a hospital and also through a process of maturation of the community. While some doctors may be attracted to new developments by the lure of a fresh market, it is more probable that large ratios of doctors will be found in well-established communities with large populations where the risks of setting up a practice are not as great.

One approach to attracting physicians that is relevant to physical planning of communities and that is suggested by these analyses is providing office space for private practice. As noted in Chapter 3, actions relating to the provision of office space were the one area of health care in which new community developers were more involved than any other. In addition, proposed hospitals in Irvine and Park Forest South were to include doctors' office facilities. The inclusion of office space in the expansion of Elk Grove Village's Alexian Brothers Hospital was a direct response to a perceived shortage of doctors.

Both new and conventional communities tended to be highly rated by professionals in terms of the quality of available office space. Physicians' office facilities were rated as excellent or good by a majority of the health professionals serving ten of the thirteen non-federally assisted new communities and ten of the paired conventional communities. Office space in federally assisted Jonathan was also rated as excellent by two of the three professionals interviewed there and as good by the other professional interviewed. (Physicians' office space was not available in Park Forest South.) The principal problem area was Columbia, where at the time of the survey there was considerable unhappiness about the lack of facilities outside the Columbia Medical Plan.[c]

UTILIZATION OF PHYSICIANS' SERVICES

Although new communities tended to have more physicians per capita than the paired conventional communities, new community development did not result in greater than average use of physicians' services. New and conventional community residents were asked whether they had a regular doctor or clinic, whether they had had a routine check-up during the previous year, and the number of times during the previous year that they had visited doctors, other than dentists, in the doctors' offices or clinics. The results are summarized in Table 4-3.

Most respondents, over 80 percent, reported that they had a regular doctor of clinic, a figure which is surprisingly high in view of the early stage of development of many of the sample communities and the relatively short period of residence of many of the respondents. Moreover, the percentage having a regular source of care was similar for new and conventional communities and among most of the individual communities. Only Lake Havasu City, with 63 percent, had a substantially lower proportion of residents with a regular doctor or clinic.

[c]Health professionals serving Columbia also pointed out that the office facilities used originally by private practitioners were not designed for medical purposes. Waiting rooms and toilet facilities were lacking and rent was high. A representative of the developer contended, however, that office facilities were not provided originally because it was assumed that private doctors would not want to come into the community.

Table 4-3.   Utilization of Physicians' Services

	Percent of Respondents		Median Number of Visits to Physicians During Previous Year [c]
New and Conventional Communities	Reported Having a Regular Doctor or Clinic [a]	Reported Having a Routine Checkup During Previous Year [b]	
Nonfederally Assisted New and Paired Conventional Communities			
Thirteen new communities	83	71	2.0
Thirteen conventional communities	86	70	2.1
New and Paired Conventional Communities			
Columbia (NC)	85	74	2.8
Norbeck-Wheaton (CC)	79	76	2.4
Elk Grove Village (NC)	86	68	1.7
Schaumburg (CC)	89	66	2.1
Forest Park (NC)	92	70	2.4
Sharonville (CC)	86	63	2.2
Foster City (NC)	87	75	1.9
West San Mateo (CC)	91	73	2.4
Irvine (NC)	78	62	1.6
Fountain Valley (CC)	83	72	2.1
Laguna Niguel (NC)	83	73	2.1
Dana Point (CC)	91	70	2.3
Lake Havasu City (NC)	63	67	2.2
Kingman (CC)	80[d]	56	2.0
North Palm Beach (NC)	81	71	1.8
Tequesta (CC)	84	83	2.9

	a	b	c
Park Forest (NC)	86	67	2.1
Lansing (CC)	75	72	1.0
Reston (NC)	78	73	2.1
West Springfield (CC)	78	82	2.3
Sharpstown (NC)	87	71	2.0
Southwest Houston (CC)	93	77	2.2
Valencia (NC)	84	69[d]	2.2
Bouquet Canyon (CC)	82	54	2.0
Westlake Village (NC)	79	72	2.2
Agoura–Malibu Junction (CC)	85	61	1.5
Federally Assisted New and Paired Conventional Communities			
Jonathan (NC)	91	75	2.2
Chanhassen (CC)	91	77	1.6
Park Forest South (NC)	83[d]	68	1.8
Richton Park (CC)	71	71	1.9

NC = New Community   CC = Conventional Community

[a] *Question:* Do you have a regular doctor or clinic you go to?

[b] *Question:* Have you had a routine check-up in the past year, that is, since (MONTH) 1972?

[c] *Question:* Altogether, how many different times have you been to see doctors, other than dentists, in their offices or in clinics about your own health in the past 12 months—that is, since (MONTH) 1972?

[d] Statistically significant difference between new community (ies) and paired conventional community (ies) at 0.05 level of confidence (percents only).

There were also few differences in the percentages of respondents who reported that they had had a regular check-up during the previous year or in the median number of visits made to see doctors during the previous year. However, the emphasis on preventive care by the Columbia Medical Plan and the plan's policy of charging only nominal fees for doctors' visits was apparent (see Chapter 7). The median number of visits to doctors by Columbia respondents was far greater than any other new community and was exceeded only by the respondents living in Tequesta (the conventional community paired with North Palm Beach), where the median age of respondents was over 60.[d]

Factors Influencing Utilization of Physicians' Services

Although there are a large number of studies dealing with factors associated with the utilization of health care services, there is relatively little concrete evidence that geographical factors such as the proximity to and availability of services result in increased rates of use.[e] One group of studies, concerned primarily with behavior in rural areas, has shown that utilization of physicians' services decreases with increasing distances from the place of residence to a physician's office.[f] In other cases, however, no such relationship was demonstrated.[g] A difficulty with a number of studies considering distance factors is that they have approached the question of utilization not in terms of overall rates of use of health care services, but in terms of use of particular facilities or types of facilities. Nearness to a specific primary care facility has been found to influence a family's selection of that facility, but not their overall use of services.[h]

[d]The mean number of visits to doctors by new community residents was similar to the national average of 4.3 (see National Center for Health Statistics 1968). Contrary to the present study, however, the national data include home visits, telephone consultations and examinations in industry and company facilities, as well as visits to doctors' offices, clinics and hospitals.

[e]For an overview of this literature, see John B. McKinlay (1972).

[f]See, for example, Antonio A. Ciocco and Isidor Altman (1954); Charles Hoffer *et al.* (1950); Paul J. Jehlik and Robert L. McNammara (1952); C.E. Lively and P.G. Beck (1927); and T. Purola *et al.* (1968).

[g]See, for example, Thomas W. Bice and R.L. Eichhorn (1972) and Harold R. Kauffman and Warren W. Morse (1945).

[h]See, for example, W.J. Abernathy and E.L. Schrems (1971). Close proximity has also been found to encourage the use of maternal health services (Andrew A. Coliver *et al.* (1967); the use of cost-free Veterans Administration facilities by elderly veterans (Arthur H. Richardson *et al.* 1967); and the nonurgent use of emergency room services by children and adolescents (G.C. Robinson *et al.* (1969).

In a study of Kaiser Plan clinics in the Portland, Oregon area, James E. Weiss, Merwyn R. Greenlick and Joseph F. Jones (1971) showed that plan members generally visited the clinic nearest to them, although this tendency decreased as the distance to the clinic increased and as the difference between the nearest and an alternative clinic decreased. The influence of proximity is also undermined by the nature of the facilities offered. For example, relatively more visits to the best staffed and equipped Kaiser Plan clinics were made by people because of the services offered than because of proximity to users' homes. Distance factors, moreover, may influence the type of care sought; persons residing farther from physicians' offices appear more likely to seek curative rather than preventive care when they do seek help (see Jehlik and McNammara 1952).[i]

There is less evidence concerning the influence of availability of resources on utilization than there is on distance to resources. The relative number of available health resources, as well as distance, can be an important determinant of the level of utilization (Purola 1968), but several studies have indicated that the number of physicians and hospital beds is either of no importance in determining the number of visits to physicians and level of hospital use or is less important than need or predisposing variables.[j]

An additional approach to the question of utilization has concerned not only the availability and location of health care facilities but also the question of whether individuals have regular sources of care on which they rely. These studies generally have shown that access to a regular source of care increases utilization.[k]

The data gathered in the present study make it possible to test the

[i]Earlier work by Weiss and Greenlick (1970) has shown that distance is a determinant of the means by which people initiate their efforts to obtain health care, although distance interacts with a more important variable, social class. At distances of fifteen to twenty miles, middle class people become more likely to use the telephone to obtain assistance than at shorter distances, while reliance on emergency rooms by working class people increased at that distance; more generalized effects of distance, however, are not apparent from the Weiss and Greenlick data.

[j]See Ronald Anderson (1968) and Linda A. Fischer (1971). A number of researchers have approached the question of availability strictly in terms of its effects on hospital utilization. They have found that the use of hospitals is encouraged by an abundance of beds (J.G. Anderson 1973; P.J. Feldstein and J.J. German 1963; M.I. Roemer 1961a; M. Shain and M.I. Roemer 1959), a scarcity of physicians (M.I. Roemer 1961a), or both (R.L. Durbin and G. Antelman 1964). One study, however, has indicated that the local availability of hospitals and physicians does not influence the percentage of the population using a hospital (Grover C. Wirick, James N. Morgan and Robin Barlow 1962).

[k]See, for example, Ronald Andersen (1968); Thomas W. Bice *et al.* (1973); and Thomas W. Bice and K.L. White (1969).

Table 4—4. Simple Correlations between Community Health Care Resources
and Visits to Physicians During Previous Twelve Months

New Community Health Care Resource Indicators	Simple Correlation Coefficients (r)
Availability of Medical Practitioners	
Number of primary care physicians	−.03
Number of gynecologists/obstetricians	.01
Number of pediatricians	.02
Availability of hospital in community	−.02
Accessibility of Health Care Facilities and Services	
Distance to nearest general practitioner	−.05
Distance to nearest hospital	−.01
Distance to nearest public health clinic	−.003
Private medical facility exists in neighborhood	−.02
Length of trip (minutes) to regular doctor or clinic	−.01

effects on utilization of both the extent of health resources within
a community and the distances residents traveled to obtain care.
With the number of visits to physicians during the previous year serving as the dependent variable, a series of analyses were performed to
determine whether the number of visits was influenced by (1) availability and distance; (2) respondents' personal characteristics; and (3)
their opinions, attitudes and perceptions. Because of the interest in
physical factors and the extent to which they are taken into account
in new community planning, the analysis was limited to new communities.

Indicators of health care availability used in the analysis included
the number of primary care physicians, number of selected specialists
and the availability of a hospital in a community. Accessibility measures included the presence of a private medical facility in the neighborhood, the number of feet to the nearest general practitioner,
hospital and public health clinic and the travel time to the doctor or
clinic where regular medical care was obtained. The simple correlations of these variables with the number of visits to physicians during
the previous year are shown in Table 4—4. As it can readily be seen,
variation in the availability and accessibility of health care facilities
and services had virtually no effect on variation in visits to physicians.

A number of personal characteristics and subjective perceptions
were also tested. Personal characteristic variables included: sex; age;
education; family income; employment status; occupation; size of
family; race; marital status; length of residence in the community;

type of dwelling unit; holding of health insurance and extent of coverage; car ownership; access to public transportation; use of a regular source of care; and degree of difficulty experienced in obtaining care. Subjective perception variables included: respondents' satisfaction with their own health; their perception that they had had check-ups as often as they should; their rating of health care in the community; and their perceptions of the availability of hospitals, emergency care facilities and sources of public assistance.

The key variables which emerged from a multivariate analysis of personal characteristics and subjective perceptions are summarized in Table 4–5. The critical factor among the variables was the assessment of personal health. People visited doctors more frequently when they experienced difficulties with their own health. Sex (women made more frequent visits), having a regular doctor or clinic and employment status (nonemployed persons made more frequent visits) also explained some of the variance in visits to doctors, but were relatively unimportant in comparison with respondents' evaluations of their own health.[1]

The importance of the personal health assessment variable suggests that one reason physical factors failed to make an impact on use was

Table 4–5. Key Variables Influencing Visits to Physicians during Previous 12 Months

Variables	Simple Correlation Coefficient	Beta	Cumulative R^2
Satisfaction with personal health status	.22	.21	.049
Sex of respondent	.07	.04	.052
Employment status of respondent	.08	.04	.054
Respondent has a regular doctor or clinic	.05	.03	.055
F-value for equation	28.45		
Sample size	1,980		

[1]The influence of these variables is also illustrated by the proportion of respondents who had made one or more visits to doctors during the previous year. Overall, 84 percent of the new community respondents had been to a doctor one or more times. However, 91 percent of those who were dissatisfied with their health (vs. 83 percent of those who were satisfied), 89 percent with a regular doctor or clinic (vs. 60 percent of those without a regular doctor or clinic), 88 percent of the women (vs. 79 percent of the men) and 87 percent of those who were not employed (vs. 81 percent of the employed respondents) had been to see a doctor one or more times during the previous year.

because physicians' services were geared to the treatment of problems; people sought curative treatment when they needed it regardless of where it was located. However, respondents were motivated to visit doctors for preventive as well as curative health care services. For example, respondents with regular sources of care visited doctors more often not because they were less well—the correlation between having a regular source of care and personal assessment of health was only $r = -.07$—but because they sought preventive services. People with their own doctor or clinic were more likely to have had a check-up in the past year than those without a regular doctor or clinic ($r = .27$). The relationship between the number of visits and satisfaction with the frequency of check-ups ($r = .14$) also reflects a tendency on the part of those concerned with preventive measures to put their values into practice by visiting doctors.

Because an interest in preventive care influenced respondents to seek physicians' services, an important question is whether increased availability of health resources encouraged individuals to have check-ups or to arrange for regular sources of care. The evidence suggests that it did not. Having a regular source of care was not related to the number of family physicians practicing in a community ($r = .02$) or to the distance to the nearest general practitioner ($r = .03$). The likelihood of having had a check-up during the previous year was not influenced by the availability of physicians ($r = -.02$) or by the distance to the nearest general practitioner ($r = .01$). Thus, regardless of respondents' motivations—whether for curative or preventive health care services—the availability and location of health resources had little impact on the frequency of visits to doctors.

A remaining issue concerns the influence of availability on distance traveled to obtain care. While many utilization studies have treated distance as an independent variable, the distance an individual is willing to travel may depend on the type of service sought, with longer trips resulting from attempts to obtain more specialized forms of care (see Isador Altman 1954). The distance traveled to obtain care has been found to be greater for whites and people with higher incomes and levels of education, primarily because people in these groups live farther away from places where physicians practice (see Rashid L. Bashur, Gary W. Shannon and Charles A. Metzner 1970, p. 51). Distances traveled to obtain care have been found to increase with increasing distance from the home to the central business district of a metropolitan area, but the reverse is true of the time spent traveling, due to such intervening factors as higher rates of speed in outlying areas. The type of service in question influences both distance and time because hospital facilities are more centrally located than physicians' and dentists' offices (see Gary W. Shannon, J.L. Skinner and Rashid L. Bashur 1973, pp. 237–244).

The distances traveled by residents of the communities studied to regular doctors or clinics were considerably greater than the distances to the nearest available general practitioners. See Table 4–6. Although the median distance to the nearest general practitioner's office was just over a mile (6800 feet), those new community respondents who had a regular doctor or clinic traveled a median distance of over five miles (28,400 feet) to obtain regular care.[m] Conventional community respondents traveled even farther to their regular sources of care, a median distance of over seven miles (38,000 feet). The only new and conventional communities in which a majority of the respondents had a regular source of care within the community were either isolated from concentrations of doctors, such as Jonathan, Kingman and Tequesta, or were large cities with an abundant supply of medical practitioners, such as San Mateo.

Among new community residents, the distance traveled to obtain regular care was almost unrelated to the distance to the nearest general practitioner ($r = -.05$) and only weakly associated with the number of primary care physicians per 100,000 population ($r = -.12$). Thus, in most cases even where the community itself offered a degree of choice, new community residents tended to look far afield for regular physicians' or clinic services which they felt were suitable for them. This suggests that developers might be able to postpone the provision of primary care health services without creating major hardships for residents if ample health care resources are available in the surrounding region.

In terms of the average time traveled to regular sources of care, new and conventional communities were similar: 18.7 minutes in new communities and 19.9 minutes in the conventional communities. Regression analysis was used to determine which factors were associated with the length of time required to reach the doctor or clinic used. As expected, the time of the trip was strongly influenced by aerial distance to the office of the physicians used ($r = .74$), which explained 55 percent of the variance in travel times. Almost no additional explanation of the variance was achieved by other variables related to distance and convenience, such as the physical size of

---

[m]The real contrast between the distance to the nearest source of care and the distance to the physician utilized is somewhat understated by these figures; distances to doctors utilized were measured in terms of straight line (aerial) distances to the community in which the doctor practiced, while distances to the nearest source of care were measured in terms of the shortest road route that could be taken.

Table 4–6. Distance Traveled to Obtain Regular Care in Comparison with Distance to Nearest General Practitioner/Internist

New and Conventional Communities	Median Aerial Distance (feet) to Regular Doctor or Clinic[a]	Median Road Distance (feet) to Nearest General Practitioner/ Internist[b]
Nonfederally Assisted New and Paired Conventional Communities		
Thirteen new communities	28,400	6,800
Thirteen conventional communities	38,000	8,800
New and Paired Conventional Communities		
Columbia (NC)	71,300	11,600
Norbeck-Wheaton (CC)	43,500	3,100
Elk Grove Village (NC)	24,200	7,200
Schaumburg (CC)	42,300	6,700
Forest Park (NC)	29,000	5,400
Sharonville (CC)	23,500	6,400
Foster City (NC)	27,500	9,800
West San Mateo (CC)	c	14,900
Irvine (NC)	34,100	5,300
Fountain Valley (CC)	49,700	5,400
Laguna Niguel (NC)	62,100	6,900
Dana Point (CC)	31,100	7,900
Lake Havasu City (NC)	100,000+	13,200
Kingman (CC)	c	8,000
North Palm Beach (NC)	30,100	6,600
Tequesta (CC)	c	3,700

Park Forest (NC)	13,800	5,200
Lansing (CC)	17,400	5,100
Reston (NC)	87,600	5,400
West Springfield (CC)	36,000	5,000
Sharpstown (NC)	52,000	9,000
Southwest Houston (CC)	52,000	15,400
Valencia (NC)	52,300	3,900
Bouquet Canyon (CC)	78,900	20,000
Westlake Village (NC)	71,300	5,800
Agoura–Malibu Junction (CC)	66,200	8,400
Federally Assisted New and		
Paired Conventional Communities		
Jonathan (NC)	47,500[c]	3,700
Chanhassen (CC)		23,000
Park Forest South (NC)	24,700	12,100
Richton Park (CC)	37,200	3,800

NC = New Community   CC = Conventional Community

[a] Aerial distance from respondent's community to community in which regular doctor or clinic was located, rounded to nearest hundred feet.

[b] Rounded to nearest hundred feet.

[c] Regular doctor or clinic located in same community as majority of respondents.

the community and the proximity of a bus stop. In contrast to previous research, there was a small positive relationship between travel time and distance from the central city (r =.08). The greater convenience in using automobiles in outlying areas was apparently outweighed by the relative scarcity of doctors' offices in those areas. Distance traveled, as with travel time, was greater at greater distances from the central city (r = .16).

Difficulties Experienced in Obtaining Medical Care

The household survey provided information not only on the level of residents' use of doctors' services, but also on any difficulties they had experienced in obtaining care. Asked whether in the past year they had ever really wanted to see a doctor but did not for some reason, 15 percent of the nonfederally assisted new community respondents reported that this was the case. See Table 4—7. About the same proportions of new and conventional community respondents reported having had such difficulties. Among new communities, the highest incidence of not seeing a doctor occurred in Columbia (22 percent), Elk Grove Village (19 percent), Lake Havasu City (21 percent) and Valencia (25 percent).

The most common reasons given for failure to see a doctor were inconvenience and the length of time it took to get to a doctor (36 percent). However, further analysis indicated that there was little systematic association between reported difficulties in seeing doctors on the one hand and personal and community characteristics on the other. Females and younger respondents reported a slightly greater degree of difficulty (r = .08 in both cases).

Respondents who had a regular doctor or clinic were asked whether on their last visit they had been annoyed by problems in arranging the appointment or in arranging transportation to get there. Getting apointments was a problem for 10 percent of the nonfederally assisted new community respondents, with about the same proportion (11 percent) of the paired conventional community respondents reporting difficulties (see Table 4—7). Reported difficulties in arranging appointments (mentioned by 15 percent or more of the respondents) were highest in the same four new communities—Columbia, Elk Grove Village, Lake Havasu City and Valencia—that had the highest proportions of respondents who had failed to see a doctor when they wanted. However, differences in the proportions of respondents who reported difficulties in each of these new communities and their paired conventional communities were not statistically significant. Also, there was little relationship between reported

difficulties in obtaining appointments and the education of the respondent, the number of hours per week the head of household
worked (where the respondent was the head of household) and the
length of residence in the community. As shown in Table 4−7, although respondents most often mentioned inconvenience as a reason
for not seeing a doctor when they wanted, few respondents experienced difficulties in arranging transportation to their regular doctor
or clinic.

In the case of the less mature federally assisted new communities,
Jonathan residents were no more likely than the residents of the nonfederally assisted communities to have failed to see a doctor when
they wanted or to have reported difficulties in arranging appointments or transportation to their regular sources of care. On the other
hand, residents living in Park Forest South, which did not have a
practicing physician, were somewhat more likely to have experienced
difficulties in obtaining medical care.

CONCLUSIONS

Several aspects of this study show that the availability of physician
care is a problem in new communities. While new communities
tended to be as well supplied with primary care physicians as the
paired conventional communities, neither compared favorably with
national averages. The availability of physician services did not appear to influence utilization, but it was a determinant of residents'
satisfaction with community health care (see Chapter 9). Moreover,
the incidence of difficulties in obtaining care was disturbingly high.
The comments of health professionals serving these communities
indicated that he scarcity of physicians was a serious matter in many
areas. Beyond the problems associated with inadequate numbers of
doctors, there were suggestions that care was difficult to obtain in
the way and at the time desired.

These problems are not unique to planned new communities, but
they do demonstrate that few new communities have exploited the
special nature of a planned environment to provide residents with a
better level of physicians' services than is generally available elsewhere. There is an apparent need for developers not only to provide
office space for doctors, but also to undertake the construction of
medical facilities at an earlier stage of development and possibly to
offer incentives to doctors in the form of reduced office rentals during the initial years of development or choice locations. It may be
useful to work more closely with physicians' groups and medical
societies to actively recruit doctors. The features of new communities which appeal to the general public should appeal to doctors

Table 4–7.   Difficulties Experienced in Obtaining Medical Care *(percentage distribution of respondents)*

New and Conventional Communities	*Failed to See Doctor when Desired During Previous Year[a]*	*Problems with Regular Doctor[b]*	
		Arranging Appointments	*Arranging Transportation*
Nonfederally Assisted New and Paired Conventional Communities			
Thirteen new communities	15	10	4
Thirteen conventional communities	18	11	4
New and Paired Conventional Communities			
Columbia (NC)	22	19	4
Norbeck-Wheaton (CC)	21	17	5
Elk Grove Village (NC)	19	18	6
Schaumburg (CC)	16	11	8
Forest Park (NC)	16	9	2
Sharonville (CC)	15	4	2
Foster City (NC)	13	6	3
West San Mateo (CC)	12	12	5
Irvine (NC)	16	6	4
Fountain Valley (CC)	9	8	3
Laguna Niguel (NC)	11	6	2
Dana Point (CC)	24[c]	7	2
Lake Havasu City (NC)	21	15	3
Kingman (CC)	29	29	1
North Palm Beach (NC)	9	9	3
Tequesta (CC)	19[c]	7	1

Park Forest (NC)	15	13	5
Lansing (CC)	14	14	7
Reston (NC)	16	11	4
West Springfield (CC)	23	8	3
Sharpstown (NC)	19	6	5
Southwest Houston (CC)	17	9	3
Valencia (NC)	25	15	5
Bouquet Canyon (CC)	20	19	10
Westlake Village (NC)	6	5	4
Agoura–Malibu Junction (CC)	14	7	3

Federally Assisted New and
Paired Conventional Communities

Jonathan (NC)	15	10	4
Chanhassen (CC)	10	5	1
Park Forest South (NC)	19	15[c]	7
Richton Park (CC)	16	2	7

NC = New Community   CC = Conventional Community

[a]*Question:* And during the last 12 months, did you ever really want to see or talk to a doctor but didn't for some reason?

[b]*Question:* The last time you went to that (doctor/clinic), did you find anything annoying or inconvenient about . . . arranging appointments? arranging transportation to get there?

[c]Statistically significant difference between new community(ies) and paired conventional community(ies) at 0.05 level of confidence.

as well. Moreover, by practicing in such communities doctors can realize an elusive goal of planned communities by being able to live, work and pursue recreational opportunities within the same community.

Alternative approaches would include planning the community with a view toward health care facilities, such as hospitals, which might help to attract doctors and toward other forms of care which might make a large number of physicians less necessary. These alternatives will be explored in succeeding chapters.

Hospital Care and Ambulance Service

No health-related matter has been the subject of so much interest in new communities as hospital care. This interest may be due not only to the continuing attention focused on hospital care throughout the country, but also to the geographic location of many of the new communities studied. Because they are outlying developments with few established sources of health care, they naturally rely on hospitals as facilities offering a number of types of care at one location. This chapter examines the characteristics of hospitals serving new communities, the assessments of residents and health professionals regarding the adequacy of care provided, and the issues that have arisen over the provision and operation of hospital facilities. In addition, attention is devoted to issues involving the ways in which emergency ambulance service to hospitals has been provided. Health professionals' evaluations of ambulance service are discussed in relation to the characteristics of and problems experienced by ambulance services in the sample communities.

AVAILABILITY OF HOSPITAL CARE

As of the spring of 1973, only three of the fifteen nonfederally and federally assisted new communities had hospitals—Elk Grove Village and Westlake Village each had one community hospital and Sharpstown had two. West San Mateo, Foster City's paired conventional community, also had two hospitals and Fountain Valley and Kingman, the conventional communities paired with Irvine and Lake

Havasu City, had one hospital each. Availability of a hospital was related to both the age of a community and its population—older communities with larger populations were more likely to have acquired such a facility.

Hospitals were in the planning or construction stage in a number of other new communities. Two community hospitals were under development in Lake Havasu City, both of which had begun operation by 1975. A hospital was opened in Columbia in July of 1973 and one was scheduled for completion in Valencia in 1975. Two additional hospitals were planned for Sharpstown and hospital proposals were pending in Irvine, Park Forest South and Reston. In Foster City, an attempt to secure a branch of the Peninsula Hospital in the community was turned down after a preliminary feasibility study showed that Foster City was adequately served by the two hospitals in San Mateo. Similarly, North Palm Beach, Laguna Niguel and Park Forest were served by hospitals in immediately adjacent communities and no efforts had been made to obtain additional hospital facilities.

In order to determine the number of hospital beds available to residents of the sample communities, health care professionals were asked to name those hospitals that served each community. Because the populations served by these hospitals were far greater than the populations of the sample communities and because the service areas of the hospitals varied considerably, it would be misleading to compare each new and conventional community on a beds-per-population basis. Nevertheless, the totals provide a rough measure of the supply of hospital beds in the vicinity of the communities. Overall, the new communities were served by an average of 650 hospital beds per community, while the conventional communities were served by an average of 620 hospital beds per community.

The variety of special facilities and services available in the hospitals serving the sample communities was ascertained from the directory of the American Hospital Association (1972). Of 42 facilities and services inventoried by the Association, the average number available at hospitals serving both the new and conventional communities was fourteen.[a] The overall number of beds and the average number of special hospital facilities and services were associated more strongly with the population of a community than with any

[a]Among the facilities most commonly found in hospitals in and near the communities studied were: postoperative recovery room, intensive care unit, pharmacy, X-ray therapy, diagnostic radioisotope facility, histopathology laboratory, inhalation therapy department, premature nursery, inpatient renal dialysis, physical therapy department, psychiatric emergency services, outpatient department, emergency department, hospital auxiliary and volunteer services department.

other community characteristic (r = .30 for beds and r = .43 for special facilities). Because a larger number of special facilities is likely to be found where a larger number of beds is available, the two variables were closely correlated with one another (r = .82).

Another approach to measuring the availability of hospital resources is to compare communities in terms of the accessibility of the nearest hospital and in terms of residents' perceptions of the availability of hospital care. Overall, the accessibility of the nearest hospital facility was somewhat better in the new communities than in the paired conventional communities. As shown in Table 5–1, the median nonfederally assisted new community resident lived about a mile and a half closer to the nearest hospital (14,800 feet vs. 22,200 feet). However, comparisons of each new community with its paired conventional community indicate that for seven of the thirteen nonfederally assisted new communities and both federally assisted communities, the paired conventional community residents were more likely to live closer to the nearest hospital. As would be expected, hospital accessibility was best in those new and conventional communities that had community hospitals in the spring of 1973 (Elk Grove Village, Sharpstown and Westlake Village among the new communities and West San Mateo, Fountain Valley and Kingman among the paired conventional communities).

New and conventional community respondents were asked whether hospital care was available in their community or its vicinity. Similar proportions of respondents in each setting, 73 percent and 72 percent, felt that hospital care was available. As with the accessibility of the nearest hospital, perceptions of the availability of care were highest in those new and conventional communities with community hospitals. In addition, residents' perceptions of the availability of hospital care also tended to be high in new communities, such as North Palm Beach, Park Forest and Valencia, where hospitals were located in adjacent communities. Finally, it should be noted that hospitals that were under construction in Columbia and Lake Havasu City, and pending in Reston and Irvine, would increase the accessibility and residents' perceptions of the availability of hospital care in those new communities with the least convenient facilities.

Characteristics of the hospitals that were most accessible to the residents of the new and conventional communities studied are summarized in Table 5–2. The measures of the number of beds and the number of special facilities and services at the nearest hospitals parallel the findings for the whole group of hospitals serving the communities. Most residents of new and conventional communities lived closest to some type of nonprofit hospital. The average cost of a semi-

Table 5–1. Accessibility of Nearest Hospital and Residents' Perceptions of the Availability of Hospital Care, Spring 1973

New and Conventional Communities	Median Road Distance (feet) to Nearest Hospital[a]	Perceived Availability of Hospital Care (percent)[b]
Nonfederally Assisted New and Paired Conventional Communities		
Thirteen new communities	14,800	73
Thirteen conventional communities	22,200	72
New and Paired Conventional Communities		
Columbia (NC)	85,400	15
Norbeck-Wheaton (CC)	32,300	49[c]
Elk Grove Village (NC)	9,600	99[c]
Schaumburg (CC)	34,300	84
Forest Park (NC)	47,600	9
Sharonville (CC)	21,600	86[c]
Foster City (NC)	20,100	68
West San Mateo (CC)	10,000	100[c]
Irvine (NC)	40,200	57
Fountain Valley (CC)	7,200	98[c]
Laguna Niguel (NC)	19,100	83[c]
Dana Point (CC)	18,100	51
Lake Havasu City (NC)	100,000+	29
Kingman (CC)	4,800	99[c]
North Palm Beach (NC)	13,200	90[c]
Tequesta (CC)	50,700	12
Park Forest (NC)	19,600	96
Lansing (CC)	21,500	96

Reston (NC)	58,200	31
West Springfield (CC)	38,300	80[c]
Sharpstown (NC)	9,200	96[c]
Southwest Houston (CC)	15,400	81
Valencia (NC)	6,200	97
Bouquet Canyon (CC)	27,300	96
Westlake Village (NC)	6,000	97[c]
Agoura/Malibu Junction (CC)	28,900	45
Federally Assisted New and		
Paired Conventional Communities		
Jonathan (NC)	44,100	51
Chanhassen (CC)	32,400	57
Park Forest South (NC)	33,900	82[c]
Richton Park (CC)	27,300	69

NC = New Community   CC = Conventional Community

[a] Rounded to nearest 100 feet.

[b] *Question:* Here is a list of services available in many communities. We'd like to know, first, if such services are available in this community or its vicinity . . . b. hospital care.

[c] Statistically significant difference between new community(ies) and paired conventional community(ies) at 0.05 level of confidence (percent only).

Table 5—2. Selected Characteristics of Hospitals Nearest to New
and Conventional Community Respondents' Homes

Characteristic	Fifteen New Communities	Fifteen Conventional Communities
Number of beds available (mean)	212	193
Number of selected facilities and services[a] (mean)	14	14
Cost of semi-private room (mean)	$57	$59
Form of control (percent)		
Government	6	12
Other nonprofit	58	53
Proprietary	36	35

[a]Mean number of facilities and services of a total possible of 42 facilities and services enumerated in American Hospital Association (1972).

private room was $58.54 in the spring of 1973. Virtually all of the hospitals situated closest to the new and conventional communities were general, short-term hospitals.

EVALUATIONS OF THE ADEQUACY OF AVAILABLE HOSPITAL CARE

Two different approaches were used to gauge the adequacy of available hospital care. See Table 5—3. Respondents in the household survey who indicated that they were aware of a hospital serving their community were asked if they would recommend the use of that facility. Responses to the question provide one indication of consumer confidence in the hospital(s) serving each community. Although a majority of the new and conventional community respondents who were aware of a hospital said that they would recommend its use, consumer confidence varied greatly from one community to another. In particular, only 22 percent of the Valencia respondents indicated that they would recommend the use of nearby hospitals. This may explain the Newhall Land and Farming Company's strong support of the Henry Mayo Newhall Memorial Hospital in Valencia, considering that the average Valencia resident lived just over one mile from the nearest existing hospital facility. In general, however, consumer confidence in hospitals tended to be highest in those new and conventional communities with a hospital within or adjacent to the community and lowest in those communities where residents had to travel relatively long distances for hospital care.

A second approach used to evaluate hospital care was to ask health care professionals serving each community whether they felt that care was adequate. In four nonfederally assisted new communities and federally assisted Jonathan each of the professionals interviewed said that hospital care was adequate to meet the needs of the community. In contrast, hospital care was unanimously judged to be adequate in eight of the paired conventional communities as well as the conventional community paired with Jonathan (see Table 5-3).

Hospital care was unanimously viewed as inadequate in four new communities (including federally assisted Park Forest South) and two conventional communities. In the remainder of the communities professional opinion regarding the adequacy of care was mixed (six new communities and four conventional communities).

ISSUES AND PROBLEMS IN THE PROVISION OF HOSPITAL CARE

A number of other questions in the health professional survey probed the attitudes of professionals toward hospital care. Since hospitals already existed, were under construction, planned or proposed in many of the new communities at the time of the health professional survey in the spring of 1973, the question of when, if ever, a community would need a hospital of its own did not elicit strong opinions in either the planned new communities or their nearby paired conventional communities. Of much more immediate concern was the question of the nature of the facility to be built and the issue of the process by which hospitals are planned and built within regional areas.

For example, none of the health professionals serving Jonathan felt that a hospital would be needed in that community in spite of the fact that Jonathan's project agreement with the Department of Housing and Urban Development called for the ultimate construction of one, and that the average Jonathan resident lived farther from a hospital (44,100 feet) than residents of twelve of the fourteen other new communities studied. A professional serving Valencia, where a hospital was planned, noted the dilemma that the community had too few people to support a hosptal, but was too far from major hospital facilities not to have one of its own.[b]

Several health care professionals, when asked about the need for additional hospital facilities, pointed out that there was overbedding

[b]Although the nearest hospital was very close to Valencia residents (the median distance to the facility from Valencia households was only 6200 feet), the hospital had only 24 beds.

Table 5–3.   Evaluations of Hospitals by Residents and Health Care Professionals

New and Conventional Communities	Percent of Respondents Who Were Aware of Hospital Serving Community[a]		Composite Professional Rating of the Adequacy of Hospital Care[b]
	Would Recommend Use of Hospital	Not Sure or Would Not Recommend Use of Hospital	
Nonfederally Assisted New and Paired Conventional Communities			
Columbia (NC)	50	50	Opinion Mixed
Norbeck-Wheaton (CC)	80	20	Adequate
Elk Grove Village (NC)	83	17	Inadequate
Schaumburg (CC)	81	19	Inadequate
Forest Park (NC)	76	24	Inadequate
Sharonville (CC)	84	16	Opinion Mixed
Foster City (NC)	63	37	Adequate
West San Mateo (CC)	82	18	Adequate
Irvine (NC)	73	27	Adequate
Fountain Valley (CC)	59	41	Adequate
Laguna Niguel (NC)	76	24	Adequate
Dana Point (CC)	80	20	Adequate
Lake Havasu City (NC)	63	37	Opinion Mixed
Kingman (CC)	56	44	Adequate
North Palm Beach (NC)	73	27	Opinion Mixed
Tequesta (CC)	67	33	Opinion Mixed
Park Forest (NC)	76	24	Opinion Mixed
Lansing (CC)	59	41	Adequate
Reston (NC)	54	46	Opinion Mixed
West Springfield (CC)	64	36	Adequate

Sharpstown (NC)	78	22	Opinion Mixed
Southwest Houston (NC)	78	22	Opinion Mixed
Valencia (NC)	22	78	Inadequate
Bouquet Canyon (CC)	30	70	Inadequate
Westlake Village (NC)	52	48	Adequate
Agoura/Malibu Junction (CC)	43	57	Adequate
Federally Assisted New and			
Paired Conventional Communities			
Jonathan (NC)	47	53	Adequate
Chanhassen (CC)	74	26	Adequate
Park Forest South (NC)	67	33	Inadequate
Richton Park (CC)	58	42	Opinion Mixed

NC = New Community   CC = Conventional Community

[a] *Question:* Here is a list of services available in many communities. We'd like to know, first, if such services are available in this community or its vicinity, and second, if you would be willing to recommend those that are here as good places to go for help . . . Hospital Care.

[b] *Question:* Considering all of the hospital facilities in the area, do you feel that hospital care available to residents of (NAME OF COMMUNITY) is adequate? If all professionals interviewed in a community responded yes, a composite rating of adequate was assigned to the community. If all professionals responded no, a composite rating of inadequate was assigned. In those cases where professionals did not agree about the adequacy of care, a rating of opinion mixed was assigned to the community.

already. This was the view of a professional in Reston who felt that
the main reason for the proposed Beverly Enterprises Hospital there
—adding beds to an already overbedded county—was the desire for a
self-contained community. Community pride was also cited as a
reason for building a local facility in Westlake Village even though
other hospitals were close by.

An official of the Greater Cincinnati Area Council of Hospitals
added that it is a mistake to plan hospitals for individual communities; the concentration of Cincinnati's hospitals in a central location
linked by expressways to satellite hospitals in outlying sections such
as the Forest Park–Sharonville area was viewed as an ideal situation.
The director of one of the branch hospitals in the system agreed that
neither Forest Park nor Sharonville would ever need its own hospital,
but contended that satellite hospitals such as his own should be
allowed to grow into subregional centers. A large central facility was
also considered preferable to numerous smaller ones by a professional serving Laguna Niguel.

In response to broader questions dealing with improvements in
hospital care for the area generally, numerous health professionals
indicated that there was already a sufficient or excessive number of
beds. Although this view was expressed in all areas in which the sample new communities were located, three stand out as examples of
the uncontrolled or apparently unnecessary proliferation of hospital
building. In Houston, the lack of a strong regional authority for
health planning had resulted in a spurt of hospital construction centered in the Sharpstown area. With two hospitals already in the community, two more were planned. One was an expanded replacement
of the existing Memorial Hospital, which was to be converted to a
long-term care facility. The second was a result of dissention among
doctors at the Sharpstown General Hospital, located across the street
from the planned hospital, and the desire of those doctors, according
to a hospital official, to control their own facility. Nevertheless,
Sharpstown General was undertaking an expansion program of its
own. New state legislation or an expanded role for the Houston-
Galveston Area Health Council were viewed as necessary means of
curbing this pattern of growth.

In the suburbs northwest of Chicago, a hospital proposed for Hoffman Estates was approved by the Illinois Hospital Licensing Board
just six months after approval was granted to the Rush-Presbyterian-
St. Luke's Medical Center branch in neighboring Schaumburg, the
conventional community paired with Elk Grove Village. The Hoffman Estates project was opposed by two area hospitals, one of them
the Alexian Brothers Hospital in Elk Grove Village, on the grounds

of overbedding. Later, plans for another project in the nearby community of Wheeling were announced. The *Comprehensive Health Survey of Elk Grove Village* (1972) noted that the four existing hospitals in the area were operating at or near capacity, thus necessitating the expansions planned by all four, and that they were careful not to duplicate each other's services. The construction of additional hospitals, however, was viewed by some health care professionals as needless expansion. What particularly miffed both the authors of the *Comprehensive Health Survey* and the health professionals who were interviewed was the fact that plans for the Rush-Presbyterian-St. Luke's Hospital in Schaumburg were announced before the completion of work by the Northwest Cook County Health Needs Study Committee. Several area hospitals and municipalities, including the Village of Schaumburg, had agreed to abide by the Committee's recommendations.

In Lake Havasu City, where two rival factions in a hospital dispute ultimately constructed their own buildings, the prospect of two hospitals operating in the community raised such issues as whether the community could financially support them both and whether their presence would preclude state authorization for hospitals in other areas of Mohave County. One instance of duplication was averted, however, when the Mohave County Health Planning Council denied approval for increased cardiology facilities at the existing Lake Havasu Community Hospital on the grounds that a cardiac care wing was already planned for the new Lake Havasu City Medical Center Hospital.

In spite of the opinions of many professionals concerning overbedding and duplication, there were also those who felt that additional facilities, either in terms of new buildings or additions to old ones, were needed. The most fundamental reasons for expanded facilities were the great demands being placed on existing hospitals and the need to respond to area-wide growth. For example, pressures put on the emergency room at the Alexian Brothers Hospital in Elk Grove Village by persons seeking routine doctors' services made the expansion of that facility one of the community's greatest needs, according to the *Comprehensive Health Survey*. Palm Beach Gardens Hospital near North Palm Beach was viewed by a neighboring hospital as having the greatest potential for growth as the northern part of Palm Beach County developed.

Improving hospital services, in the minds of health professionals, was only partly a matter of physical expansion. The administrator of the Alexian Brothers Hospital described changes in the overall aims of the facility as follows:

[The hospital] is now struggling to expand its health focus. We moved out here without full knowledge of the areas we were getting into. We had few broadly-based ideas on health care; we were just "a hospital." Now we are a regional center for some specialties. Also we are looking to health delivery outside our walls. We are concerned with the quality and scope of care and not just providing services.

Many professionals spoke not of constructing facilities but of adding services or personnel. Most of these recommendations reflected local conditions and deficiencies or the personal attitudes of professionals and do not lend themselves to generalization about hospital care in the sample communities. Illustrative of the kinds of needs mentioned were home care, alcoholism and drug treatment, ambulatory care, the addition of general practitioners and greater use of physicians' assistants and paramedics. Others felt improvement in care would come about through measures such as reducing government intervention, increasing cooperation among area hospitals, making special provisions for people unable to meet hospital expenses and correcting the underutilization of some hospitals.

Nevertheless, physical changes were prominent among the suggestions of health professionals who were seeking improvements in hospital care. As with services, few strong themes emerged among the study communities. Two types of facilities were mentioned more often than any others, however. Hospital administrators and county health officials, primarily in the Chicago area and the Southern California communities, called for additional psychiatric beds, psychiatric inpatient and outpatient clinics and improvements in mental health facilities and services generally.

A second facility that drew considerable support was a new or improved emergency room. Health professionals serving North Palm Beach, for example, were concerned about the absence of such facilities at Palm Beach Gardens Hospital. Similar views were expressed elsewhere by groups active in health care in the communities studied. The *Health Study Report* in Park Forest (see Frank C. Hostetler and Eleonor C. Prueske 1973), and the *Comprehensive Health Survey* (1972) in Elk Grove Village recommended improved emergency facilities. In Irvine, the Health Care Services Committee sought and received assurances that there would be early phasing of a 24-hour emergency room at the proposed Western World Medical Foundation Hospital. The existence of emergency facilities at the hospital under construction in Columbia and of their availability to Howard County residents not belonging to the Columbia Medical Plan was an important part of the debate as to whether an additional hospital in the county would be needed.

The construction of Westlake Hospital, which was opposed by Los Robles Hospital in nearby Thousand Oaks, was justified on the basis of emergency care provided to Westlake Village, although it offered other services as well. (Westlake Hospital was able to gain approval despite opposition from Los Robles and planners in Los Angeles and Ventura counties because the developer had secured licensing before a tougher state law took effect.)

The most intense debate concerning emergency facilities occurred in Reston. There, Gulf-Reston, Inc., the developer, supported a proposed 125-bed hospital to be constructed by a private group, Beverly Enterprises, on a ten-acre site purchased from the developer. An alternative proposal calling for a satellite facility providing emergency care was subsequently made by the Fairfax Hospital Association, which operated the main general hospital for the county. The issues involved in the debate were numerous, but they centered around the question of how best to provide a community in a relatively remote part of the county with the emergency care it felt it needed without creating hospital overbedding in the general area. The dispute also involved the issue of where authority lies for determining the type of health care facilities to be provided within a planned new community. Gulf-Reston, claiming support for the hospital project from 72 percent of the community, was nevertheless opposed by the Health Committee of the Reston Community Association, various other private and public groups and most of the health professionals interviewed for this study. This issue was resolved in February 1974 when Beverly Enterprises was denied a certificate of need by the state of Virginia, and an Ambulatory Care Center–Emergency Service System proposed by the Hospital Association was accepted in its place.

A different kind of hospital controversy, but one that also carried with it the possibility of duplication of facilities, took place in Columbia. The fact that Columbia's new hospital was intended largely for members of the Columbia Medical Plan and that the Baltimore Regional Planning Council decided that the hospital could not meet all of Howard County's needs led to consideration of rival applications for a second hospital in the county originally by three and finally by two other organizations. Although citizens' groups from the county took the early lead in calling for a second county hospital, experience with Columbia's hospital during the first months of its operation—two-thirds of its inpatients consisted of persons who were not members of the Columbia Medical Plan—led residents from outside Columbia to support the expansion of the hospital to become a general county facility; a second hospital, they felt, would be an unnecessary and expensive duplication. Ironically, several health pro--

fessionals felt that Columbia's hospital could originally have been designed with the county in mind but that this was precluded by the attitudes of both the originators of the Medical Plan and of the county's residents. The deadlock between the two factions proposing a second hospital and the possibility of an extended ban on hospital construction in the region may leave the county with only the 59 beds provided in the Columbia hospital's first phase.

Another community where a proposed hospital may result in duplication of facilities is Irvine. A major objection on the part of citizen groups toward the proposed Western World Medical Foundation Hospital has been the possibility that it may jeopardize the construction of a teaching hospital as part of the University of California at Irvine. Although the Western World project enjoyed the support of The Irvine Company, which donated part of the site, the city of Irvine's delegate to the Orange County Health Planning Council placed her highest priority on the UCI teaching hospital and would reduce the number of other hospital beds accordingly. In addition, a 1973 report by the Orange County Health Planning Council indicated that nearby Santa Ana had an excess of 1000 hospital beds and a new hospital would not be needed in Irvine before 1982. This conclusion was heatedly disputed by Irvine city officials.

AMBULANCE SERVICE

Much of the emphasis in debates over hospital building has revolved around emergency care and the view that it should be readily accessible to residents. In fact, many of the health care professionals serving the new communities studied stated that one of the greatest health care needs was emergency treatment facilities. However, there were only four new communities—Irvine, Laguna Niguel, Lake Havasu City and Park Forest South—in which a majority of the health care professionals thought that existing emergency care was inadequate. Three of these communities—Irvine,[c] Laguna Niguel and Park Forest South—were served from stations not located in the community. On the other hand, three other new communities which lacked ambulance stations—Jonathan, Valencia and Westlake Village—received consistently high ratings. The health professionals in Foster City and North Palm Beach, which also lacked ambulance stations, were divided.

Professionals' evaluations of ambulance care apparently depended

[c]In November 1973, six months after the professional survey, the city of Irvine initiated an Emergency Transportation Service that was available at no charge.

less on the presence of a station in the community than on the nature of the organization providing service and its cost. Professionals were more likely to view ambulance service favorably where service was provided by public fire departments rather than by private companies or funeral homes ($r = .46$). Since private service is more expensive, professionals' assessments were also linked to cost ($r = .54$). Location of ambulance stations in the community was only weakly related to favorable ratings ($r = .11$). The greater the distance from the metropolitan central city the more likely it was the local ambulance service was viewed as meeting community needs ($r = .19$); this finding may reflect a greater degree of attention to ambulance service in more remote areas. Location and type of service are summarized in Table 5-4.

In spite of the favorable views of professionals towards ambulance care, there was room for improvement. Health care professionals in Columbia, Park Forest South, Irvine and Foster City noted problems in achieving the basic objective of getting patients to hospitals quickly in times of emergency. Service was described as too slow or ambulance crews were said to have encountered difficulties finding locations (one of the disadvantages of convoluted street patterns that promote traffic and pedestrian safety). Improved ambulance service was also found by study groups to be among the basic health needs in North Palm Beach, Elk Grove Village and Park Forest. The Park Forest study pointed out that "most of the respondents were angry about long waits before receiving medical attention," but the complaints apparently concerned treatment at emergency facilities more often than they concerned ambulance service (see Hostetler and Prueske 1973).

Although ambulance crews received some sort of emergency care training in virtually every community in the study, the lack of ade-

Table 5-4. Characteristics of Ambulance Service in New and Conventional Communities *(number of communities)*

Characteristic	*Fifteen New Communities*	*Fifteen Conventional Communities*
Location of Station		
Within community	7	8
Outside community	8	7
Organization Providing Service		
Fire department	8	9
Funeral home	1	1
Other private company	6	5

quate training was the most widespread deficiency noted by professionals. In Palm Beach County, for example, members of ambulance crews had only eight to ten hours of Red Cross training; one professional there felt that the competing interests of different groups involved in providing emergency care militated against county-wide ambulance planning which would include an improved training program.

Ambulance services in several of the communities had become involved in programs to upgrade the training of their crews. For example, fire and rescue workers in Fairfax County, which served Reston, completed a course for emergency medical technicians and fire department members had begun similar programs in Park Forest South and Irvine. Rescue crews in Westlake Village and Valencia were reported to have undertaken an advanced paramedic program.

The community which had placed the greatest emphasis on emergency training was Elk Grove Village. The community integrated its own program employing both paramedics and emergency medical technicians with a well-established area-wide program. Although Elk Grove Village was initially reluctant to become involved in such a program on the grounds that Alexian Brothers Hospital was close at hand, it ultimately opted for advanced tele-metering and ambulance equipment. Elk Grove Village was also the site of a mock disaster sponsored by the University of Illinois Civil Defense program to help the local fire department plan for emergencies. A civil defense radio group provided communications during disasters so that the village was connected to, literally, any point in the world. Ironically, in spite of Elk Grove Village's history of concern for emergency preparedness, a tragedy occured there in the winter of 1974 when a woman living in an unincorporated enclave surrounded by Elk Grove Village died while waiting for an ambulance from the Roselle Fire Department, six miles away. Although she lived but five blocks from the Elk Grove Village ambulance station, her family subscribed to the more distant Roselle ambulance service because of its lower cost.

This highlights the issue of ambulance service cost. In Elk Grove Village ambulance service was free to residents, but $42 a year for non-residents, twice that of the Roselle ambulance service. Elk Grove Village was one of five new communities in the sample in which ambulance service was free; the others were Columbia, Reston, Park Forest and Forest Park. Typical costs elsewhere were in the range of $25 to $40 per use, but were over $50 in Laguna Niguel, Lake Havasu City and Foster City.[d] In spite of the sometimes tragic con-

[d]These costs are estimates in those cases where costs included a flat rate, plus an additional charge per mile, plus, in some cases, extra charges depending on services provided.

sequences of cost, as noted above, there was only one community, Lake Havasu City, in which the cost of ambulance service was mentioned as a problem by health professionals.

Several objections were raised, however, to the related question of the private nature of ambulance service in some areas, particularly the California communities. The ambulance systems serving all of the communities in the Washington, D.C. area, North Palm Beach and Tequesta, Kingman (paired with Lake Havasu City) and all of the communities in the Midwest except Park Forest South and Lansing (paired with Park Forest) were run by public fire or police departments. The systems serving Park Forest South and Lansing were operated by funeral homes. All systems serving the California communities and Lake Havasu City were, at the time of the survey, privately operated.

The trend in the California communities appeared to be away from privately operated ambulance care. Because of the unreliable response times of private companies, the City of Irvine reached an agreement with Los Angeles County through which the city would purchase the equipment and the county would train emergency medical technicians for the city-run system. The paramedic program for Los Angeles County firemen that served Westlake Village and Valencia raised possible conflicts, according to a health professional, with private ambulance companies whose interests were in getting the victim to the hospital as quickly as possible rather than with providing on-the-spot care.

Another problem area noted by health professionals was that of cooperation with hospitals. This was a potential difficulty in all of the sample communities, since none of the systems serving them was provided by a hospital. Paramedic programs in particular required effective communication with hospitals. The Elk Grove Village system, for example, used radio contact with Northwest Community Hospital in Arlington Heights, which had the equipment required by the paramedic system, but patients were carried to Alexian Brothers Hospital in Elk Grove Village; the two emergency rooms were also in contact with one another. Radio communication for the system serving Westlake Village presented problems because of the canyons in the area. The proposal for a satellite emergency center in Reston included close coordination of transportation services and the treatment center; the proposal called for emergency transportation to be provided by the satellite facility and for the stationing of paramedics at the facility.

Health professionals in both North Palm Beach and Lake Havasu City and their paired conventional communities expressed a need for either improved vehicles or better equipment in the ambulances serving these communities. Emphasis on emergency care and emergency transportation in remote Lake Havasu City is illustrated in a number of other ways: a mouth-to-mouth resuscitation program sponsored by the Heart Association; a plea from the fire department that residents use reflectors to make identification of their addresses easier; and a proposal for an air ambulance service.

In spite of the overall satisfaction with ambulance service in the communities studied, it is an area in which there is likely to be considerable unhappiness where deficiencies exist. The obvious interest of residents in emergency care generally and access to that care in particular suggests the importance of effective systems of emergency transportation staffed with trained personnel and offered at reasonable cost. The availability of such systems may ultimately prove to be more significant than the presence of hospitals in determining residents' satisfaction with health care.

CONCLUSIONS

The experiences of the new and conventional communities discussed in this chapter illustrate a basic dilemma in the provision of hospital services to residents of planned communities. The presence of a hospital facility within a community is closely associated with residents' satisfaction with community health care facilities and services (see Chapter 9). Moreover, the construction of hospitals in planned communities or activities supportive of hospital construction have been a favored means of involvement in health matters by developers (see Chapter 2). But the activities of developers in support of hospital projects—in communities such as Irvine, Reston and Westlake Village —may exacerbate the widely noted problems of excessive hospital beds and duplication of services. Because most new communities are satellites of metropolitan areas rather than freestanding entities, it is rarely necessary for them to have hospitals of their own. Community pride or a desire to sell property are inadequate reasons to plan hospitals for individual communities.

The planning of hospitals should be coordinated more closely with the needs of the surrounding area. Where hospitals are placed in suitable locations in the vicinity of a community and where transportation systems render those hospitals accessible to community residents, satisfaction with health care may not depend so heavily on the availability of a community hospital. Intelligent placement of hospitals in proximity to, but not necessarily within, planned communities would probably serve to attract an ample number of physicians to the community's vicinity. Meanwhile, it may be helpful for developers and others involved with community health care planning to devote greater attention to facilities which could more appropriately be planned on a community basis. These might include emergency care stations, county-operated health clinics, clinics operated in conjunction with health maintenance organizations and counseling centers for emotional problems. It may be the absence of such facilities that, in the past, has led residents to view a local community hospital as essential to the well-being of the community.

Chapter 6

Other Health and
Social Services

If physicians' services, hospital care and ambulance service represent the areas of health care requiring the most immediate attention, they hardly exhaust the community health needs that must be considered. A number of findings discussed earlier in this book suggest that one major area of neglect is the group of activities broadly described as social services. Health professionals in a number of communities, as discussed in Chapter 2, noted problems of stress and anxiety among new community residents. Yet services designed to provide assistance in these and other areas of health care—including help with emotional problems, family and marital counseling, assistance with drug and drinking problems, family planning, health care for children and prenatal care—were often perceived by residents as unavailable. In this chapter residents' awareness of the availability of various health care and social services is examined, together with health care professionals' evaluations of existing services and suggestions regarding needed social service programs. The chapter also discusses the operation of information and referral systems, the provision of nursing and convalescent care facilities and public health facilities in new and conventional communities.

RESIDENTS' AWARENESS
OF SOCIAL SERVICES

Household survey respondents were asked whether each of a number of services were available "in this community or its vicinity." The affirmative responses for six of those services—help with a drinking problem, help with a drug problem, help with an emotional problem, family and marital counseling, family planning and public assistance and welfare—are summarized in Table 6-1. The results show that in the minds of a substantial proportion of new and conventional community residents there are serious gaps in service coverage. Only two of the six services—help with a drug problem and help with an emotional problem—were perceived to be available by half or more of the new community respondents, even though health professionals indicated that most of the services were available in the immediate vicinity of each of the communities studied. Apparently either professionals' views of what constitutes availability differ greatly from those of the potential users of social services or there is a serious problem regarding public knowledge of these services.

As shown in Table 6-1, new community residents were somewhat more likely to be aware of various social services than residents of the paired conventional communities. In addition, five new communities—Park Forest, Columbia, Foster City, Reston and Elk Grove Village—stand out in terms of the relatively high proportions of residents who reported that the services were available in their community or its vicinity. Park Forest, for example, ranked first in terms of the proportion of respondents who were aware of three of the six social services—help with emotional problems, family and marital counseling and public assistance and welfare. Park Forest was one of only two new communities in which municipal governments provided direct financial support for mental health services. Park Forest's village government contracted for mental health services, including family counseling, with the Family Service and Mental Health Center of South Cook County, Inc., which was located in the adjacent city of Chicago Heights. The village also employed a social services director, while private groups manned a "hot line" crisis intervention service and a youth service center that offered counseling.

Columbia ranked among the top three new communities in terms of the proportion of its residents who were aware of each of the six services. Columbia residents, in fact, had access to a variety of social and counseling services. These included five agencies located in Columbia—the Columbia Medical Plan Clinic, Family Life Center, Grassroots, Inc. (a crisis intervention service), Planned Parenthood Association and Personal and Family Consultation Service. Additional services were available in Ellicott City, the county seat of Howard County. Although Foster City lacked the richness of social services available in Columbia—the most visible organization was a Council for the Prevention of Drug Abuse which focused its activities on public education—it was adjacent to the city of San Mateo, whose

79,000 residents had access to a full spectrum of health and social services (in this regard it is noteworthy that over 90 percent of the West San Mateo conventional community residents were aware of each of the six social services enumerated in Table 6-1). Finally, Elk Grove Village and Reston each had mental health counseling services located in the community. The Elk Grove Village–Schaumburg Townships Mental Health Center was established in 1966 with financial assistance provided, in part, by Elk Grove Village's city government. In 1974 the center had a staff of 25 persons and a budget of $300,000. In addition, the Alexian Brothers Medical Center in Elk Grove Village treated severe drug and alcoholism cases. A walk-in mental health clinic, operated by Fairfax County's Woodburn Center for Community Mental Health, was open two nights a week in Reston. Reston also had a planned parenthood clinic and a counseling and referral service was offered by the community's Common Ground Foundation.

Although residents' perceptions of social services were lower in the other new communities studied, it should not be concluded that services were entirely lacking. Activities that had received public attention in various of these communities included work in community mental health and counseling, alcoholism and drug treatment, rehabilitation and other services for the physically handicapped, child development, prenatal care, health education, mental retardation, family counseling, nutrition education, venereal disease and immunization programs.

HEALTH PROFESSIONALS' EVALUATIONS
OF SOCIAL SERVICES

On the whole, health professionals viewed social services less favorably than any other area of health care. In eight of thirteen nonfederally assisted new communities, including Columbia, Elk Grove Village, Forest Park, Foster City, Lake Havasu City, Laguna Niguel, North Palm Beach and Valencia, and in both federally assisted new communities half or more of the professionals interviewed said that social service programs were inadequate. The conventional communities fared no better—in eleven of the fifteen communities health professionals felt that improvements were needed.

Although some health and social service programs in the new and conventional communities were offered by public agencies or were supported by public funds, many others were run by church groups or voluntary associations. The variety of sources from which services were offered was viewed by health professionals as a potentially

Table 6—1. Residents' Perceptions of the Availability of Selected Health
(percentage distribution of respondents)

	Perceived Availability of Services[a]	
New and Conventional Communities	Help With a Drinking Problem	Help With a Drug Problem
Nonfederally Assisted New and Paired Conventional Communities		
Thirteen new communities	44	54[b]
Thirteen conventional communities	46	49
New and Paired Conventional Communities		
Columbia (NC)	57	78[b]
Norbeck-Wheaton (CC)	54	61
Elk Grove Village (NC)	41	65
Schaumburg (CC)	35	54
Forest Park (NC)	25	41
Sharonville (CC)	27	48
Foster City (NC)	59	63
West San Mateo (CC)	95[b]	95[b]
Irvine (NC)	26	31
Fountain Valley (CC)	37	43
Laguna Niguel (NC)	40	44
Dana Point (CC)	44	44
Lake Havasu City (NC)	53	65
Kingman (CC)	85	60
North Palm Beach (NC)	49	55[b]
Tequesta (CC)	47	22
Park Forest (NC)	59[b]	78
Lansing (CC)	35	72
Reston (NC)	51	69[b]
West Springfield (CC)	43	52
Sharpstown (NC)	46	53
Southwest Houston (CC)	46	49
Valencia (NC)	45	48
Bouquet Canyon (CC)	51	52
Westlake Village (NC)	42[b]	47[b]
Agoura/Malibu Junction (CC)	12	11
Federally Assisted New and Paired Conventional Communities		
Jonathan (NC)	36	38
Chanhassen (CC)	30	37
Park Forest South (NC)	35[b]	53[b]
Richton Park (CC)	16	31

NC = New Community   CC = Conventional Community

[a]*Question:* Here is a list of services available in many communities. We'd like to know, first, if such services are available in this community or its vicinity ... c. Family Planning; h. Public Assistance or Welfare Services; i. Family

	Perceived Availability of Services[a]		
Help With an Emotional Problem	Family and Marital Counseling	Family Planning	Public Assistance and Welfare
50[b]	43[b]	33	37
42	38	30	37
69	56	51	46
59	49	42	52
57	52	33	46
45	42	21	61[b]
32	27	10	15
29	29	18	18
60	59	57	60
93[b]	91[b]	91[b]	97[b]
30	22	21	20
41	32	35[b]	39[b]
44	36	37[b]	32
37	34	19	22
48	33	10	31
62[b]	34	29[b]	84[b]
57[b]	45[b]	24[b]	30[b]
18	19	6	6
73[b]	63[b]	40[b]	64[b]
42	37	27	37
49	43	30	31
48	31	25	33
57	43	36	29
53	41	46	37
40	34	28	45
37	36	25	51
49[b]	45[b]	38[b]	36[b]
12	15	14	9
43	38	34	70
35	27	23	61
51[b]	40[b]	19[b]	39
24	11	8	39

and Marital Counseling; j. Help with a legal problem; k. Help with a drug problem; l. Help with an emotional problem; m. help with a drinking problem.
[b]Statistically significant difference between new community(ies) and paired conventional community(ies) at 0.05 level of confidence.

serious problem. For example, one Elk Grove Village health professional described social services there as "fractured" and lamented the
lack of coordination between the Alexian Brothers Hospital, with its
medical approach, and the Elk Grove Community Services (parent
organization of the Elk Grove–Schaumburg Townships Mental Health
Center), with its social work orientation.

Of greater concern to professional respondents, however, was simply the inadequate level of services being offered. By far the greatest
number of comments had to do with emotional care. Health professionals serving two-thirds of the communities studied made comments along these lines. In Norbeck-Wheaton, for example, a county
health official described the most urgent needs as a 24-hour crisis
interventional center, additional psychiatrists in newly developed
sections of the county, halfway houses for after-treatment care for
psychiatric and retarded patients and outpatient services for emo-
tionally disturbed children.

Strong feeling was also expressed concerning the need for education and treatment programs for alcoholism and drug abuse. Other
areas requiring attention were numerous. The flavor of professional
comments regarding general needs for health and social programs is
illustrated by a partial list: adoption services; abortion referral; youth
programs and youth centers; home health care; suicide prevention;
augmented social work programs; and programs for prenatal and
child health care. As one Columbia health professional stated, "There
is a need for an all-purpose social service program which would include advocacy, referral, jobs, a friendship exchange, and liaison with
government agencies."

Even as these deficiencies were described by professionals, respondents in the household survey indicated a surprising lack of familiar-
ity with the programs that did exist. It also appeared that some
residents may not fully have understood their own needs for help.
For example, health professionals serving North Palm Beach described
the area as being "unsophisticated," in spite of its affluence, in terms
of social services. As an example, one professional noted that, "Drinking is a problem because in areas like these drinkers don't believe
they have a problem." Perhaps an overriding need in the communities studied was for a way to increase residents' awareness of both
the nature of their own problems and the availability of programs to
assist them.

INFORMATION AND REFERRAL

Sources of information about health services and referral mechanisms
were available in most of the communities in the sample. In many of

the new communities, information about health services was provided by community developers, multi-unit complex builders or developer-controlled community associations.[a] In others, similar material was made available by local governments, as in Park Forest, or by organizations such as the Junior Chamber of Commerce, as in Elk Grove Village. The *Comprehensive Health Survey* of Elk Grove Village also provided residents with a great deal of information. In or near Park Forest South and Irvine, "health fairs" had been used for the same purpose. In Jonathan, a two-way cable television system was developed, in part, to provide a "telemedicine" system which enabled doctors to communicate with both patients and other doctors.

The referral systems described by health professionals were operated primarily by county or municipal health departments or by county medical societies (usually known as Tel-Med programs, which direct callers to the types of physicians they need). Other organizations that sometimes provided referral services were hospitals and voluntary agencies.

In spite of the existence of such programs, the provision of suitable mechanisms for information and referral within the fragmented systems of health care serving the sample communities appeared to be an important problem area. Residents' relatively low perceptions of the availability of many services was one indication of this. Health professionals cited inadequacies in information and referral as major deficiencies in health care in Forest Park and its paired conventional community, Sharonville, and in Reston's paired conventional community, West Springfield. Residents' groups placed high priority on improving information and referral in Columbia, Elk Grove Village and Park Forest. Even in an affluent community such as Norbeck-Wheaton, "gaining entry into the health care system is a real problem" according to a health professional.

NURSING AND CONVALESCENT CARE FACILITIES

Nursing and convalescent facilities were not generally located in the sample communities nor were they usually perceived as available by residents.[b] Sharpstown was the only new community with such a

---

[a]These communities included Columbia, Elk Grove Village, Forest Park, Foster City, Jonathan, Laguna Niguel, North Palm Beach, Reston, Sharpstown, Valencia and Westlake Village.

[b]Forty-four percent of the new community and 50 percent of the conventional community respondents were aware of convalescent or nursing home care in their community or its vicinity. While there are important distinctions among

facility; among the paired conventional communities, convalescent care facilities were available in Kingman and West San Mateo. On the whole, health professionals did not see a great need for additional convalescent and nursing home facilities. Lake Havasu City, where about 20 percent of the household heads were retired, and Park Forest South were the only new communities in which health professionals were unanimous about the need for such facilities. In contrast, a majority of the professionals who were serving eight of the new communities and ten of the conventional communities felt that additional convalescent and nursing home facilities were not needed.

Some health professionals felt quite strongly about the need for such facilities, however, and placed them among the highest health care priorities facing the community. These views were expressed in Columbia, Lake Havasu City and Reston. A Reston health professional pointed out that the presence of nursing home facilities would make it easier for two-generation families to live within Reston, thereby helping to make Reston a more complete community. (A proposal for a combined convalescent care and emergency facility in Reston died when Gulf-Reston Inc. refused to cosponsor a rezoning application. A representative of Gulf-Reston pointed out that the land in question had been earmarked for church use and that there would be too much traffic at that location.)

In the vicinity of Elk Grove Village, nearly all types of nursing facilities were at or near capacity and the provision of additional facilities was recommended by the *Comprehensive Health Survey* (1972). Ironically, a facility existed within the community at one time, but went bankrupt because there was insufficient need to justify its 200 beds.

Nursing or extended care facilities were envisioned by the developer of Forest Park and are mentioned in the Department of Housing and Urban Development's project agreement with Park Forest South. Facilities of this type were to be added to a hospital in Lake Havasu City and one of Sharpstown's hospitals was being converted to a long-term care facility.

In Columbia, a proposed private nursing home was granted a certificate of need by the Maryland State Comprehensive Health Planning Agency and awaited approval by the Baltimore Regional Planning Council. Health professionals from the Council indicated that an

---

convalescent care facilities, long-term or extended care facilities and nursing or old-age homes, this study, in seeking an overview of facilities along these general lines, did not attempt to distinguish among them. In practice, moreover, it would appear that distinctions among these types of institutions are not always sharp.

earlier application had been rejected because of inadequate financing and because the applicants had failed to propose a "continuum of care," combining institutional services with outreach and home support. Park Forest also was seeking intermediate care service for convalescents and the elderly in their own homes.

PUBLIC HEALTH FACILITIES

Facilities offering public health services were not only absent from most of the new and conventional communities studied, but were also quite distant from them. Only Park Forest and Valencia and the conventional communities of Sharonville, West San Mateo and Kingman had public health facilities or programs located within the community. For all new communities the median distance to the nearest public health clinic was over seven miles (37,000 feet). Conventional community residents had to travel even farther for public health services, the median distance to the nearest facility being over nine miles (47,600 feet).

Health professionals had divided opinions as to whether existing public health facilities were of any use to new community residents. In eight new communities, including both federally assisted communities, half or more of the professionals interviewed thought such facilities were of value to residents, while in seven new communities a majority of the professionals thought public health facilities were of no use. In contrast, public health facilities were viewed as a useful source of care by half or more of the professionals serving thirteen of the fifteen paired conventional communities.

In explaining their reasons for these evaluations, some professionals stated that existing public health facilities were the only available sources of care for the community or the only sources of care serving low- and moderate-income residents. Several pointed out that people use public facilities only for certain types of services—most commonly immunization and, less frequently, social services. However, the Howard County Health Department offices were said to also be used by "gray area" Columbia residents who could not afford to join the Columbia Medical Plan but who were ineligible for state medical assistance.

Among professionals who stated that public sources of care were not useful, two explanations predominated: (1) because such services were geared to lower income people, residents of the new communities reputedly considered them to be inappropriate for their own use or believed that they were ineligible for public services; and (2) public health facilities were too far away or too difficult to reach. Others were critical of the quality of the facilities, which were described as poorly equipped, or disapproved of their methods of dispensing care, observing that clinics "treat categories of diseases, not people."

The combination of large distances to public health facilities and the sometimes negative attitudes toward them, especially in new communities, means that these facilities could not be considered a significant health resource for community residents. This situation contributed to the lack of variety in the types of health care available in planned new communities, with few alternatives to traditional private fee-for-service practice. It also could have contributed to the lack of diversity in the population of these communities, since few residents, other than those who had the means and the inclination to rely on private sources for most of their health needs, could find low-cost sources of care in the community.

SUMMARY

A serious deficiency in the provision of health services in the sample communities is the range of care available to residents. Although needs in such areas as emotional care and assistance with drinking or drug problems are great, residents' awareness of services in these areas was low and health professionals viewed the availability of services as inadequate. These difficulties were compounded by problems in the coordination of services. Existing information and referral programs left the problems largely unresolved. Convalescent care facilities were rarely found in the sample communities and in some areas health professionals felt the need for additional nearby facilities was urgent. Public health clinics were usually distant from the new communities and were often regarded by health professionals as resources that were of little use to community residents.

Chapter 7

Health Insurance and Health Maintenance Programs

Although new communities have not established an outstanding record in the provision of health care services, the
Federal Health Maintenance Organization (HMO) Act of
1974 (PL 93–222)[a] may stimulate more comprehensive approaches
to health care by making grants available for feasibility studies, planning and initial development of health maintenance organizations.
This chapter presents a brief summary of the pattern of membership
in prepaid medical plans and other kinds of medical or hospital insurance and examines the prospects for the development of prepaid
plans or health maintenance organizations in new communities. The
experience of Columbia, the only new community with a prepaid
health plan organized on a community basis, is analyzed in depth.

HEALTH INSURANCE AND PREPAID HEALTH PLANS

Well over 90 percent of the new and conventional community respondents held some type of health insurance. See Table 7–1. The new
and conventional communities were almost identical in this respect
(only 6 percent of the nonfederally assisted new community respondents and 5 percent of the paired conventional community respondents did not hold insurance or belong to a prepaid plan). Among
individual new communities, the proportion of respondents who did

[a]This act authorized $375 million in fiscal 1974–1978 to assist approxi-
mately 100 groups offering comprehensive health care for set fees on a monthly
or annual basis.

Table 7–1. Residents with Health Insurance and/or Membership in a Prepaid Health Plan
(percentage distribution of respondents)

New and Conventional Communities	Type of Plan[a]			
	Health Insurance Only[b]	Health Insurance and Prepaid Health Plan	Prepaid Health Plan Only	Neither Health Insurance nor Prepaid Health Plan
Nonfederally Assisted New and Paired Conventional Communities				
Thirteen new communities	85	2	7	6
Thirteen conventional communities	86	1	8	5
New and Paired Conventional Communities				
Columbia (NC)	54	10	29[c]	7
Norbeck-Wheaton (CC)	81[c]	2	6	11
Elk Grove Village (NC)	97	2	0	1
Schaumburg (CC)	98	0	0	2
Forest Park (NC)	93	0	4	3
Sharonville (CC)	97	0	1	2
Foster City (NC)	74	0	23	3
West San Mateo (CC)	72	2	21	5
Irvine (NC)	75	8	7	10
Fountain Valley (CC)	78	0	15	7
Laguna Niguel (NC)	77	6	6	11
Dana Point (CC)	79	3	10	8
Lake Havasu City (NC)	84	1	2	13
Kingman (CC)	78	1	0	21

Community				
North Palm Beach (NC)	91	2	1	6
Tequesta (CC)	93	1	1	5
Park Forest (NC)	95	1	0	4
Lansing (CC)	93	0	0	7
Reston (NC)	90[c]	1	7	2
West Springfield (CC)	76	0	19[c]	5
Sharpstown (NC)	94	0	1	5
Southwest Houston (CC)	92	0	0	8
Valencia (NC)	79	1	17	3
Bouquet Canyon (CC)	73	0	24	3
Westlake Village (NC)	85	3	5	7
Agoura–Malibu Junction (CC)	86	0	9	5
Federally Assisted New and Paired Conventional Communities				
Jonathan (NC)	88	1	2	9
Chanhassen (CC)	91	2	3	4
Park Forest South (NC)	95	1	0	4
Richton Park (CC)	95	0	1	4

NC = New Community   CC = Conventional Community

[a] *Question:* Do you belong to a prepaid medical plan or have any other kind of medical or hospital insurance?

[b] Includes respondents with either medical or hospital insurance.

[c] Statistically significant difference between new community(ies) and paired conventional community(ies) at 0.05 level of confidence.

not have insurance was greatest in Lake Havasu City (13 percent) and its paired conventional community, Kingman (21 percent).

Although the proportion of respondents who held health insurance or belonged to a prepaid health plan did not vary widely among new communities, it did vary among different groups of new community residents. As would be expected, income had a strong influence on insurance coverage. The proportion of respondents who had some type of insurance ranged from 83 percent of those with incomes under $5,000 per year to 94 percent of those with incomes of $25,000 or more. While 88 percent of the respondents who had not attended high school held health insurance, 97 percent of those with some post-college education were covered. In addition, renters (90 percent) were less likely to hold insurance than homeowners (95 percent); younger persons under 30 years old (92 percent) were less likely than the elderly (97 percent) to be covered, and persons who were separated (86 percent) or divorced (89 percent) were less likely to hold insurance than respondents who were married (95 percent). On the other hand, the proportion of new community respondents who held health insurance or belonged to a prepaid health plan did not vary by the race of the respondent, in part, because the income of black households living in new communities was as high as that of white households.

Relatively few new community or conventional community respondents (9 percent in each case) were members of prepaid health plans.[b] Membership in prepaid health plans was much higher in Columbia, where the Columbia Medical Plan was available (39 percent of the Columbia respondents belonged to a prepaid health plan), and in California, where the Kaiser Foundation Health Plan, Inc. concentrated its activities. Membership in the Kaiser Plan was highest in Foster City (23 percent of the respondents were members), Valencia (18 percent) and their paired conventional communities, West San Mateo (23 percent) and Bouquet Canyon (24 percent).

If current membership in prepaid plans was low, interest was not. Outside Columbia, health professionals in every new community other than Forest Park, Lake Havasu City and North Palm Beach indicated that consideration had been given to some type of prepaid plan. The same was true in most conventional communities. Most health professionals, however, did not have community-based plans in mind and many were speaking in terms of possibilities rather than concrete proposals. Still, there was reason for professionals to feel

---

[b]In the nation as a whole less than 5 percent of the population is enrolled in prepaid plans (see Robert M. Heyssel 1971).

that the sample communities were suitable areas for prepaid plans even where no formal consideration had been given to them. For example, it was pointed out that such a plan might work in the vicinity of North Palm Beach because of the presence of a large employer, Pratt Whitney, through which a plan could be made available and because a large number of young families with children lends itself to a prepaid program stressing preventive medicine. At the same time, however, health professionals felt that the "negativism" of the medical profession would have made the implementation of a prepaid health plan almost impossible in the near future. In Park Forest, a prepaid group practice was recommended as an approach that combined improved medical practice and improved financial coverage (see Hostetler and Prueske 1973).

Interest in prepaid plans had progressed further in several new communities. Park Forest South and Jonathan were both committed through their project agreements with the Department of Housing and Urban Development to investigate community-wide health plans. As early as 1971, discussions with a number of major insurance companies had been undertaken by the developer of Park Forest South toward that end, while Jonathan's planners envisioned a system modeled after the Kaiser or Columbia plans. In Westlake Village, a private prepaid program was established at Westlake Hospital strictly for Medi-Cal patients. The program allowed patients more than the two visits per month they could make under Medi-Cal while sparing doctors paperwork and increasing their profits. Service was free to enrollees and physicians were reimbursed by the state.

In 1973 Georgetown University operated a clinic in Reston which offered services on a fee-for-service basis. However, beginning in the spring of 1974 Reston residents could participate in the Georgetown University Community Health Plan through membership in the Reston Community Association. Initial rates were set at $20.96 for an individual and $63.95 for a family. Services included routine visits to the Reston-Georgetown Medical Center (located in Reston's Hunters Woods Village Center), various specialists' services, preventive health care, family planning and counseling, 24-hour emergency service, ambulance coverage and 365 days of hospital care per confinement.

The respondent representing the Georgetown Clinic in the professional health survey described the project as a comprehensive program emphasizing preventive care. He pointed out that as was not true of the Columbia Medical Plan there would be no geographical limits to service and estimated an eventual enrollment of 7000. Other professionals in the survey, however, were skeptical of the program. A representative of Gulf-Reston, Inc. regarded the project as a "money-loser," which could not survive without a hospital. Representatives of both the county health department and the county medical society raised basic objections to the HMO concept.[c]

THE COLUMBIA MEDICAL PLAN

The only new community where a community-based prepaid program can be judged on the basis of experience is Columbia. The Columbia Medical Plan is similar in concept to other prepaid health plans, such as the Kaiser Foundation plan, but its origins, structure, sponsorship, finances and organization are different. As noted in Chapter 2, James Rouse, the developer of Columbia, was concerned from the outset that the new community provide a full complement of community services. In 1964 Rouse approached The Johns Hopkins School of Medicine to explore its participation in the provision of health care services in the proposed new community. Since Johns Hopkins was at that time exploring ways of expanding its training program in family medicine, it agreed to collaborate in establishing a family-oriented group practice in Columbia. After four and one-half years of analysis and planning, a decision to proceed was made in February 1969 and the following October the Columbia Medical Plan was established.

The Columbia Medical Plan was initiated with three component entities: (1) The Johns Hopkins Medical Partnership, a financially independent physician partnership associated with the School of Medicine, was to be responsible for the provision of professional services; (2) The Columbia Hospital and Clinics Foundation, a nonprofit private hospital corporation controlled by The Johns Hopkins Hospital and The Johns Hopkins University, was to own facilities, employ nonphysician personnel and perform other duties of any hospital; and (3) Private health insurance carriers were to underwrite the risk.[d] These three entities were bound together by a contractual agreement

---

[c]The health department respondent described HMOs as "fadish" and "political." The medical society official objected to the Georgetown project because: (1) he disliked medicine offered through clinics; (2) there would be a lack of choice of physicians; (3) "Any doctor over 30 who is in the plan probably isn't very good"; and (4) health maintenance organizations competed unfairly because they could advertise and private doctors could not. Even a representative from the Reston Community Association, which had supported the Georgetown program from the outset, pointed out that the clinic would be a "well-staffed doctor's office," which would not meet emergency needs.

[d]For a full discussion of the history and organization of the Columbia Medical Plan, see Robert M. Heyssel (1971) and William F. Towle (1972). In order to establish its credibility as the general hospital for Howard County (see Chapter 4), in the spring of 1974 control of the Columbia Medical Center hospital was

that, according to William F. Towle (1972, p. 47), included: "(1) mutual agreement to the benefits to be provided, (2) agreement as to the number of members to be enrolled during any period and (3) negotiation of operating budgets." The contract guaranteed services through the plan and "cement(ed) the physician, the hospital and the insurer in a relationship ensuring the guarantee."

In 1973 the Columbia Medical Plan offered comprehensive health services to persons living in or near Columbia. Families could enroll in the plan either through employer groups or through special groups, such as the Columbia Park and Recreation Association. In addition to the back-up resources of Johns Hopkins Hospital, the 59-bed first phase of the Columbia Medical Center hospital became available in July of 1973, after the completion of the household survey. While premium rates differed somewhat depending on the group involved and the specific benefits, representative rates in 1973 were $20.75 for an individual, $39.00 for a family of two and $68.00 for a family of three or more. In addition to the basic premium, there were copayments of $2 for each prescription, $100 for maternity care and $10 for each psychiatric visit after the first fifteen (see Towle 1972, p. 49). Benefits covered by the plan included unlimited ambulatory visits for physicians' services, periodic health review, emergency care, laboratory and radiology services, immunizations and injections, referrals for consulation with specialists at Johns Hopkins, prescription drugs, full acute hospitalization with no limit on stay and at no charge, maternity services, psychiatric services (with a 30-day limit each year on hospitalization), home visits, ambulance service and out-of-area emergency services.

Enrollment in March 1973 was about 13,500, which by the fall of 1975 had increased to more than 18,000. As originally envisioned, the plan would require a membership of 25,000 to 30,000 before it could operate without financial subsidies.[e] In 1970 approximately 45 percent of Columbia's residents were enrolled in the plan (see Clifton Gaus 1971). As shown in Table 7–1, 39 percent of the 1973 Columbia household survey respondents reported that they belonged to a prepaid health plan, of which 92 percent indicated that they

---

transferred from the Columbia Hospital and Clinics Foundation to the hospital's own board of trustees. In July 1974 the hospital's name was changed to Howard County General Hospital, Inc. and by September 1974 enough new board members had been appointed so that control and ownership of the facility was in the hands of Howard County residents.

[e]Connecticut General Life Insurance Company and other insurance carriers assumed 100 percent of all operating losses of the plan during its first five years of operation and 90 percent of all losses thereafter, repayable from premiums paid by plan members (see E. Frank Harrelson and Kirk M. Donovan 1975).

belonged to the Columbia Medical Plan (36 percent of all Columbia respondents).

Characteristics of Columbia Medical Plan Members

Selected characteristics of the members of the Columbia Medical Plan are summarized in Table 7−2. In comparison with Columbia residents who had not joined the plan, members of the Columbia Medical Plan tended to be more affluent. For example, members of the plan were only about half as likely to have incomes under $10,000 per year (9 percent) as households who had not joined the plan (20 percent). On the other hand, members of the plan were much more likely (32 percent vs. 19 percent) to have annual incomes of $25,000 or more. These findings tend to substantiate the feelings of a number of health professionals that cost was an important barrier to membership in the Columbia Medical Plan.

Membership in the Columbia Medical Plan did not vary greatly by race. However, the plan tended to attract proportionately more members among married households with older household heads and/or spouses. Eighty-two percent of the plan members living in Columbia were married versus 72 percent of the residents of Columbia who had not joined the plan. Twenty-nine percent of the plan members were under 30 years old versus 51 percent of the nonplan Columbia residents. Plan members tended to have larger households and were much more likely than nonplan members to own their homes (74 percent) than to rent (26 percent). In contrast, a majority (54 percent) of the Columbia respondents who had not joined the Columbia Medical Plan were renters. Finally, members of the plan tended to have more formal education than nonplan Columbia residents.

Similar findings were reported by Clifton Gaus (1971) based on the results of a 1970 survey of 340 Columbia households. Gaus found that families who had joined the Columbia Medical Plan had higher annual incomes, larger families, older family heads and slightly greater educational attainment than families who had not enrolled in the plan. Gaus also reported that families who had moved to Columbia from outside of the Baltimore-Washington area were more likely to have joined the plan than families who had moved from within the area. The latter group apparently found it easier to retain their former sources of medical care after moving to Columbia and, as a result, plan membership was a less attractive alternative. The data summarized in Table 7−2 suggest that while in the short run residents may retain their former sources of care, over time there is a tendency to

Table 7–2. Characteristics of Members and Nonmembers of the Columbia Medical Plan, Spring 1973 *(percentage distribution of respondents)*

	Membership in Columbia Medical Plan[a]	
Characteristic	*Members*	*Nonmembers*
Race		
White	80	82
Nonwhite	20	18
Age of Respondent (household head or spouse)		
Under 30	29	51[b]
30–39	43	30
40–49	14	9
50–64	10	6
65 or older	3	4
Marital Status		
Married	83	72
Single, never married	5	15[b]
Widowed, divorced or separated	13	13
Household Size		
One person	10	10
Two persons	16	25
Three or more persons	74	65
Education of Respondent		
High school graduate or less	10	24[b]
Some college	26	20
College graduate	26	23
Graduate or professional training	38	33
Family Income (1972)		
Under $5,000	5	7
$5,000–$9,999	4	13
$10,000–$14,999	18	23
$15,000–$24,999	41	38
$25,000 or more	32	19
Tenure		
Owns (or buying)	77[b]	46
Rents	23	54[b]
Year First Moved to Community		
1967	4	0
1968	6	4
1969	25[b]	8
1970	15	15
1971	32	28
1972	18	45[b]
Sample Size	70	129

[a] Residents of Columbia, Maryland only.

[b] Statistically significant difference between members and nonmembers of the Columbia Medical Plan at 0.05 level of confidence.

switch to the Medical Plan alternative. For example, while a majority (51 percent) of the household survey respondents who were members of the plan had lived in Columbia for two or more years, only 27 percent of the nonplan respondents had lived in the community that long. While only 18 percent of the members of the Columbia Medical Plan had moved to Columbia the previous year (1972), 45 percent of the Columbia respondents who were not members of the plan had moved to the community in 1972. The effect of length of residence on residents' tendencies to join the Columbia Medical Plan is further illustrated in Table 7−3. Over 60 percent of the respondents who had moved to Columbia prior to 1970 were members of the plan versus 36 percent of those who moved to the community in 1970, 38 percent of those who moved in 1971 and only 17 percent of those who moved in 1972. In sum, the data indicate that as Columbia matures and as residents adjust to their new surroundings, the proportion of households who join the plan should gradually increase.

Medical Care Utilization

If some Columbia residents chose not to join the plan because they retained family physicians elsewhere, it was nevertheless the case that a far greater proportion of subscribers to the plan reported that they had a regular doctor or clinic than nonplan members (99 percent vs. 78 percent). See Table 7−4. In spite of nearly unanimous reports of a regular doctor or clinic by members of the Columbia Medical Plan and the emphasis on preventive care by the plan, the proportion of plan members who had had a routine check-up in the year previous to the survey did not differ greatly from the proportion of nonmembers who had had a routine check-up (77 percent vs. 72 percent).

Analysis of the mean number of physician visits in a one-year period by Columbia residents shows that members of the Columbia

Table 7−3. Length of Residence in Columbia and Membership in Columbia Medical Plan *(percentage distribution of respondents)*

	Year Household Moved to Columbia				
Membership	*1967−1968*	*1969*	*1970*	*1971*	*1972*
Membership in Columbia Medical Plan, Spring 1973					
Enrolled in plan	61	64	36	38	17
Not enrolled in plan	39	36	64	62	83
Sample size	12	27	29	57	70

Table 7–4. Health and Medical Care Utilization and Evaluations by Members and Nonmembers of the Columbia Medical Plan, Spring 1973 *(percentage distribution of respondents)*

Indicators	Membership in Columbia Medical Plan[a]	
	Members	Nonmembers
Utilization of Physicians' Services		
Regular Doctor or Clinic		
Yes	99[b]	78
No	1	22[b]
Routine Check-up during Past Year		
Yes	77	72
No	23	28
Visits to Doctors and/or Clinics during Past Year		
Mean	5.4	4.2
Median	3.6	2.4
Difficulties Experienced during Last Visit to Doctor		
Arranging appointment	29[b]	12
Arranging transportation	3	5
Cost in relation to treatment received	4	8
Failed to See or Talk to Doctor When Desired during Past Year		
Yes	21	23
No	79	77
Evaluations of Health and Medical Care		
Satisfaction with Regular Doctor or Clinic		
Completely satisfied	55	70
Satisfied	33[b]	17
Neutral or dissatisfied	12	13
Aware of and Willing to Recommend Health Services Located Within Community and its Vicinity		
Convalescent or nursing home care	4	2
Dental care	61[b]	41
Emergency medical care	65[b]	27
Family and marital counseling	38[b]	17
Family planning	37[b]	14
Health care for children	89[b]	45

(Table 7–4 continued overleaf . . .)

Table 7-4. continued

Indicators	Membership in Columbia Medical Plan[a]	
	Members	Nonmembers
Help with a drinking problem	44[b]	19
Help with a drug problem	55	42
Help with an emotional problem	60[b]	28
Hospital care	12	5
Prenatal care	59[b]	25
Public assistance and welfare	19	19
Overall Evaluation of Community Health Care Facilities and Services		
Excellent	37[b]	11
Good	44	34
Average	11	26[b]
Below average/poor	8	29[b]
Sample size	70	129

[a]Residents of Columbia, Maryland only.
[b]Statistically significant difference between members and nonmembers of the Columbia Medical Plan at 0.05 level of confidence.

Medical Plan were less reluctant to visit doctors than were Columbia residents who did not belong to the plan (5.4 visits compared to 4.2 visits). M.L. Peterson (1971) reported an even more dramatic difference in a 1971 comparison of Columbia Medical Plan members (8.0 visits) with the national average for a population of comparable income, age, sex and race (4.6 visits). Peterson's finding that 40 percent of the visits by Columbia Medical Plan members were for well-person care suggests, in a way not indicated by the new communities household survey, that the plan encouraged preventive care.

Peterson also reported that hospital utilization was lower than national averages, an interesting finding in view of the greater frequency of hospital use by early enrollees in the five-year period prior to joining (see Gaus 1971). While the greater use of ambulatory services, particularly preventive services, and the decreased use of hospital services may be viewed as an encouraging outcome of the Columbia Medical Plan, some observers have become concerned about the tendency of subscribers to overutilize services.[f] Moreover, the presence of the Howard County General Hospital in Columbia could result in increasing rates of hospitalization.

[f]According to Heyssel (1971, p. 70), the tendency toward overutilization may occur, "in part because they are testing us to see if we are delivering what we promised and probably because they believe that because the services are there, they should be used."

While utilization of physicians' services was greater for members of the Columbia Medical Plan, obtaining those services was not accomplished without difficulty. Among the Columbia respondents with a regular doctor or clinic (see Table 7−4), more than twice as many plan as nonplan members reported problems in arranging appointments (29 percent vs. 12 percent). Cost was somewhat less of an obstacle to members of the Columbia Medical Plan. Only 4 percent complained of the cost of treatment compared to a surprisingly low 8 percent of those who did not belong to the plan. Concerning the nonplan group, it appears that cost was more of a barrier to joining the Columbia Medical Plan that it was to seeking physicians' services on a given occasion. Also of great concern in terms of the operation of the Columbia Medical Plan was the fact that 21 percent of the respondents who belonged to the plan reported not seeing a doctor on at least one occasion when they wanted to during the previous year. See Table 7−4. If members of the plan were not much worse off in this respect than other Columbia residents (23 percent of the nonplan Columbia respondents had failed to see a doctor when wanted), neither did they seem to be doing much better in a plan with an objective of guaranteeing around-the-clock access to medical care.[g]

Columbia residents who belonged to the Columbia Medical Plan were more likely than nonplan members to be aware of and willing to recommend the use of a variety of health and social services in the community, including dental care, emergency medical care, family and marital counseling, family planning, health care for children, help with a drinking problem, help with an emotional problem and prenatal care. In addition, plan members gave much higher ratings to the overall quality of health care facilities and services in Columbia. They were more than three times as likely (37 percent vs. 11 percent) to rate facilities and services as excellent (see Table 7−4). While 55 percent of the Columbia respondents who did not belong to the plan rated health care facilities and services as average, below average or poor, this was true of only 19 percent of the respondents who were members of the Columbia Medical Plan.

Columbia health professionals generally felt that the Medical Plan was serving its enrollees well, but their comments were laced with qualifying remarks and indications of problem areas. The most frequently mentioned drawback of membership was its cost. There were also references to long waiting periods for service (although improve-

[g]A guiding principle of the plan is that "enrollees are guaranteed access to high quality medical care 24 hours a day, seven days a week" (Towle 1971, p. 48).

ments were anticipated when the hospital opened), inadequate preventive care and the small size of the full-time staff.

The comments of some of the professionals pointed to limitations in the suitability of the Columbia Medical Plan for many residents. Several health professionals felt that the plan worked well for those who could afford it, that it was economical "for a family of five seeing the doctor at least three times a week" and that members, as a self-selected group, were bound to be satisfied. Health professionals believed that the plan was unlikely to serve as a source of care for the whole community, however. In addition to the frequently mentioned obstacle of cost, residents' lack of awareness of the plan, the fact that many residents already had personal physicians and a preference for fee-for-service practice were cited as reasons. The plan was faulted by several health professionals for not making special accommodations for low- and moderate-income residents. Gaus (1971), in analyzing the results of a 1970 survey of residents, found that the most important reasons for not enrolling in the plan were excessive cost, satisfaction with present medical care arrangements and the limited selection of physicians (enrollees joined the plan chiefly for the large range of services available, the association with Johns Hopkins University and the convenience of the clinic).

Several doctors who held positions with physicians' organizations stated that the Columbia Medical Plan competed unfairly with private practice and lured the best-paying patients away from private practitioners; however, doubts were expressed that the plan would be able to compete as successfully with fee-for-service practice once office facilities and opportunities were available in Columbia for private doctors.

One area of contention at the time of the survey concerned the Columbia Medical Center hospital, which was then under construction. It was not clear whether hospital privileges would be made available to doctors outside the Columbia Medical Plan and to what extent nonemergency hospital services would be made available to persons who did not belong to the plan (both fears proved to be unfounded). Although the early experience of the hospital showed that two-thirds of the inpatients consisted of non-participants in the plan, it may still be true, as one professional stated, that the Columbia Medical Plan "made a major error in not broadening its base through the hospital," by deciding initially that the hospital should not serve as a general county facility.[h]

[h]This professional felt that the Columbia Medical Plan had in effect given its opponents in the county a veto over future hospital expansion, since expansion of the Columbia Medical Center hospital might have to be "wedded" to the

Writing in 1972, William F. Towle, the administrator of the Columbia Hospital and Clinics, identified the adjustment of physicians to an unfamiliar role in a health maintenance organization as one of the issues that had yet to be faced. By the time of the health professional survey, most professionals felt that physician participation in the Columbia Medical Plan had been successful from the point of view of the doctors involved and that doctors had become accustomed to working with a health maintenance organization. However, professionals who represented private physicians' groups indicated that the advantages the plan held for staff doctors were shorter hours, less responsibility and the opportunity to improve private practices on the side.

Towle (1972, p. 49) also described some of the steps required to bring about public acceptance of the Columbia Medical Plan:

> Only as a result of full establishment of options of medical care availability, extension of the markets to all residents of the enrollment area, adoption of a true dual choice for all residents, and acceptance of the services offered will it be possible to evaluate the degree of success of the endeavor.

Health professionals had a number of thoughts about the specific measures that would increase public acceptance and membership in the plan and that would increase its effectiveness for those who joined. A Columbia Medical Plan spokesman felt that additional services—including dental care, extended care and home care—should be added and emphasis should be placed on members' awareness of programs and on general health education. However, most professionals felt that more critical problems were the costs of membership and the corresponding lack of realistic opportunities for low- and moderate-income residents of Columbia to join. A change suggested by several health professionals would have allowed subscribers some latitude in selecting services and would not have required that all services be covered through a monthly premium.

While the health professional interview was designed to elicit comments regarding the experiences of physicians and patients with a community-based prepaid health plan, it is apparent that the Columbia Medical Plan had to contend with difficulties not discussed in these interviews. Heyssel (1971), for example, described the problems involved in attempting to market the plan through a multiplicity of employers working with a multiplicity of insurers. Towle (1972), pointed out the difficulties of developing effective working

---

plans of a second hospital and that the Columbia hospital had cut itself off from sources of capital financing, thereby driving up membership rates for subscribers.

relationships among a hospital, a private physicians' group, insurance carriers and consumer groups. Harrelson and Donovan (1975) discussed problems and successes of consumer participation in management of the plan. At the same time, the Columbia Medical Plan has had the advantage, particularly in its early years, of operating in a captive market, in which residents of a new, relatively isolated community had few alternatives to a prepaid plan that was being encouraged by the developer.

CONCLUSIONS

Based on the Columbia experience, new communities seem to be particularly appropriate settings in which to establish prepaid health plans. The community-based health maintenance organization (HMO) is an attractive way to provide comprehensive health services in locations where few other sources of care are available; the absence of competing forms of care may increase the chances for the successful operation of the HMO. But the real lesson of Columbia's experience is not that plans such as the Columbia Medical Plan should be the exclusive source of health care in the area, but that they should be designed to be available to all members of a balanced community who wish to join and to use them. The unhappiness resulting from developer actions which initially tended to exclude fee-for-service practice suggests the advisability of providing options for more than one type of service where prepaid plans are introduced. Moreover, much of the value of a prepaid plan is lost if it fails to serve all members when needed, as appeared to be the case in Columbia, or if, as was also the case, the cost of membership tends to exclude a significant portion of the community.

Chapter 8

Health Care for
Target Populations

Planned new communities are widely regarded as environments that can, or should, attract diverse populations, including low- and moderate-income persons, racial minorities, the elderly and families with teenage as well as younger children—in short, all of the groups whose presence is required to form a socially balanced community. In order to accomplish this task, it is necessary not only to remove practical and economic barriers to residence in the community, but also to provide the services and facilities required by the special needs of these groups.

Relatively few members of target populations resided in new communities in 1973.[a] Only 12 percent of new community respondents

[a]Some new communities had gone much farther than others in attracting low- and moderate-income persons, racial minorities and the elderly. With the exception of Elk Grove Village, each of the older new communities had a somewhat higher than average proportion of families with incomes under $10,000—Sharpstown, 22 percent; Park Forest, 16 percent; North Palm Beach, 16 percent; and Forest Park, 13 percent. This was also true of the five new communities with some form of subsidized housing for moderate-income families—Lake Havasu City, 33 percent; Columbia, 16 percent; Park Forest, 16 percent; Reston, 14 percent; and Forest Park, 13 percent as noted above. Among the federally assisted new communities, 40 percent of the Jonathan respondents had annual incomes of less than $10,000, while the proportion of lower income respondents in Park Forest South was 12 percent. For an analysis of income integration in new communities, see Helene V. Smookler (1976).

Both Columbia and Reston had developed nonexclusionary reputations and, as a result, had attracted higher than average black populations. Nineteen percent of the Columbia respondents and 4 percent of the Reston respondents were black. In addition, black in-migration into previously white neighborhoods had been occurring in Park Forest (6 percent black), Sharpstown (5 percent black)

reported annual family incomes of less than $10,000 (12 percent
of the respondents in conventional communities were also in this
income group). Black respondents comprised 3 percent of the sample
of new community residents (and only 0.6 percent of the conventional community sample).

Persons 65 years old and older repre-
sented less than 5 percent of the population of the sample new
communities—less than half the proportion of elderly persons in the
general population—while the proportion of elderly persons in the
conventional communities was only 2 percent. This low level of
representation creates difficulties in assessing the experiences of such
groups. Nevertheless, health professionals serving the new and conventional communities identified health care for the elderly, lower
income or teenage residents as one of the most critical areas of unmet
needs. Moreover, the lack of social diversity in the communities may
itself be a reflection of an inadequate provision of services for these
groups.

This chapter evaluates the extent to which health and social programs and facilities have been directed toward target populations and
examines the level of satisfaction with health care, utilization of
health services and obstacles to obtaining health care experienced by
these population groups. The analysis also focuses on comparisons
between target populations residing in new communities with those
who were residing in conventional suburban communities.

FACILITIES AND SERVICES FOR
TARGET POPULATIONS

It has already been seen that the new communities were not noted
for the availability of certain facilities that can be of particular importance to various target populations. Public health clinics, potentially
useful for lower income families, if not for all residents, were distant
from respondents' homes. Nursing homes, the availability of which
might give a community long-term appeal for older residents or those
concerned about the care of parents, were not found in most of the

and Forest Park (9 percent black). Jonathan had attracted few black households
(2 percent) but matched the Twin Cities metropolitan racial profile. Park Forest
South had attracted a significantly higher proportion of black households (10
percent at the time of the household survey) and was one of the few suburbs
south of Chicago with a racially mixed population.

Because elderly households (age 65 and older) are much less residentially
mobile than younger households, the underrepresentation of elderly persons in
the new communities studied is not surprising. Until these communities have had
a greater opportunity to mature, they are not likely to accumulate elderly persons proportionate to the nation as a whole. Over half of the respondents who
were 65 years old or older lived in three new communities located in warmer
climates—Lake Havasu City, Arizona; Laguna Niguel, California; and North Palm
Beach, Florida.

communities, and residents rarely felt they were available nearby. While drug problems are by no means limited to teenagers, programs to provide assistance with drug problems are clearly a basic need for people in this age group. Although most health care professionals indicated that drug programs were available to the new and conventional communities, only about half of the household survey respondents were aware of them. Among teenagers themselves, only 42 percent felt that there was someone other than family or friends they could turn to for advice about drugs or sex; in new communities, 40 percent knew of a source of assistance compared to 49 percent in the conventional communities.

Questioned about the existence of programs for target populations within the communities, health professionals found the communities to be better supplied with programs for the elderly than for the other groups and most poorly supplied with those for low-income residents. All thirteen nonfederally assisted communities, both of the federally assisted new communities and thirteen of the fifteen paired conventional communities were reported to have one or more health or social program designed for older residents. Programs for teenagers were identified in twelve new communities, including one federally assisted community and nine conventional communities. Only five new communities and six conventional communities were reported to have programs for lower income residents.

The exact comments of professionals depict a less encouraging picture of special services. Many of the services described as being intended for target populations were either not specific to a sample community (and usually not located within it), not directed at the particular target population in question or not concerned primarily with health care or social services. Typical responses for all three groups had to do with the availability of general county-wide programs or welfare departments, or with such important, but nonhealth, activities as youth employment services or senior citizens' organizations. The general programs described may well be useful to subgroups in the community population; but there is reason to doubt that a program which is not geared to a particular group will reach that group, since individuals may either be unaware of the program's applicability to them or may feel uncomfortable participating in it. Moreover, since teenagers, older persons and low-income residents are all likely to have difficulty arranging transportation, services located outside the community may not do them much good.

Most of the health professionals' remarks regarding programs for lower income people were references to often distant public health clinics or to such programs as Medicare or, in California, Medi-Cal. There were also occasional descriptions of the activities of volunteer or church groups, special hospital programs and, in a number of areas, nearby programs for lower-income people sponsored by medical societies. The five new communities with subsidized housing—Columbia, Forest Park, Jonathan, Lake Havasu City and Reston—were not noteworthy for the existence of health services designed to reach families with low incomes. Health professionals in those communities were evenly divided as to whether the nearest public health clinics were useful sources of care for community residents.

In the case of elderly residents, health professionals mentioned a few county services planned specifically for older people, such as a senior citizens' information service (Foster City) and a community mental health center specializing in the problems of aging (North Palm Beach), or programs likely to be relied on more heavily by older people than other age groups, including home-care services and mobile medical programs.

Health professionals' references to programs for teenagers were more specific with respect to the group in question than was the case for the other groups. These comments often concerned drug counseling or related services, such as crisis hotlines sponsored by a variety of agencies, including local and county governments, schools, hospitals, churches and volunteer groups. Some of the same groups sponsored programs in sex counseling, venereal disease prevention and treatment and emotional counseling. But even in Columbia, which was stronger than many communities in terms of youth-oriented programs, one health professional commented that "overall, teenagers represent Columbia's greatest failure."[b]

A survey of the activities publicized in local newspapers indicated that several additional programs for target populations, including some that were not mentioned by health professionals, were available in the new and conventional communities.[c] However, this survey also indicated that there was considerably less activity and interest in such programs than in any other area of health care.

[b]This professional and others who elaborated on the situation of teenagers in new communities was not thinking primarily in terms of health care, however. Their comments related to widespread feelings of boredom, alienation and hostility on the part of teens in new communities and other suburban areas. Drug problems and the need for services to deal with them are a manifestation of these deeper-seated problems. In one example, in the spring of 1974 Irvine became the scene of one of the largest drug raids in California history and most of the nearly 100 arrested were teenagers.

[c]Examples of programs for lower income people attracting notice from late 1972 to early 1974 include the counseling work of Elk Grove Village Community Services, the prepaid health plan set up for Medi-Cal patients at Westlake Hospital and the use of a sliding scale for patients at the Woodburn Center for Community Mental Health, which operated a branch in Reston. For teenagers, there was a VD clinic at Elk Grove Village's Alexian Brothers Hospital for all persons over the age of twelve, a program of drug seminars including both police

Two remaining questions concerning health care facilities and services for target populations are (1) whether target populations enjoy greater access to basic health services in new communities than in other types of communities and (2) whether target populations are as aware of available health and social services as the general populations of new communities and target populations living in conventional communities. To answer these questions comparisons were made among three sets of communities. In the case of low- and moderate-income residents, the comparisons focused on the residents of subsidized housing living in five new communities—Columbia, Forest Park, Jonathan, Lake Havasu City and Reston—and two specially selected conventional communities—Laurel, Maryland and Richton Park, Illinois—that had subsidized housing projects. The availability of health care resources for black residents was examined in five new communities with substantial black populations—Columbia, Forest Park, Park Forest, Park Forest South and Reston—in comparison with specially selected convetnional suburban communities—Markham, Illinois and Seat Pleasant, Maryland—that had large predominantly black residential areas. Finally, comparisons were made among the elderly residents (age 65 or older) who were living in the thirteen nonfederally assisted new communities, thirteen paired conventional communities and two retirement communities—Rossmoor Leisure World, California and Sun City Center, Florida—that were designed specifically for the elderly.

As shown in Table 8–1, the new communities with subsidized housing had fewer primary care physicians (general practitioners, internists, osteopaths, pediatricians and obstetrician-gynecologists) than the two specially selected conventional communities with subsidized housing. However, in terms of the accessibility of the nearest sources of care, the new community subsidized housing residents fared somewhat better than those living in the two conventional communities. Within the five new communities, subsidized housing residents lived somewhat farther from the nearest general practitioner than nonsubsidized housing residents, but were marginally closer to the nearest hospital and public health clinic.

None of the new or conventional communities with substantial black populations was well supplied with primary care physicians.

---

and teenagers in Foster City and, in Reston, a church-sponsored walk-in clinic providing teen counseling. Programs directed toward the elderly included free bus service to doctors' offices and elsewhere for older people in Elk Grove Township. There were other programs mentioned that provided assistance of a general nature to persons in need, but on the whole there was far less comment and less activity in these areas than there was regarding hospitals, ambulances, physicians' services and other health and social services.

Table 8–1. Availability of Basic Health Resources for Target Populations

Communities and Population Groups	Primary Care Physicians per 100,000 Population	Median Road Distance to Nearest: (feet)		
		General Practitioner	Hospital	Public Health Clinic
Communities with Subsidized Housing Residents				
Five new communities[a]				
Nonsubsidized housing residents	54	6,300	47,100	22,000
Subsidized housing residents	54	7,500	45,600	20,100
Two conventional communities[b]				
Subsidized housing residents	102	11,000	55,500	31,500
Communities with Black Residents				
Five new communities[c]				
Nonblack residents	39	7,100	45,600	26,500
Black residents	39	7,600	52,700	34,800
Two conventional communities[d]				
Black residents	26	5,200	9,700	100,000+
Communities with Elderly (age 65 or older) Residents[e]				
Thirteen nonfederally assisted new communities				
Nonelderly (under age 65) residents	68	7,000	14,800	36,400
Elderly residents	68	6,300	12,600	44,800
Thirteen conventional communities				
Elderly residents	63	5,100	48,000	97,200

Two retirement communities (elderly residents)				
Rossmoor Leisure World	100	6,100	27,200	60,100
Sun City Center	67	7,200	100,000+	56,300

[a] Five new communities with subsidized housing subsamples (N = 271) include: Columbia, Forest Park, Jonathan, Lake Havasu City and Reston.

[b] Two conventional communities with subsidized housing samples (N = 133) include: Laurel, Maryland and Richton Park, Illinois.

[c] Five new communities with black subsamples (N = 246) include: Columbia, Forest Park, Park Forest, Park Forest South and Reston.

[d] Two conventional communities with black samples (N = 201) include: Markham, Illinois and Seat Pleasant, Maryland.

[e] The samples of elderly (age 65+) residents included: Thirteen nonfederally assisted new communities (N = 155); thirteen paired conventional communities (N = 97); Rossmoor Leisure World (N = 87); and Sun City Center (N = 68).

The five new communities had only 39 physicians per 100,000 population, while the two conventional communities were even worse off with only 26 physicians per 100,000 population (see Table 8–1). However, the accessibility of the nearest physicians and nearest hospital (but not the nearest public health clinic) tended to be better in the two conventional communities. Among the new community respondents, nonblack residents tended to live somewhat closer to health care resources than black residents.

In the case of elderly residents, those living in new communities tended to have better access to health care facilities and services than elderly residents of the retirement communities and younger new community residents. Although elderly residents of the paired conventional communities tended to live closer to the nearest general practitioner, new community elderly residents lived closer to the nearest hospital and public health clinic.

Target populations' awareness of community health and social services is summarized in Tables 8–2 (subsidized housing residents), 8–3 (black residents) and 8–4 (elderly residents). Low- and moderate-income residents of subsidized housing were likely to be as aware of health care and social services available to them as nonsubsidized housing residents of the same new communities. In fact, in three instances—family planning, hospital care and public assistance and welfare—higher proportions of subsidized housing than nonsubsidized housing residents were aware of the services. For seven of the twelve facilities and services summarized in Table 8–2, new community subsidized housing residents were significantly more likely to be aware of available services than subsidized housing residents living in the two conventional communities.

In comparison with nonblack residents, black residents of the same five new communities were in many cases significantly less likely to be aware of health and social services and facilities (see Table 8–3). For example, fewer blacks than nonblacks indicated that they knew about convalescent and nursing home care, dental care, family or marital counseling or help with a drug problem in their communities or their vicinities. In addition, black new community residents were no more likely to be aware of various services than black residents of the predominantly black sections of the two specially selected conventional communities. New community black respondents were significantly more likely to be aware of dental care, family and marital counseling, health care for children and help with a drug problem, but were significantly less likely to be aware of convalescent or nursing home care, hospital care and public assistance and welfare services. In the case of the remaining services summarized

Table 8–2.   Awareness of Community Health and Social Services: Subsidized Housing Residents[a]
(percentage distribution of respondents)

Service	Five New Communities[b]		Two Conventional Communities[c]
	Nonsubsidized Housing Residents	*Subsidized Housing Residents*	*Subsidized Housing Residents*
Convalescent or nursing home care	9	13[e]	23
Dental care	82	85[e]	69
Emergency medical care	69	74	75
Family and marital counseling	38	44[e]	21
Family planning	25	34[d]	33
Health care for children	70	76[e]	54
Help with a drinking problem	45	45[e]	23
Help with a drug problem	60	56[e]	31
Help with an emotional problem	48	49[e]	26
Hospital care	24	35[d]	36
Prenatal care	56	61[e]	43
Public assistance and welfare	34	53[d]	45
Sample size	883	271	143

[a]*Question*: Here is a list of services available in many communities. We'd like to know, first, if such services are available in this community or its vicinity . . .

[b]Five new communities with subsidized housing subsamples include: Columbia, Forest Park, Jonathan, Lake Havasu City and Reston.

[c]Two conventional communities with subsidized housing samples include: Laurel, Maryland and Richton Park, Illinois.

[d]Difference between subsidized housing and nonsubsidized housing new community respondents statistically significant at 0.05 level of confidence.

[e]Difference between subsidized housing new community respondents and subsidized housing conventional community respondents statistically significant at 0.05 level of confidence.

Table 8–3.   Awareness of Community Health and Social Services: Black Residents[a]   (percentage distribution of respondents)

Service	Five New Communities[b]		Two Conventional Communities[c]
	Nonblack Residents	Black Residents	Black Residents
Convalescent or nursing home care	27[d]	19[e]	31[e]
Dental care	84[d]	73[e]	49
Emergency medical care	73	68	60
Family and marital counseling	47[d]	36[e]	26
Family planning	30	31	39
Health care for children	77	72[e]	43
Help with a drinking problem	46[d]	41[e]	21
Help with a drug problem	64[d]	53[e]	25
Help with an emotional problem	51	48[e]	23
Hospital care	44[d]	35	59[e]
Prenatal care	59	52	44
Public assistance and welfare	39	32	45[e]
Sample size	1,035	290	203

[a]Question: Here is a list of services available in many communities. We'd like to know, first, if such services are available in this community or its vicinity . . .

[b]Five new communities with black subsamples include: Columbia, Forest Park, Park Forest, Park Forest South and Reston.

[c]Two conventional communities with black samples include: Markham, Illinois and Seat Pleasant, Maryland.

[d]Difference between black and nonblack new community respondents statistically significant at 0.05 level of confidence.

[e]Difference between black new community respondents and black conventional community respondents statistically significant at 0.05 level of confidence.

Table 8-4. Awareness of Community Health and Social Services, Elderly Residents (Age 65+)[a]
(percentage distribution of respondents)

Service	New Communities[b]		Conventional Communities[c]	Retirement Communities Age 65 or Older	
	Under Age 65	Age 65 or Older	Age 65 or Older	Sun City Center	Rossmoor Leisure World
Convalescent or nursing home care	44	41	31	0[f]	98[f]
Dental care	86[d]	74	80	94[f]	97[f]
Emergency medical care	83[d]	68	74	99[f]	99[f]
Help with a drinking problem	45[d]	32	41	5[f]	39
Help with a drug problem	55[d]	37[e]	22	6[f]	38
Help with an emotional problem	51[d]	34[e]	19	3[f]	40
Hospital care	73	75[e]	40	5[f]	97[f]
Public assistance and welfare	37[d]	27[e]	15	3[f]	36
Sample size (average)	2,414	154	97	68	87

[a] Question: Here is a list of services available in many communities. We'd like to know, first, if such services are available in this community or its vicinity . . . .

[b] Residents of thirteen nonfederally assisted new communities.

[c] Residents of thirteen nonfederally assisted paired conventional communities.

[d] Difference between new community respondents under 65 years old and age 65 years old and over statistically significant at 0.05 level of confidence.

[e] Difference between new and conventional community respondents age 65 years old and older statistically significant at 0.05 level of confidence.

[f] Difference between new community and Sun City Center or Rossmoor Leisure World respondents age 65 years old and older statistically significant at 0.05 level of confidence.

in Table 8−3, differences in levels of awareness of health care and social services were not statistically significant.

In most instances, new community elderly residents were less likely to be as aware of available health and social services than younger new community residents (see Table 8−4). The most serious gap in awareness was emergency service. Only about two-thirds (68 percent) of the elderly new community residents indicated that they knew of such a service in their community or its vicinity versus 83 percent of the younger new community residents. For the most part, however, elderly new community residents were just as likely to know of available health and social services as elderly residents of the conventional communities. In fact, they were significantly more likely to be aware of hospital care, public assistance and help with a drinking and a drug problem in their communities or their vicinities. Finally, the elderly residents of one of the reitrement communities, Rossmoor Leisure World, tended to be well informed about available health care services. The Rossmoor Leisure World residents' awareness of health and social services can be attributed to the activities of the Leisure World Foundation, which had established an Office of Medical Administration to assist residents with their health care needs. Among other activities, the Office of Medical Administration supervised a medical center, provided home-support services with nurses and doctors on 24-hour call, operated an ambulance service and sponsored a weekly closed circuit television series that dealt with personal health. In the other retirement community, Sun City Center, most residents were aware of dental care and the resident-operated emergency ambulance service, but very few felt that convalescent or nursing home care, help with a drug problem, hospital care or public assistance and welfare services were available to their community.

In summary, it has been shown that although new community development has been viewed as one means of attaining social balance in the suburbs, as of 1973 few new communities were providing health care and social services designed to meet the needs of target populations. On the other hand, low- and moderate-income residents, blacks and the elderly were no worse off in new communities than they were in nearby less planned conventional communities. In fact, subsidized housing residents of new communities tended to live closer to various health care facilities and services and were more likely to be aware of available services than subsidized housing residents living in conventional communities. New community black residents lived somewhat farther from and were less aware of health and social services than non-black residents of the same new communities, but tended to be no worse off in this regard than residents of predominantly black sections of conventional suburban communities. Finally, elderly residents of new communities were somewhat less likely than younger residents to be aware of various health and social services, but were no worse off than elderly residents living in conventional communities. In comparison with the elderly residents of the new and conventional communities, elderly residents of Rossmoor Leisure World were much better informed about available health and social services because a special institution, the Leisure World Foundation, had been formed specifically to address the needs of the elderly living in that community.

UTILIZATION OF HEALTH CARE FACILITIES AND SERVICES

Although the literature on the subject of health care utilization indicates that persons in low- and moderate-income groups and blacks utilize health care services less frequently than the general population,[d] there is little evidence that this was the case among target populations who were living in the sample new and conventional communities. As shown in Table 8—5, low- and moderate-income residents of subsidized housing were just as likely as nonsubsidized housing residents to have had a regular doctor or clinic and to have had a routine annual check-up during the previous year. The median number of visits to doctors during the previous year, 2.3, was the same for both new community subsidized housing and nonsubsidized housing residents. Subsidized housing residents living in the conventional communities were somewhat more likely than those living in new communities to have had a regular doctor or clinic and to have visited a doctor.

It would be encouraging to report that the lack of variation in utilization measures by income was due to the attention given to the placement of health resources in new communities. It has already been seen, however, that new communities were not noteworthy for the planning of health care facilities, that they did not have more health care resources than the conventional communities with subsidized housing and that utilization was as frequent in the conventional communities as in the new communities. A more probable explanation is, as has been contended recently by Monteiro (1973), that differences between income groups in terms of physician visits are diminishing on a national basis.

It is possible that these patterns of utilization can be explained by

[d]See National Center for Health Services Research and Development (1972, pp. 20, 23).

Table 8–5.   Utilization of Physicians' Services by Target Populations

Target Population	Percent of Respondents Who during Past Year Had		Median Number of Visits to Doctor During Past Year
	Regular Doctor or Clinic	Routine Annual Check-up	
Subsidized Housing Residents			
Five new communities[a]			
Nonsubsidized housing residents	81	71	2.3
Subsidized housing residents	83	75	2.3
Two conventional communities[b]			
Subsidized housing residents	86	73	2.8
Black Residents			
Five new communities[c]			
Nonblack residents	84	69	2.2
Black residents	91	84	2.4
Two conventional communities[d]			
Black residents	85	76	2.1
Elderly (Age 65 or older) Residents[e]			
Thirteen nonfederally assisted new communities			
Nonelderly (under age 65) residents	83	71	2.0
Elderly residents	82	74	2.3

Thirteen conventional communities			
Elderly residents	89	83	2.9
Two Retirement Communities			
(elderly residents)			
Rossmoor Leisure World	85	68	3.4
Sun City Center	87	65	2.0

[a]Five new communities with subsidized housing subsamples (N = 271) include: Columbia, Forest Park, Jonathan, Lake Havasu City and Reston.

[b]Two conventional communities with subsidized housing samples (N = 135) include: Laurel, Maryland and Richton Park, Illinois.

[c]Five new communities with black subsamples (N = 246) include: Columbia, Forest Park, Park Forest, Park Forest South and Reston.

[d]Two conventional communities with black samples (N = 201) include: Markham, Illinois and Seat Pleasant, Maryland.

[e]The samples of elderly (age 65+) residents include: thirteen nonfederally assisted new communities (N = 155); thirteen paired conventional communities (N = 97); Rossmoor Leisure World (N = 87); and Sun City Center (N = 68).

a greater awareness by residents of subsidized housing of assistance in obtaining care or by a greater need for care. In new communities with subsidized housing, subsidized housing residents were more familiar with sources of public assistance (as shown in Table 8−2, 53 percent knew of such sources compared with 34 percent of the nonsubsidized housing group). However, there was little difference between the two groups in terms of their assessments of their own health (85 percent of the subsidized housing residents were satisfied with their health status compared to 88 percent of the residents who did not live in subsidized housing). Residents of subsidized housing in the two conventional communities, for their part, were more familiar with sources of public assistance than nonsubsidized housing new community residents (45 percent vs. 34 percent), and rated the status of their own health less favorably (83 percent were satisfied with their health status compared to 88 percent of the nonsubsidized housing new community respondents).

Black respondents in the five new communities with significant black populations were more likely than nonblacks to have a regular doctor or clinic (91 percent compared to 84 percent) and were far more likely to have had a check-up in the past year (84 percent compared to 69 percent). Racial differences in the number of doctors visits per year were insignificant (medians of 2.2 visits per year for nonblacks compared to 2.4 visits per year for blacks). Since it has been suggested that racial differences in health services utilization can be attributed to the greater representation of blacks in lower socioeconomic groups (Geraldine A. Gleeson and Elijah L. White 1965), the present findings may be explained by the fact that blacks in the sample new communities tended to be as well educated, as likely to be employed in professional occupations and as affluent as nonblacks who were living in the same communities.

The tendency of older people to require and use physicians' services more frequently than younger persons is well substantiated.[e] This pattern generally held in the sample communities. See Table 8−5. Respondents who were 65 years old or older made more doctor visits than any other age group living in new communities. However, the 65 and over group living in the conventional communities made considerably more visits than was the case in new communities. Respondents in Rossmoor Leisure World visited doctors the most frequently. There were no pronounced differences among age groups or communities in terms of the proportions of respondents who reported that they had a regular doctor or clinic. The new and retire-

[e]See Ronald Anderson and Odin W. Anderson (1967) and Odin W. Anderson (1963).

ment communities were similar in terms of the proportions of respondents who had had a routine check-up during the previous year. In contrast, the conventional community elderly residents were significantly more likely to have had an annual check-up.

OBSTACLES TO OBTAINING
HEALTH CARE SERVICES

In the five new communities with subsidized housing, 22 percent of the subsidized housing respondents failed to see a doctor when desired compared to 18 percent of the respondents who were not living in subsidized housing (see Table 8—6). Subsidized housing respondents with regular doctors had greater difficulty arranging appointments (17 percent vs. 14 percent), arranging transportation (9 percent vs. 3 percent) and also had more difficulties with cost (11 percent vs. 8 percent). Respondents living in subsidized housing in the conventional communities had more difficulty in seeing a doctor when they wanted than new community subsidized housing residents (26 percent vs. 22 percent had failed to see a doctor when desired during the previous year). However, among the subsidized housing residents with their own regular sources of care, smaller proportions of those who were living in the conventional communities reported difficulties in arranging appointments and transportation or the cost of seeing a doctor.

With respect to race, black respondents living in new communities were somewhat more likely to have neglected visiting a doctor than were nonblack respondents who were living in the same communities (21 percent compared to 18 percent) and were more likely to have neglected seeing a doctor than black respondents in the two suburban conventional communities (14 percent). In particular, black residents in two new communities had problems. The percentages in Reston and Park Forest South, respectively, were 27 percent and 29 percent for blacks compared to 15 percent and 20 percent for nonblacks. The major obstacle to seeing a doctor when desired was the inconvenience involved in obtaining care.

New community blacks had no more difficulty with visits to doctors than nonblacks where a regular source of care was involved. The only complaint voiced more often by black respondents was arranging transportation (6 percent compared to 4 percent). It was in the two conventional communities that blacks had difficulties when they attempted to utilize regular sources of care. Markham, in particular, was a community in which blacks seemed to experience numerous obstacles in receiving care. Twenty-seven percent of the black respon-

Table 8–6. Difficulties in Obtaining Medical Care Experienced by Target Populations (percentage distribution of respondents)

Target Population	Failed to See Doctor When Desired	Difficulties during Last Visit to Doctor[a]		
		Arranging Appointment	Arranging Transportation	Cost
Subsidized Housing Residents				
Five new communities[b]				
Nonsubsidized housing residents	18	14	3	8
Subsidized housing residents	22	17	9	11
Two conventional communities[c]				
Subsidized housing residents	26	7	8	9
Black Residents				
Five new communities[d]				
Nonblack residents	18	13	4	11
Black residents	21	10	6	8
Two conventional communities[c]				
Black residents	14	19	15	21
Elderly (age 65 or older) Residents[f]				
Thirteen nonfederally assisted new communities				
Nonelderly (under age 65) residents	16	10	4	12
Elderly residents	10	8	8	12
Thirteen conventional communities				
Elderly residents	11	8	2	4

Two retirement communities
(elderly residents)

Rossmoor Leisure World	5	4	0	11
Sun City Center	8	5	2	2

a Respondents with a regular doctor or clinic only.

b Five new communities with subsidized housing subsamples (N = 271) include: Columbia, Forest Park, Jonathan, Lake Havasu City and Reston.

c Two conventional communities with subsidized housing samples (N = 133) include: Laurel, Maryland and Richton Park, Illinois.

d Five new communities with black subsamples (N = 246) include: Columbia, Forest Park, Park Forest, Park Forest South and Reston.

e Two conventional communities with black samples (N = 201) include: Markham, Illinois and Seat Pleasant, Maryland.

f The samples of elderly (age 65+) residents include: thirteen nonfederally assisted new communities (N = 155); thirteen paired conventional communities (N = 97); Rossmoor Leisure World (N = 87); and Sun City Center (N = 68).

dents who were living in Markham complained of problems with arranging appointments, 20 percent complained of transportation difficulties and 27 percent complained of the cost. Thus, if blacks in the two conventional communities, especially Markham, were more successful in seeing doctors when needed than new community blacks, it was largely through their own persistence in overcoming these obstacles.

Older people had fewer difficulties obtaining health care than other target populations and fewer than other age groups in the sample communities. Those living in retirement communities had the least difficulty of all. Of the new community respondents 65 years of age or older, 10 percent failed to see a doctor on at least one occasion, compared to 16 percent of those under 65 years old. The incidence was about the same in the conventional communities. Only 5 percent of the Rossmoor Leisure World elderly residents and 8 percent of those living in Sun City Center had failed to see a doctor when desired during the previous year.

Among respondents with regular sources of care, older residents generally experienced no more difficulties than younger ones. An exception was transportation. In new communities persons 65 years old and older were twice as likely as those in younger age groups to report problems of this kind, although the proportion that experienced difficulty (8 percent) was small. With respect to almost every type of difficulty, a lower proportion of retirement community residents reported problems than did the older residents of new communities.

CONCLUSIONS

These findings present an inconclusive picture of the performance of new communities with respect to target populations. On the whole, members of racial and income subgroups were indistinguishable from other new community residents in terms of the use of health care facilities and services and incidence of difficulties in obtaining care. Older people appeared to fare somewhat better in new communities than did those in other age groups.

The success—or, more correctly, the lack of failure of new communities—cannot be attributed to any particular effort on their part. As shown in this chapter, there was very little that was noteworthy about these environments in terms of improved health care delivery to special population groups. The apparent superiority of new communities over less planned conventional communities was probably due to difficulties in accessibility or quality of care in the conventional areas, or to general dissatisfaction with the latter environments on the part of their residents. In instances where comparisons could be made between target populations living in new communities and those living in less planned environments nearby, there were few important differences; household responses seemed to reflect the general state of health care in affluent suburban areas, which was about the same in new communities as in other suburbs housing comparable populations.

Where planned environments do devote attention to special needs, as was the case in Rossmoor Leisure World, the results were evident in greater resident awareness of services and health care utilization. Should new communities choose to emphasize programs and facilities for target populations, it is reasonable to expect that they would be more successful in attracting diverse populations.

Chapter 9

Residents' and Professionals' Overall Evaluations of Health Care in New Communities

Earlier it was noted that planned new communities have been regarded as ideal settings in which to develop better ways of providing health care facilities and services. Various aspects of the health care system, from primary care to services for target populations, were examined in the preceding chapters. Here the focus shifts to residents' and professionals' overall evaluations of health care in new communities and to our conclusions regarding the performance of health care systems.

Residents' satisfaction with community health care facilities and services is examined from two perspectives: first, residents were asked to evaluate health and medical services in their communities in comparison with the communities from which they had moved. Second, residents were asked to evaluate the overall quality of health care facilities and services on a five-point scale as excellent, good, average, below average or poor. The analysis of the responses focused on identifying those health care systems that received the highest ratings from the residents and on identifying those aspects of health care systems that contributed to residents' satisfaction. Additional insight into the quality of health care in new communities was sought through the survey of professional health personnel. As with the residents, health care professionals were asked to rate community health care systems as excellent, good, average, below average or poor. The analysis in this case focused on the association between objective characteristics of health care systems and the health professionals' ratings.

HEALTH CARE IN COMPARISON WITH
THE PREVIOUS COMMUNITY

On an aggregate level, new community residents were somewhat more likely than residents of the paired conventional communities to rate health and medical services as better than those in the communities from which they had moved (see Table 9-1). Twenty-five percent of the new community respondents rated services as better versus 20 percent of the conventional community respondents, a difference that is small but statistically significant. However, almost as many new community respondents (24 percent) rated services as not as good in their communities as rated them as better than where they had lived before.

There were no new communities in which a majority of the respondents thought that health and medical services were better than in their former communities. Columbia, with 47 percent of the respondents rating services as better, ranked first, followed by Sharpstown (45 percent better) and Elk Grove Village (40 percent better). The only other new communities in which more than a third of the respondents rated health and medical services as better than those in their previous communities were Park Forest (34 percent better) and federally assisted Jonathan (36 percent better). The three new communities that received the highest ratings—Columbia, Sharpstown and Elk Grove Village—each had a well-developed health care system. Columbia, as discussed in Chapter 7, was the only new community studied that had a community-based health maintenance organization. Sharpstown exceeded national standards for the number of primary care physicians per capita and had two community hospitals. Elk Grove Village had only an average number of physicians per capita, but had a large hospital and an active community mental health agency.

In almost half of the new communities—Irvine, Laguna Niguel, Lake Havasu City, Reston, Valencia and federally assisted Park Forest South—residents were more likely to have rated health and medical services as not as good as in their previous communities as to have rated services as better. Residents' dissatisfaction with services was greatest in Lake Havasu City (84 percent rated health and medical services as not as good as those in their previous communities) and Valencia (56 percent not as good). However, in both of these new communities hospital projects, the completion of which would improve households' ratings, were under way at the time of the household survey in the spring of 1973. Similarly, the improvements in emergency care, opening of another medical building and completion of a proposed hospital in Irvine, extension of a prepaid health plan to

Reston and implementation of the proposed comprehensive health care system in Park Forest South should also result in better ratings from the residents of these communities.

In addition to the ratings given by the general population of new community residents, ratings by various target populations were also examined. In the five new communities in which subsamples of subsidized housing residents were interviewed, subsidized housing residents were significantly more likely than either nonsubsidized housing residents of the same new communities (36 percent vs. 25 percent) or subsidized housing residents of conventional communities (36 percent vs. 19 percent) to feel that health and medical services were better than those of their previous communities. Black residents of new communities (27 percent) were just as likely as non-blacks living in the same communities (28 percent) and blacks living in conventional communities (24 percent) to feel that health and medical services were better than in their former communities. However, a somewhat larger proportion of new community black respondents (33 percent) felt services were not as good as where they had lived before. Fewer nonblacks living in new communities (25 percent) or blacks living in conventional communities (27 percent) rated health and medical services as not as good as those in their previous communities. Elderly (age 65 and older) new community residents were significantly more likely than the elderly residents of conventional communities (23 percent vs. 13 percent) to rate health and medical services as better than those in the communities from which they had moved. However, a sizable proportion of the respondents in both settings (19 percent and 33 percent, respectively) felt services were worse in their present communities. Elderly persons in Sun City Center, the Florida retirement community, were no more likely than new community elderly residents (21 percent vs. 23 percent) to rate services as better than those of their former communities. On the other hand, more than two-thirds (72 percent) of the elderly residents living in the California retirement community, Rossmoor Leisure World, rated health and medical services there as better than in their previous communities. As noted in Chapter 8, the Leisure World Foundation's Office of Medical Administration provided an extensive array of services designed to serve the health care needs of older persons.

RESIDENTS' OVERALL EVALUATIONS OF HEALTH CARE FACILITIES AND SERVICES

Later in the interview, following a series of questions regarding their awareness and utilization of health care services, the new and con-

Table 9-1. Rating of Health and Medical Services in Relation to Services in Previous Community[a]
(percentage distribution of respondents)

New and Conventional Communities	In Comparison with Previous Community, Present Community's Health and Medical Services Are:		
	Better	About the Same	Not as Good
Nonfederally Assisted New and Paired Conventional Communities			
Thirteen new communities	25[b]	51	24
Thirteen conventional communities	20	52	28[b]
New and Paired Conventional Communities			
Columbia (NC)	47[b]	30	23
Norbeck-Wheaton (CC)	16	69[b]	15
Elk Grove Village (NC)	40[b]	47	13
Schaumburg (CC)	20	46	34[b]
Forest Park (NC)	21	58	21[b]
Sharonville (CC)	27	63	10
Foster City (NC)	16	67	17[b]
West San Mateo (CC)	21	78	1
Irvine (NC)	17	48	35[b]
Fountain Valley (CC)	18	71[b]	11
Laguna Niguel (NC)	11	71[b]	19
Dana Point (CC)	26[b]	44	30
Lake Havasu City (NC)	5	11	84[b]
Kingman (CC)	22[b]	36[b]	42
North Palm Beach (NC)	25[b]	57	18
Tequesta (CC)	8	50	42[b]

Community			
Park Forest (NC)	34	53	13
Lansing (CC)	22	60	18
Reston (NC)	25	38	37[b]
West Springfield (CC)	18	68[b]	14
Sharpstown (NC)	45	50	5
Southwest Houston (CC)	35	59	6
Valencia (NC)	13	31	56
Bouquet Canyon (CC)	8	30	62
Westlake Village (NC)	29[b]	53[b]	18
Agoura–Malibu Junction (CC)	16	38	46
Federally Assisted New and *Paired Conventional Communities*			
Jonathan (NC)	36[b]	48	16
Chanhassen (CC)	18	55	26
Park Forest South (NC)	11	52	37[b]
Richton Park (CC)	13	66[b]	21

NC = New Community   CC = Conventional Community

[a]*Question:* Now, I'd like you to compare this community to the one you lived in just before you moved here. For each item . . . please tell me if where you are living now is better, not as good, or about the same as where you lived before.

[b]Statistically significant difference between new community(ies) and paired conventional community(ies) at 0.05 level of confidence.

ventional community respondents were asked to rate the absolute quality of health care facilities and services for people in their communities. About two-thirds of the new community respondents rated health care as excellent (26 percent) or good (40 percent), significantly more than the 54 percent (18 percent excellent and 36 percent good) of the conventional community respondents who rated facilities and services that highly (see Table 9—2).

An examination of residents' evaluations in individual communities, however, reveals that most of the advantage in favor of new communities was contributed by relatively few communities. In particular, the residents of Westlake Village, Laguna Niguel and North Palm Beach gave strikingly higher ratings to community health care than did residents in their paired conventional communities. Although differences in ratings from their paired conventional communities were not as sharp, respondents in four other new communities—Elk Grove Village, Jonathan, Park Forest and Sharpstown—were also highly satisfied with health care facilities and services.

Columbia ranked first in terms of the proportion of respondents who felt that health and medical services there were better than those in their former communities. In terms of absolute ratings, however, Columbia ranked eighth, with only 58 percent of the Columbia respondents rating health care facilities and services as excellent or good. In large part this slippage was due to the dissatisfaction of Columbia residents who had not enrolled in the Columbia Medical Plan. As reported in Chapter 7, 81 percent of the Columbia respondents who belonged to the plan rated Columbia's health care facilities and services as excellent or good. In contrast, only 45 percent of the Columbia respondents who were not members of the plan rated facilities and services that highly.

Less than a majority of the respondents in five new communities— Irvine (39 percent), Lake Havasu City (24 percent), Reston (47 percent), Valencia (30 percent) and federally assisted Park Forest South (48 percent)—rated community health care facilities and services as either excellent or good. However, as noted above, residents' evaluations of health care in these communities should improve when health facilities under construction at the time of the household survey are completed.

In the case of the target populations, there was little difference in the ratings of health care facilities by subsidized housing and nonsubsidized housing respondents (50 percent and 51 percent, respectively, rated facilities as excellent or good in the five new communities where subsamples of subsidized housing residents were obtained).

New community subsidized housing residents were somewhat more satisfied with facilities and services, however, than subsidized housing residents living in the conventional communities (51 percent vs. 44 percent rated facilities and services as excellent or good). In the five new communities where subsamples of black residents were interviewed, black respondents rated health care facilities and services about as high as nonblack respondents (56 percent vs. 57 percent excellent or good). New community black residents were much more satisfied with health care facilities and services than blacks living in the conventional communities (only 22 percent of the black residents of Markham and Seat Pleasant rated health care facilities and services in those communities as excellent or good). Finally, the elderly (age 65 years old or older) residents of new communities were more likely to rate facilities and services as excellent or good than younger new community respondents (73 percent vs. 47 percent). As could be expected from the previous discussion, however, the most satisfied elderly respondents lived in Rossmoor Leisure World, where 92 percent rated health care facilities and services as excellent or good.

In order to gain a better understanding of factors associated with residents' evaluations of health care facilities and services in their communities, their ratings were analyzed in relation to (1) personal and household characteristics, (2) residents' evaluations of selected attributes of the health care system and (3) objective characteristics and professionals' evaluations of selected attributes of the health care system. The results of these analyses are summarized in Tables 9-3, 9-4 and 9-5.

As shown in Table 9-3, residents' personal and household characteristics, including patterns of use of health services, were not strongly related to their overall evaluations of health care facilities and services. Among these variables, the key factors influencing evaluations were the length of residence in the community (longer residence was associated with better evaluations of facilities and services), the ability to see doctors when desired during the previous year, time spent in traveling to a regular source of care (residents who spent less time in travel to their doctors evaluated facilities and services higher) and use of a regular doctor or clinic. In combination, however, these variables explained only 3 percent of the variance in residents' overall evaluations of new community health care facilities and services.

New community residents' evaluations of selected attributes of the health care system had a stronger effect on their overall evaluations of facilities and services. In this case, key attributes of the health care

Table 9–2.　Residents' Ratings of the Overall Quality of Community Health Care Facilities and Services[a]
(percentage distribution of respondents)

	Rating			
New and Conventional Communities	*Excellent*	*Good*	*Average*	*Below Average/Poor*
Nonfederally Assisted New and Paired Conventional Communities				
Thirteen new communities	26[b]	40[b]	20	14[b]
Thirteen conventional communities	18	36	26[b]	20[b]
New and Paired Conventional Communities				
Columbia (NC)	20	38	20	22[b]
Norbeck-Wheaton (CC)	19	52[b]	19	10
Elk Grove Village (NC)	42[b]	39	17	2
Schaumburg (CC)	24	45	15	16[b]
Forest Park (NC)	13	42	29	16[b]
Sharonville (CC)	14	47	35	4
Foster City (NC)	28	31	16	25[b]
West San Mateo (CC)	48[b]	41	11	0
Irvine (NC)	11	28	26	35[b]
Fountain Valley (CC)	24[b]	49[b]	21	6
Laguna Niguel (NC)	26[b]	49	19	6
Dana Point (CC)	14	36	29	21[b]
Lake Havasu City (NC)	3	21	24	52[b]
Kingman (CC)	7	18	54[b]	21
North Palm Beach (NC)	31[b]	52[b]	14	3
Tequesta (CC)	8	29	33[b]	30[b]

Community				
Park Forest (NC)	21[b]	53	21	5
Lansing (CC)	12	58	18	12
Reston (NC)	9	38	34[b]	19[b]
West Springfield (CC)	35[b]	53[b]	8	4
Sharpstown (NC)	39	43	16	2
Southwest Houston (CC)	27	46	23	4
Valencia (NC)	3	27	30	40
Bouquet Canyon (CC)	2	18	30	50
Westlake Village (NC)	47[b]	42[b]	10	1
Agoura–Malibu Junction (CC)	11	21	17	51[b]
Federally Assisted New and Paired Conventional Communities				
Jonathan (NC)	26[b]	47	21	6
Chanhassen (CC)	9	41	31	19[b]
Park Forest South (NC)	11	37[b]	25	27
Richton Park (CC)	4	20	53[b]	23

NC = New Community   CC = Conventional Community

[a] *Question*: Overall, how good would you say health care facilities and services are for people who live in this community—excellent, good, average, below average or poor?

[b] Statistically significant difference between new community(ies) and paired conventional community(ies) at 0.05 level of confidence.

Table 9—3.   Multivariate Analysis of Residents' Personal and Household Characteristics and Overall Evaluations of Community Health Care Facilities and Services[a]

Variables[b]	Simple Correlation Coefficient	Beta	Cumulative R^2	F-Value[c]
Length of residence in community	.10	.08	.01	10.8
Inability to see doctor when desired	−.09	−.08	.02	11.2
Time (minutes) of journey to regular doctor or clinic	.10	.08	.03	13.4
Use of regular doctor or clinic	.10	.06	.03	7.2
Family income	−.08	−.07	.04	8.5
Health insurance coverage of doctors' bills	−.04	−.05	.04	2.9
Routine check-up during past year	.06	.04	.04	2.8
Satisfaction with status of own health	.05	.04	.04	3.3

[a]This analysis was performed with data from 2596 respondents who were living in thirteen nonfederally assisted new communities.

[b]The following variables, with F-values of 2.0 or less, were not included in this table (simple correlation coefficients with overall ratings are in parentheses): employment status of respondent ($r = -.03$); respondent's marital status ($r = .001$); respondent's sex ($r = .04$); number of children living in household ($r = -.01$); hospital insurance coverage ($r = .01$); respondent's age ($r = -.05$); and respondent's education ($r = -.01$).

[c]F-value of 4.0 in partial regression equation is statistically significant at the 0.05 level of confidence.

system in terms of residents' evaluations were hospital care, emergency medical care, health care for children, dental care and residents' satisfaction with their own regular sources of medical care (see Table 9—4). In general, residents' awareness of and willingness to recommend the use of various social services had less effect on their overall evaluations.

The associations between objective characteristics of the health care system and residents' evaluations paralleled the findings for residents' evaluations of system attributes (see Table 9—5). Health care facilities and services tended to receive higher ratings in new communities which had a community hospital, where health professionals rated the quality of physicians' office space highly and felt public health facilities were a useful source of care for community residents and where there were large numbers of pediatricians and general

Table 9–4. Multivariate Analysis of Residents' Evaluations of Selected Attributes of the Health Care System and Overall Evaluations of Community Health Care Facilities and Services[a]

Variables[b]	Simple Correlation Coefficient	Beta	Cumulative R^2	F-Value[c]
Aware of and would recommend use of available hospital care	.40	.32	.16	170.3
Satisfaction with regular source of medical care	.13	.13	.18	38.8
Aware of and would recommend use of available emergency medical care	.31	.10	.19	17.0
Aware of and would recommend use of available health care for children	.22	.06	.20	4.8
Aware of and would recommend use of available dental care	.22	.06	.20	5.9
Aware of and would recommend use of available convalescent care	.13	-.04	.20	3.5
Aware of and would recommend use of available help with emotional problems	.17	.06	.20	3.7
Aware of and would recommend use of available help with drinking problems	.11	-.06	.20	4.4
Aware of and would recommend use of available public assistance services	.09	-.06	.20	4.9

[a]This analysis was performed with data from 2596 respondents who were living in thirteen nonfederally assisted new communities.

[b]The following variables, with F-values of 2.0 or less, are not included in this table (simple correlation coefficients with overall ratings are in parentheses): aware of and would recommend use of available family planning services ($r = .14$); family and marital counseling ($r = .15$); help with a drug problem ($r = .13$) and prenatal care ($r = .18$); difficulties experienced in arranging transportation to personal doctor ($r = -.03$); and difficulties with cost of treatment ($r = .01$).

[c]F-value of 4.0 in partial regression equation is statistically significant at the 0.05 level of confidence.

Table 9–5. Multivariate Analysis of Characteristics of Health Care System
and Overall Evaluations of Community Health Care Facilities and Services[a]

Variables[b]	Simple Correlation Coefficient	Cumulative		
		Beta	R^2	F-Value[c]
Availability of hospital in community	.32	.31	.11	181.1
Quality of physicians' office space in community[d]	.20	.06	.14	4.2
Usefullness of public health facility for community residents[d]	.22	.19	.18	63.4
Number of pediatricians practicing in community	.26	.17	.19	49.4
Number of gynecologists/ obstetricians practicing in community	−.05	−.21	.20	41.5
Adequacy of nursing and convalescent facilities[d]	.11	.13	.20	26.5
Number of general practitioners, internists and osteopaths practicing in community	.21	.08	.21	9.9

[a]This analysis was performed with data from 2596 respondents who were living in thirteen nonfederally assisted new communities.

[b]Other characteristics of community health care systems that were associated with residents' overall ratings of health care facilities and services included: number of dentists practicing in community ($r = .21$), adequacy of emergency service ($r = .07$), adequacy of social services programs ($r = .16$), road distance to nearest hospital ($r = .10$), adequacy of hospital care available to community ($r = .01$), road distance to nearest public health facility ($r = .21$), and road distance to nearest general practitioner or internist ($r = −.05$).

[c]F-value of 4.0 in partial regression equation is statistically significant at the 0.05 level of confidence.

[d]Based on health care professionals' evaluations.

practitioners, internists and osteopaths practicing in a community. Other aspects of the health care system that were positively associated with residents' ratings included the number of dentists practicing in a community, adequacy of nursing and convalescent facilities available to a community, adequacy of social services programs and accessibility of public health facilities.

PROFESSIONALS' OVERALL EVALUATIONS OF HEALTH CARE FACILITIES AND SERVICES

Additional insight into the quality of health care in new communities was sought through the survey of professional health care personnel.

Health professionals were asked to rate health care facilities and services in the same manner as household survey respondents. Frequency distributions of their ratings are summarized in Table 9−6.

On an aggregate level, health care professionals gave higher ratings to community health care facilities and services than the household survey respondents. For example, while 19 percent of the nonfederally assisted new community respondents rated facilities and services as excellent, 19 of 55 professionals (35 percent) rated facilities and services that highly. Two-thirds of the household survey respondents versus three-fourths of the professionals rated facilities and services as either excellent or good. However, whereas the new community household survey respondents were more likely than conventional community respondents to rate facilities and services as excellent or good (66 percent vs. 54 percent), the conventional communities received a somewhat higher proportion of excellent or good ratings (77 percent) from the health care professionals.

Health care professionals gave the highest proportions of excellent or good ratings to Foster City (three of four professionals interviewed), Irvine (three of four professionals), Laguna Niguel (three of four professionals), Sharpstown (two of three professionals) and Westlake Village (two of four professionals). In three of these communities— Foster City, Irvine and Laguna Niguel—professionals tended to be much more satisfied with the quality of health care facilities and services than the residents. On the other hand, in Sharpstown and Westlake Village both the professionals and residents gave the communities high ratings.

In five new communities—Elk Grove Village, Forest Park, Reston, Valencia and federally assisted Park Forest South—half or more of the professionals interviewed rated health care facilities and services as average, below average or poor. With the exception of Elk Grove Village, which was rated very highly by the residents, the professionals' and residents' evaluations tended to agree. For example, in Reston, three of six professionals and 53 percent of the household survey respondents rated health care facilities and services as average or below; three of four Valencia professionals and 70 percent of the Valencia household survey respondents rated facilities and services in that new community poorly; in Park Forest South, two of four health care professionals and 45 percent of the household survey respondents rated facilities and services as average, below average or poor.

Analyses of health care professionals evaluations of community health care facilities indicated that their ratings were associated with both objective characteristics of the health care system and their subjective evaluations of various attributes of community health care.

Table 9–6. Health Care Professionals' Ratings of the Overall Quality of Community Health Care Facilities and Services[a]
(frequency distribution of respondents)

New and Conventional Communities	Rating					
	Excellent	Good	Average	Below Average/Poor	No Response	Total
Nonfederally Assisted New and Paired Conventional Communities						
Thirteen new communities	19	22	7	7	5	60
Thirteen conventional communities	18	15	6	4	5	48
New and Paired Conventional Communities						
Columbia (NC)	1	7	0	0	0	8
Norbeck-Wheaton (CC)	1	0	1	0	0	2
Elk Grove Village (NC)	0	0	2	0	1	3
Schaumburg (CC)	0	1	1	0	1	3
Forest Park (NC)	0	1	1	1	1	4
Sharonville (CC)	0	2	0	1	2	5
Foster City (NC)	3	1	0	0	0	4
West San Mateo (CC)	3	1	0	0	0	4
Irvine (NC)	3	1	0	1	1	6
Fountain Valley (CC)	3	1	0	0	1	5
Laguna Niguel (NC)	3	1	0	0	1	5
Dana Point (CC)	3	1	0	0	1	5
Lake Havasu City (NC)	1	2	0	1	0	4
Kingman (CC)	0	3	0	0	0	3
North Palm Beach (NC)	1	2	1	0	0	4
Tequesta (CC)	0	2	1	1	0	4

Park Forest (NC)	1	2	0	1	0	4
Lansing (CC)	1	2	0	0	0	3
Reston (NC)	2	1	2	1	1	7
West Springfield (CC)	3	1	1	0	0	5
Sharpstown (NC)	2	1	0	0	0	3
Southwest Houston (CC)	2	0	1	0	0	3
Valencia (NC)	0	1	1	2	1	4
Bouquet Canyon (CC)	0	1	1	2	2	4
Westlake Village (NC)	2	2	0	0	0	4
Agoura–Malibu Junction (CC)	2	0	0	0	0	2

Federally Assisted New and Paired Conventional Communities

Jonathan (NC)	0	3	0	0	0	3
Chanhassen (CC)	0	3	0	0	0	3
Park Forest South (NC)	1	1	1	1	0	4
Richton Park (CC)	2	1	0	0	0	3

NC = New Community   CC = Conventional Community

[a] *Question:* Overall, how good would you say health care facilities and services are for people who live in (NAME OF COMMUNITY)—excellent, good; average; below average or poor?

For example, professionals tended to give higher ratings to communities with hospitals ($r = .32$), more primary care physicians per 100,000 population ($r = .39$), a greater variety of medical specialists ($r = .34$) and a larger number of special facilities in hospitals serving the community ($r = .29$).

Health care professionals' ratings were also associated with their views about the adequacy of hospital care ($r = .59$) and with their ratings of doctors' office facilities ($r = .63$). Strangely, however, there were negative associations between professionals' overall ratings of community health care facilities and services and their ratings of the adequacy of health care planning ($r = -.22$) and of developer initiative in this field ($r = -.49$). These associations may be due to instances in which planning and developer initiative, though well regarded, had yet to result in better than average health care facilities and services, as in Park Forest South, and to cases where excellent facilities were not viewed as the result of a particularly laudable planning process, as in Sharpstown.

CONCLUSIONS: HEALTH CARE IN NEW COMMUNITIES

Depending on how one chooses to read them, the findings discussed in this and the preceding chapters can lead to complacency or concern with regard to the status of health care in planned new communities. The residents of new communities appeared to be satisfied with their own health. Both residents and health professionals tended to rate health care facilities highly, and new communities compared well with less planned conventional communities. Professionals also tended to view hospital care, ambulance service and doctors' offices as adequate. The use of regular sources of care and the practice of having annual check-ups were common, and the level of utilization of physicians' services was comparable to national figures. There was little distinction among target populations, in terms of satisfaction with facilities or utilization of services, and new communities generally performed better with respect to these groups than did less planned conventional communities.

If the availability of health care resources, particularly primary care physicians, was not impressive in new communities, it could be argued that it was somewhat better than in nearby conventional communities. While there was little extensive involvement by developers, it would be difficult to demonstrate on the basis of these communities that such involvement yielded a significantly greater amount of health care resources. Moreover, the inactivity of developers was paralleled by the attitudes of residents, for whom health care was a relatively insignificant aspect of their quality of life; who rarely moved to or from new communities on the basis of the availability of health care or cited health care as an important community problem; and whose ratings of health facilities had little bearing on their overall satisfaction with the community as a place to live. An additional point to consider is that the location and extent of health care resources had almost no effect on their utilization by individuals.

On the other hand, satisfaction with health care was by no means high in all communities. In a number of locations, many residents settled for health care facilities which they regarded as inferior to those that were available to them before they moved to a new community. Although utilization of health services was not influenced by the availability of resources, satisfaction with care was affected. Where the level of resources was low, residents tended to be unhappy about health care in the community.

The availability of primary care physicians in new communities, while on a par with their availability in the conventional communities, was not impressive in comparison with national averages. A relatively large proportion of residents experienced difficulties in obtaining care. Health care professionals often expressed the view that the number of physicians was either inadequate or was not keeping pace with community growth.

The apparent shortage of physicians in planned new communities was especially pronounced because of the absence of other forms of care. There were few public health facilities in new communities and few near them. Only one of the fifteen new communities studied had a long-term care facility. Very little had been done to develop programs specifically designed for elderly, teenage, or low- and moderate-income residents. Although blacks and residents in subsidized housing were more satisfied with health care in new communities than in the conventional communities, retirement communities appeared to be a better form of planned environment for elderly persons than either new or conventional communities. Only one new community had a health maintenance organization designed to operate on a community basis, and its performance has been characterized by the exclusion of other types of care, difficulties in obtaining services and a premium structure that made it difficult for lower income residents to join. Health professionals indicated numerous other deficiencies in the availability of services and facilities in and near new communities. Even where they felt that appropriate resources were generally available in the vicinity of a community, as with emotional care and other types of counseling, they described resources as being inadequate or of poor quality.

Residents, moreover, were alarmingly unaware of the programs that were available to them, even where the need was strong. Although health professionals noted that emotional difficulties were among the major health problems facing the residents of new communities, only about half of the new community respondents were familiar with sources of assistance in this area. Perceptions of numerous other services were low as well, even where the health professional survey indicated that the resources in question were close at hand. These findings indicate that a major unmet need in new communities is improving ways to inform individuals about available health care resources and to refer them to appropriate types of care.

In addition to problems relating to the availability of care and to perceptions of services, there is abundant evidence in the material discussed in this book of problems in quality, delivery or appropriateness of services offered in such areas as hospital care, ambulance service and public health facilities.

Planning for health care in new communities was not, on the whole, highly regarded by health professionals. With a few major exceptions, developers made few significant contributions toward improving health care resources. Although there was little evidence that developer involvement in the health field had a major impact on the level of health resources, this could be attributed to the fact that few developers were involved in comprehensive approaches to community health care. The emphasis on hospital building in a number of communities contributed to the irrational and wasteful process by which these facilities were planned and developed, and failed to meet the more immediate needs of residents. In some locations where developers acknowledged extensive responsibilities in health care, implementation was lacking. Federally assisted new communities, where a high degree of commitment was accompanied by a low level of health resources, appear to be illustrative of this problem, especially during the early years of the community development process.

Deficiencies in planning for health care in new communities and inadequacies in the resources available suggest that there is an important role in health care planning that can be played by developers. It would be a mistake to assume that all problems in a field as complex as health care can be solved on a community level or that developers should bear full responsibility for solving them. But the developer, as the single entity in control of a tract of land large enough to be called a community, is in a unique position to influence events. The need for such action is likely to be great, since new communities tend to be isolated from existing facilities and often lack resources of their own, at least in the initial stages of development. Moreover, the developer is likely to have made claims concerning the creation of a "community," a concept that implies the presence of basic services. The heightened responsibilities of the developer are matched by heightened opportunities. In the large areas under development, he is clearly the prime mover of events. The contacts that a developer necessarily has with public bodies and private institutions put him in a position to facilitate health projects. Moreover, developers should find motivation for this kind of involvement in the added appeal attention to health planning would lend the community. Although health care is much less important than other mobility factors, potential residents will want to consider where they can take care of their family's health needs should they move to a new community. Conveniently located health care facilities, no less than those for shopping and recreation, should be regarded favorably.

On the other hand, while new community developers have an appropriate role to play in health care planning, their focus should not be restricted solely to the community. The data presented in this book indicate that developers and planners should tie their communities into the regions in which they are located rather than attempt to build all needed health facilities in their community. The study has also demonstrated the need for greatly improved programs of information and referral which would, in effect, bring resources in the vicinity "closer" to community residents. Moreover, since difficulties in obtaining care can often be attributed to problems of transportation and convenience, particularly for such groups as the elderly, teenagers and lower income persons, increased attention to transportation systems within and near a new community would help to make health care easier to obtain.

While resisting the temptation to plan for a community as an isolated unit that is separate from its surroundings, developers do need to consider locating certain types of resources within the community. Because conditions differ in each community, it is impossible to establish a firm set of priorities. However, the topics treated in this study indicate particular areas of need. These include more primary care physicians, more sources of assistance for emotional problems, more public health facilities, a greater range of social services, more health and social programs designed—in terms of costs, training of personnel and problems emphasized—with lower income residents, the elderly and teenagers in mind. The development of health maintenance organizations and of community-based clinics to support them also appears to be a promising way of providing care to new community residents. On the whole, one of the most serious deficiencies in the health resources within planned communities is their lack of variety. Future planning needs to provide residents with a greater selection of types of care, closer to home.

Although an eventual goal of health planning should be the provision of readily accessible comprehensive health services, it must be recognized that a first step should be to assure that basic care is available when it is most urgently needed. To link the community with nearby resources and to provide care that is close to home, increased emphasis should be placed on developing efficient, well-equipped ambulance services operated by thoroughly trained personnel. As facilities are built within a community, an appropriate first project might be an emergency care station. Less urgent facilities may also be developed at an early stage of community growth, but the highest priority should be placed on steps which establish the new community as a safe place in which to live.

Appendixes

Data Collection Procedures

The data reported in this study were collected in a sample of 36 new and conventional communities in the United States. Three data collection procedures were used. These included a household survey, surveys of developers and professional personnel who were involved in the provision of health care facilities and services, and field inventories and map measurements. This appendix describes the methods used in conducting the various surveys and field measurements.

THE HOUSEHOLD SURVEY

Residents living in the 36 new and conventional communities were interviewed during the period from February through May 1973. Portions of the interview schedule that were used for the analyses in this book are reproduced in Appendix B. The number of households interviewed in each community is shown in Table A—1.

Selection of Sample Households
and Respondents
The universe sampled for the household survey included family heads and their spouses living in the 36 sample communities. The sample was selected in such a manner that every head or spouse who had moved into his or her dwelling before January 1, 1973 had a known probability of selection. The method of selecting the household sample was as follows.

Table A–1. Number of Household Interviews

| | | | Number of Interviews | | | |
| | | | | Subsamples | | |
Communities	Total	Basic Sample	Subsidized Housing Residents	Black Residents	Young Adults
Total	6,485	5,087	274	150	974
Thirteen Nonfederally Assisted New Communities	3,546	2,619	219	131	577
Thirteen Paired Conventional Communities	1,585	1,321	NA	NA	264
Federally Assisted New Communities and Paired Conventional Communities					
Jonathan, Minn. (NC)	219	152	55	NA	12
Chanhassen, Minn. (CC)	118	100	NA	NA	18
Park Forest South, Ill. (NC)	247	200	NA	19	28
Richton Park, Ill. (CC)	104	101	NA	NA	4
Two Retirement New Communities (NC)	204	204	NA	NA	NA
Two Subsidized Housing Conventional Communities (CC)	215	187	NA	NA	28
Two Black Conventional Communities (CC)	246	203	NA	NA	43
Nonfederally Assisted New Communities and Paired Conventional Communities					
Columbia, Md. (NC)	341	213	61	37	30
Norbeck-Wheaton, Md. (CC)	151	123	NA	NA	28

Community					
Elk Grove Village, Ill. (NC)	258	199	NA	NA	59
Schaumburg, Ill. (CC)	116	102	NA	NA	14
Forest Park, Oh. (NC)	374	202	53	51	68
Sharonville, Oh. (NC)	145	115	NA	NA	30
Foster City, Calif. (NC)	202	176	NA	NA	26
West San Mateo, Calif. (CC)	112	93	NA	NA	19
Irvine, Calif. (NC)	239	202	NA	NA	37
Fountain Valley, Calif. (CC)	117	102	NA	NA	15
Laguna Niguel, Calif. (NC)	245	208	NA	NA	37
Dana Point, Calif. (CC)	139	105	NA	NA	34
Lake Havasu City, Ariz. (NC)	324	209	47	NA	68
Kingman, Ariz. (CC)	108	93	NA	NA	15
North Palm Beach, Fla. (NC)	245	202	NA	NA	43
Tequesta, Fla. (CC)	126	111	NA	NA	15
Park Forest, Ill. (NC)	253	200	NA	16	37
Lansing, Ill. (CC)	78	64	NA	NA	14
Reston, Va. (NC)	331	197	58	27	49
West Springfield, Va. (CC)	114	95	NA	NA	19
Sharpstown, Tex. (NC)	248	203	NA	NA	45
Southwest Houston, Tex. (CC)	134	108	NA	NA	26
Valencia, Calif. (NC)	235	202	NA	NA	33
Bouquet Canyon, Calif. (CC)	124	103	NA	NA	21
Westlake Village, Calif. (NC)	251	206	NA	NA	45
Agoura/Malibu Junction, Calif. (CC)	121	107	NA	NA	14

NC = New Community
CC = Conventional Community
NA = Not Applicable

Visits were made to all 36 sample communities between mid-October 1972 and mid-January 1973 to identify all occupied dwellings on large-scale maps showing lot lines for each community. These maps, with the location and number of occupied dwellings delineated, were used to outline clusters of from five to seven dwelling units. The number of units to be included in a cluster was chosen on the basis of projected field costs, expected response rate and the number of clusters needed to generate a household sample representative of the sample communities. The eventual analysis of housing clusters was considered in delineating sample clusters. Accordingly, the clusters were outlined so as to include dwellings that faced one another across a street or common court. Dwellings strung out in a row were rarely defined as clusters.

For apartment buildings where the location of individual dwellings was unknown, the total number of units in the building was divided into a designated number of five-, six- or seven-dwelling clusters. For buildings containing fewer than ten apartments, two or three neighboring buildings were grouped together and clusters were designated for all units in the group. Where the location of apartments within a building was known it was possible to cluster these units directly as in the procedure described above.

After clusters were defined for a community, a probability sample of clusters was selected. The samples in paired conventional communities that had more than one type of dwelling unit available were stratified by dwelling unit type (single-family detached houses, townhouses or apartments) so that the proportion of selected clusters of each dwelling type approximated the proportions of dwelling unit types found in the paired new community. Overall, the selection of sample clusters was designed to obtain 200 interviews in each of the thirteen nonfederally assisted new communities and two federally assisted new communities and 100 interviews in each of the paired conventional communities, retirement new communities and conventional communities used to obtain interviews with subsidized housing and black residents.

Subsample of new community households occupying subsidized housing. Five of the sample new communities (Columbia, Forest Park, Jonathan, Lake Havasu City and Reston) had FHA Sections 235 (owner) and/or 221(d)3 or 236 (rental) subsidized housing occupied at the time of the sampling process. In each of these communities the sampling frame was divided into two strata, one of subsidized housing units and one of nonsubsidized housing units. Separate random probability cluster samples were drawn from each stratum in the manner described above. Selection of clusters was designed to produce 50 interviews with households occupying subsidized housing and 200 interviews with households occupying non-subsidized housing in each of the five communities.

Subsample of new community black households. In each of the five sample new communities known to have more than 100 resident black households (Columbia, Forest Park, Park Forest, Park Forest South and Reston) a special subsample of black households was selected to supplement those falling into the regular cluster samples. Lists suitable for use as sampling frames were not available in all five of the communities. Therefore, sampling frames were constructed by referrals from the random sample respondents. Addresses generated by the referral procedure were listed and duplications were eliminated. The five resulting lists were used as the sample frames from which simple random samples of addresses were drawn, aimed at producing 50 additional interviews with black households in each of the five communities.

It should be noted that because it is a referral sample this subsample of black households does not constitute a random sample representative of the population of black family heads and their spouses in these communities. However, comparison of black subsample respondent characteristics and attitudes with those of black respondents from the random sample in the five communities indicated that the two groups were very similar. See Table A−2. Therefore, responses from the black subsample were included with those of random sample blacks in the analysis presented in Chapter 8 to increase the reliability of estimates for new community blacks without introducing substantial sampling error. Interviews obtained from the black subsample are not included in community totals presented in other chapters.

Subsample of new community and conventional community young adults. The universe for the young adult subsample included all persons fourteen through twenty years old (other than family heads and their spouses) who were found to be living in sample dwellings. If one such young adult was found at a sample dwelling, this person was selected for the young adult sample. If two or more were found, the interviewer selected one of these at random using a random selection table stamped on the young adult questionnaire. Thus, choice of young adult respondents was specified for interviewers rather than left to their discretion.

Table A-2. Comparison of Responses from Random Sample Blacks and the Nonrandom Black Subsample in Five Sample Communities

	Percent of Black Respondents from[a]	
Characteristic or Attitude	Random Sample	Nonrandom Black Subsample
Number of Persons in Respondent's Household		
One	2.2	2.7
Two	23.7	10.0
Three to five	62.6	70.7
Six or more	11.5	16.7
Number of Children in Respondent's Household		
None	23.5	12.7
One	28.2	24.0
Two	28.3	30.0
Three or more	20.0	33.3
Age of Family Head		
Under 35	50.4	45.0
35-44	32.1	37.6
45-54	14.1	16.1
55 or older	3.5	1.3
Marital Status of Household Head		
Married	89.9	86.7
Widowed	0.1	2.0
Divorced or separated	9.0	6.0
Never married	1.0	5.3
Education of Household Head		
High school graduate or less	39.7	33.6
Some college to college graduate	34.5	33.6
Graduate or professional training	25.9	32.9
Employment Status of Household Head		
Employed	95.8	97.3
Retired	1.3	0.0
Not employed (not retired)	2.8	2.7
Family's Total Income in 1972 (before taxes)		
Under $10,000	13.2	15.6
$10,000-$14,999	23.9	13.6
$15,000-$24,999	42.1	44.9
$25,000 or more	20.8	25.9
Tenure		
Owns or buying	67.3	85.8
Rents	32.1	13.5
Other	0.6	0.7

Table A—2. continued

Characteristic or Attitude	Percent of Black Respondents from[a]	
	Random Sample	Nonrandom Black Subsample
Length of Residence in the Community		
One year or less	47.2	32.4
Two or three years	31.8	30.4
Four or five years	17.2	27.0
Six or more years	3.9	10.1
Rating of Health Care Facilities		
Excellent	10.8	12.6
Good	40.0	45.9
Average	30.2	22.2
Below average or poor	19.1	19.2
Rating of the Community Overall		
Excellent	38.0	31.5
Good	44.6	58.4
Average	15.2	10.1
Below average or poor	2.2	0.0

[a] The responses of blacks falling into the random cluster sample in five sample communities known to have more than 100 resident black households at the time the sample was drawn are shown in the first column; the percentages are based on 95 interviews. Responses from blacks in the nonrandom referral subsamples in the same five communities are shown in the second column; the percentages are based on 150 interviews. The five communities are: Columbia, Md.; Forest Park, Oh.; Park Forest, Ill.; Park Forest South, Ill.; and Reston, Va. To be statistically significant, differences between percents in the table that are around 50 percent need to be at least 14.8 percent; differences between percents around 30 percent or 70 percent need to be at least 13.6 percent; and differences between percents around 10 percent or 90 percent need to be at least 8.9 percent.

Designation of the household survey respondent. The prospective respondent was randomly designated as either the head of the family residing at the address or the spouse of the family head for each address in the regular cluster sample, the subsidized housing subsample and the black subsample prior to assignment of addresses to interviewers. The head was designated as the respondent for half of the addresses sampled in each community; the spouse was designated as the respondent for the remaining half. Interviews were allowed only with the designated respondent except where the spouse was designated and there was no spouse of family head living in the household. In such situations the interview was to be taken with the family head. If a household was occupied by more than one family unit, the head or spouse of the head of each family unit was to be interviewed.

These procedures left no freedom to interviewers in the choice of respondents. The dwellings at which interviews were to be taken and the individuals to be interviewed within the dwellings were specified.

Interviewing Methods

Interviewers were instructed to ask questions using the exact wording appearing in the questionnaire. When probing was necessary to obtain full answers to open-end questions, interviewers were to use nondirective probes (such as, "How do you mean?" or "Could you tell me more about that?") to avoid influencing the responses.

When recording responses to open-end questions, interviewers were to write the actual words spoken as nearly as possible and to indicate when they had probed for additional information. Recording of responses to closed-end questions simply required checking the appropriate precoded response in most cases.

In situations where the respondent could not be contacted on the first call at a sample household, interviewers were required to call back at the household up to six times in order to obtain the interview. These call-backs were to be made at different times of day and on different days of the week to maximize the chance of a contact. Addresses at which the designated individuals refused to be interviewed were generally reassigned to a second interviewer who contacted the individuals and attempted to persuade them to be interviewed.

No substitutions for sample households or sample respondents were allowed. The addresses of sample households (including apartment designations) were listed for each cluster, and the proper respondent (head or spouse of head) was designated for each address listed prior to assignment of clusters to interviewers. Interviewers were required to interview the designated individuals at the addresses listed.

Reliability of the Data

Sample surveys, even though properly conducted, are liable to several kinds of errors. These include response errors which arise in the reporting and processing of the data; nonresponse errors, which arise from failure to interview some individuals who were selected in the sample; and sampling errors, which arise from the choice by chance of individuals for the sample who may make the sample unrepresentative of the population from which it was drawn. Some evaluation of each of these types of error is necessary for the proper interpretation of any estimates from survey data.

Response errors. Such errors include inaccuracies in asking and answering questions in the interview, recording responses, coding the recorded responses, and processing the coded data. They can be reduced by thoroughly pretesting field procedures and instruments, training interviewers and coders and exercising quality controls throughout the data collection, coding and editing phases of the research process.

The questionnaires and field procedures used in the household survey were pretested in the autumn of 1972.[a] Pretesting was carried out in a planned community, Crofton, Md., in the Washington, D.C. metropolitan area, with respondents similar to the populations in the sample. Analysis of pretest interviews resulted in some revisions, such as the rewording of questions to make their meaning more clear to respondents and interviewers.

Interviewer training included a question-by-question review of the household interview instrument, the taking of a practice interview and discussion of this interview with the interviewer's supervisor. Supervisors reviewed interviewers' work with them throughout the field period.

The coding operation involved two procedures. Responses to closed-end questions were scored directly on the household interview and young adult questionnaire forms which had been printed so that the scored responses could be machine read directly from the forms onto computer tape. Responses to open-end questions were hand coded onto coding forms and keypunched from these forms. Coders were trained as to the codes and coding conventions used prior to the beginning of this work. Hand coding was checked by coding 10 percent of the interviews and questionnaires twice and comparing the two codings for discrepancies. Errors found were corrected.

Data tapes were checked for inconsistencies and incorrect codes and indicated corrections were made.

Nonresponse errors. Some proportion of the sample in any survey fails to respond, usually because of refusals or the failure of the interviewers to contact potential respondents despite repeated attempts. In the random sample for the 36 communities there were a total of 7626 addresses at which there was an eligible respondent after elimination of those addresses whose occupants had moved in on January 1, 1973 or later, as well as addresses that were vacant, commercial establishments and others at which no one lived perma-

---

[a]The field and coding operations for the household survey were conducted by The Research Triangle Institute, Research Triangle Park, N.C. Members of the research team monitored all phases of these operations.

nently. Interviews were obtained with the selected respondent at 5361 of these addresses—an overall response rate of 70.3 percent. Response rates varied somewhat from community to community.

Because response rates were lower than anticipated (80 to 85 percent overall), a study was conducted to assess the extent to which nonrespondents differed systematically from respondents. First, response rates were computed by dwelling unit type and found to differ. Households living in higher density housing were somewhat underrepresented. Since residents in higher density areas tended to have fewer children, for example, and were thought likely to view the community and its facilities from a different perspective than residents of single-family detached homes, interviews in each of the sample communities were weighted to give responses from residents of each of the three dwelling unit types a weight proportional to that of the dwelling unit type in the community's original sample.

In addition, a survey of nonrespondents was conducted to gather basic demographic and attitude data.[b] Analyses of these data in comparison with household survey data revealed no significant differences between respondent and nonrespondent households for eight of thirteen demographic items (including race, income, marital status and employment status). For five of seven community and quality of life rating items there were no significant differences between respondents and nonrespondents (including their overall rating of community livability, ratings of schools and recreational facilities and satisfaction with life as a whole). The major differences which occurred between respondent and nonrespondent households included age of household, length of residence and ratings of health care and shopping facilities. Since most differences which occurred could be explained by the length of time which elapsed between the original survey and the nonrespondent follow-up survey, it is estimated that the lower than expected response rates obtained for the original household survey do not bias the study findings.

Sampling errors.   If all family heads or their spouses living (as of January 1, 1973) in new communities and conventional communities fitting the inclusion criteria noted earlier had been interviewed, the percentages and other values reported in the text would be population values. Because a sample of persons was interviewed in a sample of communities, the reported statistics are estimates of the population values. Any distribution of individuals selected for a sample will

---

[b]The nonrespondent follow-up survey, involving telephone interviews and mailback questionnaires, was carried out during February and March of 1974 by Chilton Research Services, Radnor, Pa.

differ by chance somewhat from the population from which it was drawn. If more than one sample was used under the same survey conditions, the estimates from one sample might be larger than the population value for a given variable while the estimates from another sample might be smaller. The magnitude of random variability of sample statistics from population values (sampling error) can be calculated for any sample providing it is known exactly how and with what probability the sample was selected.

Sampling errors associated with observed differences in percentages between subgroups (e.g., between individual new communities and their paired conventional communities) indicate the minimum size of a percentage difference required for the difference to be considered statistically significant—i.e., for it to reflect a true difference between the subgroups in the population rather than chance variation because of sampling. Statistically significant differences between subgroups are noted in most tables and in the text of this book. Estimates of average sampling errors based on experiences with other studies in urban areas were adjusted for the clustering in the sample to estimate the statistical significance of percentage differences. Conservative estimates of the sampling error in the sample have been used.

DATA WEIGHTS

Before combining the nonfederally assisted new community and paired conventional community samples to produce estimates presented in this book, cases were weighted by factors that include adjustments for each community's probability of selection and expected number of interviews in the community (200 for new communities, 100 for less planned suburban conventional communities and 50 for subsidized housing subsample). Cases in the five communities having subsidized housing subsamples (Columbia, Forest Park. Jonathan, Lake Havasu City and Reston) have also been weighted to adjust for over-sampling of households in subsidized housing in the community. In addition, each case is weighted by the proportion of its dwelling unit type (single-family detached, townhouse/rowhouse or apartment) in the original sample for its community to adjust for differential response rates among the three dwelling unit types.

Data presented for combined nonfederally assisted new communities and combined paired conventional communities are weighted to make all the adjustments listed above: each community's probability of selection, dwelling unit type, disproportionate selection of subsidized housing and expected number of interviews. Data presented for individual communities exclude the weight for the community's probability of selection. Weights for subsidized housing have been applied only for the five new communities with a subsidized housing subsample and only when data for this sample are presented in combination with those from the basic random sample.

THE SURVEYS OF PROFESSIONALS AND DEVELOPERS

Information about the organization of health care service systems, objective characteristics of health care resources and professionals' evaluations of the adequacy and quality of facilities and services were collected during the spring of 1973 through interviews with health care professionals serving each of the 36 communities studied. Additional data about health care service systems and developers' activities were collected during the summer of 1974 through interviews with new community developers and their staffs.

The health professional survey questionnaire (see Appendix C) was pretested in Forest Park and Sharonville in February 1973 and was revised on the basis of the pretest. Health was conceptualized broadly in this study to include mental health as well as physical health and related social services. A judgmental sample of respondents considered to be most knowledgeable about such health matters was identified in each community. Most health professionals interviewed were officials of county or community health offices, officers of county medical societies or hospital administrators. The breakdown of professional health respondents by affiliation was as follows:

Hospital or hospital association	51
County health department	23
County medical society	17
Community health agency or community health plan	12
Private medical clinic	6
Community social service agency	5
Health planning council	5
Visiting nurse association	4
Group medical practice	3
New community developer's staff	3
Regional health agency	3
Other	12
Total	144

The interviews were structured and generally required about an hour for administration, which was done by appointment with the respondent. Interviewers were instructed to ask questions exactly as worded and in the order presented in the questionnaire. Interviewing was carried out primarily by members of the study team. Each interview was taken with specific reference to a particular new or conventional community. Some professionals (e.g., county health officials) had responsibility for facilities or services in more than one sample community. In such cases separate questionnaires were filled out for each community involved. Table A−3 shows the number of interviews obtained for each community in the sample. The interviews were hand coded by coders on the project staff. One tenth of the coding was completely checked. Consistent errors involving a misunderstanding of the code were corrected in all interviews before the coded data were keypunched. In addition, all responses to open-end questions were recorded on index cards for use in the analysis.

In July and August of 1974 a series of informal interviews was conducted by members of the study team with the developers of the ten sample new communities where active development began after 1960. The purpose of these interviews was to determine what actions developers had taken in providing community health care facilities and services, especially those that seemed particularly successful or problematic in their own communities on the basis of preliminary analyses of the household survey data. Additional objectives were to obtain developers' interpretations of their residents' responses to the household survey and to learn what changes had occurred in the communities after completion of the household survey and other data collection procedures in the spring of 1973.

The developer interviews were limited to the sample communities that began active residential development after 1960 in order to reduce or eliminate problems of recall and staff turnover. The ten communities included in the survey were: Columbia, Foster City, Irvine, Jonathan, Laguna Niguel, Lake Havasu City, Park Forest South, Reston, Valencia and Westlake Village. Although the developers of the five sample new communities begun in the 1940s and 1950s (Elk Grove Village, Forest Park, North Palm Beach, Park Forest and Sharpstown) were not included in the developer interviews, letters soliciting reactions to the findings of the household survey were sent to them as well as to various institutional officials, such as mayors, city councilmen, city managers, planning directors and leaders of homes associations in their communities.

Developer interviews were based on a series of community profiles

Table A-3. Professional Personnel and Developer Interviews

Community	Number of Interviews		
	Total	Health Care Personnel	Developers
Total	156	144	12[a]
Thirteen Nonfederally Assisted New Communities	70	60	10[a]
Thirteen Paired Conventional Communities	48	48	NA
Federally Assisted New and Paired Conventional Communities			
Jonathan, Minn. (NC)	4	3	1
Chanhassen, Minn. (CC)	3	3	NA
Park Forest South, Ill. (NC)	5	4	1
Richton Park, Ill. (CC)	3	3	NA
Two Retirement New Communities (NC)	7	7	NA
Two Subsidized Housing Conventional Communities (CC)	9	9	NA
Two Black Conventional Communities (CC)	7	7	NA
Nonfederally Assisted New Communities and Paired Conventional Communities			
Columbia, Md. (NC)	9	8	1
Norbeck-Wheaton, Md. (CC)	2	2	NA
Elk Grove Village, Ill. (NC)	3	3	a
Schaumburg, Ill. (CC)	3	3	NA
Forest Park, Oh. (NC)	4	4	a
Sharonville, Oh. (CC)	5	5	NA
Foster City, Calif. (NC)	5	4	1
West San Mateo, Calif. (CC)	4	4	NA
Irvine, Calif. (NC)	8	6	2
Fountain Valley, Calif. (CC)	5	5	NA
Laguna Niguel, Calif. (NC)	6	5	1
Dana Point, Calif. (CC)	5	5	NA
Lake Havasu City, Ariz. (NC)	5	4	1
Kingman, Ariz. (CC)	3	3	NA
North Palm Beach, Fla. (NC)	4	4	a
Tequesta, Fla. (CC)	4	4	NA
Park Forest, Ill. (NC)	4	4	a
Lansing, Ill. (CC)	3	3	NA
Reston, Va. (NC)	8	7	1
West Springfield, Va. (CC)	5	5	NA

Table A–3. continued

| | Number of Interviews | | |
Community	Total	Health Care Personnel	Developers
Sharpstown, Tex. (NC)	3	3	a
Southwest Houston, Tex. (CC)	3	3	NA
Valencia, Calif. (NC)	5	4	1
Bouquet Canyon, Calif. (CC)	4	4	NA
Westlake Village, Calif. (NC)	6	4	2
Agoura/Malibu Junction, Calif. (CC)	2	2	NA

NC = New Community
CC = Conventional Community
NA = Not Applicable
[a]Developer interviews were not conducted with the developers of communities that began development prior to 1960.

that summarized residents' evaluations of various aspects of the community. Prior to the interview the developer was sent copies of the profile for his community, which showed the new community residents' responses in comparison with the responses from residents of the paired conventional community and with the combined responses of residents of the thirteen nonfederally assisted new communities in the sample. In addition, a document summarizing the strengths and weaknesses of each community, as revealed by the household survey, was prepared for discussion during the interview.

The interviews themselves were informal and unstructured. Respondents were the developer (i.e., president of the development corporation) and those members of his staff whom he asked to participate. The interviews were arranged by prior appointment and conducted in the developers' offices. They took from 90 to 120 minutes to complete. Each interview was taped.

THE COMMUNITY INVENTORIES AND MAP MEASUREMENTS

Community-level data were collected in the community inventories. The inventory in each sample community was made concurrently with the field work for the professional personnel survey in that community. The inventory served both as a listing of facilities and services available in the community upon which selection of health professionals could be based and as an independent data set. Among other data, information collected in each inventory included: (1) location and population data for the sample community and for the county and SMSA in which it was located; (2) developer characteristics; (3) name and location of general practitioners, internists and osteopaths practicing in community; (4) availability of each of fourteen medical specialists in community; (5) name, location and selected characteristics of all hospitals serving community; (6) selected characteristics of emergency ambulance service serving community; (7) availability of selected social services in community; (8) availability of nursing or convalescent care in community; (9) availability of health and social programs for low- and moderate-income households, young adults and the elderly; (10) availability of information and referral services; and (11) existence of procedures for citizen participation in health care planning. This information was gathered from public records, questioning of knowledgeable persons, field observations and from the professional health care personnel survey. Because of the complexity of the data, a summary form was prepared using data taken from the professional survey and from the community inventory.

Two phases of map measurements were carried out. The first was designed to measure accessibility of general practitioners and internists, hospitals and public health facilities for household survey respondents. The second was to measure the distance from these respondents to the doctors they used most frequently.[c] The procedures used were the same for both phases.

Two maps were used for each community: a plat map of the community showing property lines and a regional map of the area within which the community was found. The locations of all household survey sample clusters that had yielded interviews for the community were shown on the community plat map.[d] The locations of doctors, hospitals and public health facilities found in the community inventory were marked on the map. Inventoried facilities lying outside the community were located and marked on the regional map. For the

[c]To help the study team locate these facilities respondents were asked for the name of the facility, the names of the streets of the intersection nearest the facility and of the community in which it was located. Since respondents could not always remember precise names and intersection locations, not all facilities they mentioned could be found. However, the fact that a number of respondents in a community often used a given facility and some could give the name and location precisely helped in determining which facilities were used by those who could remember only the name or only the location. Thus, a high proportion of the facilities used by the respondents was located.

[d]The community plat maps used were the same as those used in selecting the household survey sample. Therefore, they showed the location of all housing in the community that had been occupied as of the fall of 1972, as well as the location of clusters sampled for the survey.

phase two measurements, any doctors mentioned by household survey respondents that had not already been located on a map were added to the appropriate map. Virtually all such additions involved doctors who were located outside the community and were therefore additions to the regional map.

Facility location markers were placed on the maps at the location of the building containing or associated with the doctor's office, hospital or public health facility if its location was known. Otherwise they were placed at the center of the parcel containing the building.

The initial procedures for phase one, and the only procedures for phase two, were those associated with measuring distances from sample clusters to particular facilities.

For phase one, road distances were measured from the center of each sample cluster to the center of the marker locating the nearest available doctor, hospital or public health facility. Distances were measured in inches (to the nearest fraction of an inch shown on the map-measuring wheel used), and converted to feet in accordance with the scale of the map. All distances measured in phase one were road distances, and were measured along the shortest street route from the sample cluster to the marker locating the facility. When two or more available facilities were equidistant from a cluster, the facility accessible by the route that could accommodate the largest amount of traffic (i.e., arterial streets rather than residential and local streets) took precedence. Where a cluster was adjacent to a facility, the straight-line distance from the center of the cluster to the center of the marker was used.

For phase two (distances to doctors or clinics used by household respondents) the same procedures were used as for phase one with one exception. It was necessary to locate the doctor or clinic each respondent said he or she used most often rather than the doctor or clinic nearest the housing cluster. Because of the extreme number of different doctors and clinics that were used by respondents, aerial (straight-line) distances (rather than road distances) were calculated from the center of the respondents' communities to the center of the towns where the respondents' doctors were located.

One worker did the measurements for all sample clusters in a community for at least one phase of the work on that community. Measurements were independently checked for at least 10 percent of the clusters in each community. Where consistent errors were found, all such measurements for all clusters in the community were checked and corrected.

Appendix B

Household Survey Questionnaire

**Face Sheet and Selected
Health Care Questions
Nos. 40–48**

I. D. NUMBER

⓪ⓞⓞⓞⓞⓞⓞ
①①①①①①①
②②②②②②②
③③③③③③③
④④④④④④④
⑤⑤⑤⑤⑤⑤⑤
⑥⑥⑥⑥⑥⑥⑥
⑦⑦⑦⑦⑦⑦⑦
⑧⑧⑧⑧⑧⑧⑧
⑨⑨⑨⑨⑨⑨⑨

A NATIONAL STUDY OF ENVIRONMENTAL PREFERENCES AND THE QUALITY OF LIFE
JANUARY – APRIL 1973

OFFICE USE ONLY

Supporting Agency	National Science Foundation Research Applied to National Needs Division of Social Systems and Human Resources Research Grant Number GI-34285		
Research Organization	Center for Urban and Regional Studies, University of North Carolina at Chapel Hill	Field Work Subcontractor	Research Triangle Institute Research Triangle Park, North Carolina

A. Sample Cluster Number: _____ – _____   B. Sample Line Number: _____

C. Street Address: _____

D. City or Town: _____

E. Respondent Designated on Cluster Listing Sheet: ○ Head   ○ Spouse

F. Hello, I'm _____ representing the Research Triangle Institute, a not-for-profit national research organization and the University of North Carolina. We are conducting a survey about the attitudes, preferences, living conditions, and activities of people in a number of communities across the United States. Since your household falls into our sample in this community, I would like to ask you a few questions. All the answers you give will be strictly confidential and will be used only in statistical tables where your name can in no way be connected with your answers. Of course, no one is required to participate, but I hope very much that you will, and I think you'll find it interesting.

G. Before we start, however, I need to know if you and your family have moved to this address since the first of the year (1973) or if you've been living here longer than that.
○ SINCE FIRST OF YEAR - - THANK RESPONDENT AND TERMINATE INTERVIEW
○ "LONGER THAN THAT" - - CONTINUE WITH HOUSEHOLD LISTING

H. Time is now: _____

I. Good. Now first, I need some information about the people who live here with you. I don't need the names, just the relationships of the people who live here. Let's start with the adults. What is the age of the head of household? (PAUSE. OBTAIN ALL INFORMATION ABOUT HEAD OF HOUSEHOLD AND CONTINUE WITH OTHER HOUSEHOLD MEMBERS.) Have we missed anyone -- a roomer, someone who lives here but who is away right now?

IF HEAD AND SPOUSE ARE LIVING IN A HOUSEHOLD, INTERVIEW PERSON INDICATED ON CLUSTER LISTING SHEET (AND TRANSFERRED TO ITEM E ABOVE). IF HEAD IS NOT NOW MARRIED, OR SPOUSE IS NOT LIVING IN HOUSEHOLD, INTERVIEW HEAD.

ADULTS

All Persons:
* 21 or Older
  or
* Married, any Age
  or
* Under 21 and Living Away From Parents

NCS Trans-Optic S388C-321

List All Adults By Relation to the Head	Sex	Age	Marital Status	Indicate R "X"
1. Head of Household				
2.				
3.				
4.				

40. Now we have some questions about your health and health care. Of course, most people get sick now and then, but overall, how satisfied are you with your own health? **(HAND CARD E)** Here is a card I'd like you to use to answer this question. If you are completely satisfied with your health, you would say "one." If you are completely dissatisfied, you would say "seven." If you are neither completely satisfied nor completely dissatisfied, you would put yourself somewhere from two to six; for example, four means that you are just as satisfied as you are dissatisfied.

   Completely Satisfied ① ② ③ ④ ⑤ ⑥ ⑦ Completely Dissatisfied

41. Have you had a routine check-up in the past year, that is, since **(MONTH) 1972**?
   ① Yes   ⑤ No

42. Do you have routine check-ups as often as you feel you should?
   ① Yes   ⑤ No

43. Do you have a regular doctor or clinic you go to?
   ① Doctor   ③ Clinic   ⑤ No -- Go to Q. 44

   43a. Where is (his/her office/the clinic) located?
   NAME OF DOCTOR/CLINIC: _____

   NEAREST INTERSECTION: _____ TOWN: _____
                              (Street)   (Cross Street)

   43b. How long does it usually take to
        get there from here?   _____MINUTES ⊙⊖②③④⑤⑥⑦⑧⑨
                                                            ⓪①②③④⑤⑥⑦⑧⑨

   43c. The last time you went to that (doctor/clinic), did you find anything annoying or inconvenient about · · · · ·
        Yes No
        ①   ⑤ Arranging appointments?
        ①   ⑤ Arranging transportation to get there?
        ①   ⑤ The way you and other patients were treated?
        ①   ⑤ The cost of the visit for treatment received?

   43d. Overall, how satisfied are you with the quality of the medical care you usually receive from that (doctor/clinic)?
        (HAND CARD E) Which number comes closest to how you feel?
        Completely Satisfied ① ② ③ ④ ⑤ ⑥ ⑦ Completely Dissatisfied

   ---

44. Altogether, how many different times have you been to see doctors, other than dentists, in their offices or in clinics about your own health in the past 12 months -- that is, since **(MONTH) 1972**?

   _____ TIMES   ⓪①②③④⑤⑥⑦⑧⑨
                         ⓪①②③④⑤⑥⑦⑧⑨

45. And during the last 12 months, did you ever really want to see or talk to a doctor but didn't for some reason?
   ⊙ Yes   ⑤ No -- Go to Q. 46.

   45a. The last time that happened, why didn't you?
   _____
   _____

   ---

46. Do you belong to a prepaid medical plan or have any other kind of medical or hospital insurance?

　○ Yes – Prepaid plan only　　　③ Yes – Both　　　　　　　⑤ No – Go to Q. 47.
　② Yes – Insurance only　　　　④ Yes – Not sure/don't know which

46a. What is the name of the (plan/insurance)?

　NAME(S): _____

46b. (Does this/Do these) cover your doctor's bills in full, in part, or not at all?
　① In full　　　③ In part　　　⑤ Not at all

46c. (Does it/Do they) cover your hospital expenses in full, in part, or not at all?
　① In full　　　③ In part　　　⑤ Not at all

---

47. Here is a list of services available in many communities. (HAND CARD F) We'd like to know, first, if such services are available in this community or its vicinity, and second, if you would be willing to recommend those that are here as good places to go for help.

	SERVICE AVAILABLE			SERVICE NOT AVAILABLE	DON'T KNOW IF SERVICE AVAILABLE
	Would Recommend	Not Sure	Would Not Recommend		
a. Emergency medical care	①	②	③	⑤	⑧
b. Hospital care	①	②	③	⑤	⑧
c. Family planning	①	②	③	⑤	⑧
d. Prenatal care	①	②	③	⑤	⑧
e. Health care for children	①	②	③	⑤	⑧
f. Dental care	①	②	③	⑤	⑧
g. Convalescent or nursing home care	①	②	③	⑤	⑧
h. Public assistance or welfare services	①	②	③	⑤	⑧
i. Family and marital counseling	①	②	③	⑤	⑧
j. Help with a legal problem	①	②	③	⑤	⑧
k. Help with a drug problem	①	②	③	⑤	⑧
l. Help with an emotional problem	①	②	③	⑤	⑧
m. Help with a drinking problem	①	②	③	⑤	⑧

48. Overall, how good would you say health care facilities and services are for people who live in this community – excellent, good, average, below average, or poor?
　① Excellent　　　② Good　　　③ Average　　　④ Below average　　　⑤ Poor

Health Professional
Survey Questionnaire

Community:_____   Interview No._____

CONFIDENTIAL

PERFORMANCE CRITERIA FOR NEW COMMUNITY
DEVELOPMENT: EVALUATION AND PROGNOSIS
NSF RESEARCH GRANT GI-34285

Health Survey

Respondent's Name:_____   Interviewer's Name:_____

Address:_____   Date of Interview:_____

City:_____ State:_____   Place of Interview:_____

Telephone Number:_____   _____

Respondent's Position:_____   City:_____ State:_____

Name of Organization:_____

Address:_____

City:_____ State:_____

Telephone Number:_____

* * * * * * * * * * *

Hello. I'm from the Center for Urban and Regional Studies at the
University of North Carolina. We are conducting a study of residential
living conditions in communities across the United States. One of the
most important aspects of this study concerns the health needs of community residents and the planning of health services and facilities.
Any information you can provide in these areas would be greatly appreci-
ated. As you answer the following questions, please keep in mind that
we will not use direct quotes of your opinions on the matters we discuss
without your permission. Of course, you are not required to participate,
but I hope very much that you will and I think that you will find it
interesting.

* * * * * * * * * * *

Center for Urban and Regional Studies
University of North Carolina at Chapel Hill

February, 1973

Introduction

In this interview, I would like to discuss the health care services and facilities available to residents of (NAME OF COMMUNITY), along with your views on the health needs and problems of the community and on the way in which facilities and programs for health care have been planned and developed.

General

1. In your opinion, what are the most important health or health-related problems currently facing (NAME OF COMMUNITY)?

    | 0 | NONE

    _____

    _____

    _____

    _____

    _____

    _____

    _____

Private Medical Practice

2. Now I would like to turn to the health care facilities and services available in (NAME OF COMMUNITY). First, can you tell me how many of each of the following medical practitioners are practicing in (NAME OF COMMUNITY)? What about...

    a. General practitioners and internists, either in solo or group practice?

        _____

    b. Pediatricians?   _____

    c. Gynecologists and/or obstetricians?   _____

    d. Dentists?   _____

3. Can you tell me which of the practitioners listed on this card have practices within (NAME OF COMMUNITY)? HAND RESPONDENT CARD A.

YES	NO		
1	5	a.	Child psychologist
1	5	b.	Chiropractor
1	5	c.	Dermatologist
1	5	d.	Ophthalmologist
1	5	e.	Optometrist
1	5	f.	Orthodontist
1	5	g.	Orthopedist
1	5	h.	Osteopath
1	5	i.	Otolaryngologist
1	5	j.	Podiatrist
1	5	k.	Psychiatrist
1	5	l.	Urologist

4. What additional types of practitioners, if any, do you think will be needed in (NAME OF COMMUNITY) during the next five years?

| 0 | NONE

_____

_____

_____

5. Next, I would like to get an idea of the way in which private medical care is organized in (NAME OF COMMUNITY). Are there any organized medical practices in the community, such as a private clinic or a group practice including more than one specialty?

| 1 | YES | 5 | NO

5a. Can you describe these?   _____

_____

_____

_____

6. How would you rate the office facilities available for private medical
    practice in (NAME OF COMMUNITY)? Would you say they were excellent,
    good, average, below average, or poor?

    | 1 | EXCELLENT | 2 | GOOD | 3 | AVERAGE | 4 | BELOW AVERAGE | 5 | POOR

    6a. Why do you say that?

    _____

    _____

    _____

7. In your estimation, about what percent of the population of (NAME OF
    COMMUNITY) have a family doctor?

    PERCENT WITH FAMILY DOCTOR: _____%

Hospital Facilities

8. The next group of questions concerns hospital facilities available to the
    residents of (NAME OF COMMUNITY). Is there a hospital in (NAME OF
    COMMUNITY)?

    | 5 | NO | 1 | YES

    8d. What is its (are their) name(s)?

    | 1 | NAME:_____

            LOCATION:_____
                     Street   Cross Street

    | 2 | NAME:_____

            LOCATION:_____
                     Street   Cross Street

            GO TO Q. 8c

    8a. Is there a hospital in the planning stage or under construction in
    (NAME OF COMMUNITY)?

    | 5 | NO | 1 | YES

    8e. What is its name?

         NAME:_____

         LOCATION:_____
                  Street   Cross Street

         GO TO Q. 8c

↓

8b.   At what point in the development of (NAME OF COMMUNITY), if any, do you think a hospital will be needed in the community?

_____

_____

_____

8c.   What (other) hospitals serve a significant number of people from (NAME OF COMMUNITY)?   IF MORE THAN THREE, GET THREE WHICH SERVE MOST RESIDENTS.

| 1 | NAME:_____

LOCATION:_____
         Street   Cross Street

         _____
         Town

| 2 | NAME:_____

LOCATION:_____
         Street   Cross Street

         _____
         Town

| 3 | NAME:_____

LOCATION:_____
         Street   Cross Street

         _____
         Town

9.   Considering all of the hospital facilities in the area, do you feel that hospital care available to residents of (NAME OF COMMUNITY) is adequate?

| 1 | YES | 5 | NO

9a.   In what ways might existing hospital services be improved?

_____

_____

_____

_____

9b.   What additional facilities, services, or personnel are needed?

_____

_____

_____

_____

_____

_____

Emergency Service

10.   Is emergency ambulance service provided to residents of (NAME OF COMMUNITY)?

| 1 | YES | 5 | NO |

10a.   Who provides this service?

| 1 | Fire department, police department, or rescue squad

| 2 | Hospital (specify:_____)

| 3 | Funeral home

| 4 | Private company

| 5 | Other (specify:_____)

10b.   From what location is service provided?

LOCATION:_____
         Street   Cross Street   Town

10c.   What is the basic cost for emergency service?

EMERGENCY SERVICE COST: $_____

10d.   Are attendants trained to provide emergency care?

| 1 | YES | 5 | NO |

10e.   In your view, does this service meet the needs of the community?

| 5 | NO | 1 | YES |

10f.   In what ways is it deficient?

_____

_____

_____

Other Health and Social Services

11. In addition to the private medical practices we discussed earlier, are
    there any organizations in (NAME OF COMMUNITY) or the immediate vicinity
    which provide assistance in the following areas?   HAND THE RESPONDENT
    CARD B.

    YES   NO

    | 1 | | 5 | a.   Family planning

    | 1 | | 5 | b.   Prenatal care

    | 1 | | 5 | c.   Health care for children

    | 1 | | 5 | d.   Family and marital counseling

    | 1 | | 5 | e.   Help with a drug problem

    | 1 | | 5 | f.   Help with an emotional problem

    | 1 | | 5 | g.   Help with a drinking problem

12. Considering these types of health and social services, would you say
    that present facilities and programs are adequate to deal with the
    needs of (NAME OF COMMUNITY) residents?

    | 5 | NO | 1 | YES

    12a. What improvements or additions in facilities, services, or
         personnel are needed most?

    _____

    _____

    _____

    _____

    ---

13. Is supervised home care or visiting nurse service available to
    residents of (NAME OF COMMUNITY)?

    | 1 | YES | 5 | NO

14. Where is the nearest nursing or convalescent home?

    LOCATION: _____
                  Street   Cross Street

              _____
                  Town

14a. Is there a need for additional nursing facilities in or near (NAME OF COMMUNITY)?

| 1 | YES | 5 | NO |

Services for Low-income Persons, Teenagers, and Elderly Persons

15. One of the primary interests of this study concerns facilities for low and moderate income persons, especially in the area of health care. With this in mind, could you tell me the location of the nearest public health clinic or similar facility. PROBE FOR NEIGHBORHOOD CLINICS, HOSPITAL CLINICS AND EMERGENCY ROOMS, AND OTHER POTENTIAL SOURCES OF LOW-COST PRIMARY HEALTH CARE.

LOCATION:_____
          Street   Cross Street

_____
          Town

15a. In your opinion, is this facility a useful source of health care for residents of (NAME OF COMMUNITY)?

| 1 | YES | 5 | NO |

15b. Why do you say that?

_____

_____

_____

16. Have any health or social programs been undertaken within (NAME OF COMMUNITY) specifically for low and moderate income persons? PROBE FOR INFORMAL ACTIVITIES UNDERTAKEN BY PRIVATE PHYSICIANS OR OTHER INDIVIDUALS OR GROUPS.

| 1 | YES | 5 | NO |

16a. What are they? _____

_____

_____

17. We are also interested in the health and social problems of teenagers and of elderly persons. Have any special programs been developed in (NAME OF COMMUNITY) for teenagers?

| 1 | YES | 5 | NO |

17a. What are they? _____

_____

_____

18. What about for elderly persons? Have any activities in the area of health care been undertaken especially for them?

☐ 1   YES   ☐ 5   NO

┌───┐
│ 18a. What are they?   _____   │
│   │
│   _____   │
│   │
│   _____   │
└───┘

Information and Referral Services

19. Are any of the following aids found in (NAME OF COMMUNITY) to assist residents in locating health care facilities? What about...

YES	NO		
☐ 1	☐ 5	a.	Organized health information service?
☐ 1	☐ 5	b.	Newcomer's guide issued by developer?
☐ 1	☐ 5	c.	Newcomer's guide issued by local government?
☐ 1	☐ 5	d.	Any other? (Specify:_____
			_____)

20. Are there any agencies in (NAME OF COMMUNITY) which assist in referring patients to appropriate health care services in and near the community?

☐ 1   YES   ☐ 5   NO

┌───┐
│ 20a. What agency is that?   │
│   │
│   _____   │
│   │
│ 20b. What are its most important activities in the area of health   │
│   services referral?   │
│   │
│   _____   │
│   │
│   _____   │
│   │
│   _____   │
│   │
│   _____   │
│   │
│   _____   │
└───┘

Pre-Paid Community Health Plans

(COLUMBIA - GO TO Q. 22)

21. Has any thought been given to implementing a pre-paid health plan in (NAME OF COMMUNITY)?

| 1 | YES | | 5 | NO - GO TO Q. 27 |

21a. Please explain what you have in mind.

_____

_____

_____

_____

GO TO Q. 27

22. I am familiar with the general design of the Columbia Medical Plan, but could you tell me whether any recent changes have been made in the way the program works?

_____

_____

_____

INTERVIEWER: ASK FOR RECENT PRINTED MATERIAL ABOUT THE PROGRAM.

23. I would also be interested in getting your evaluation of the way the program has been working so far. Do you feel that the program has been successful from the standpoint of the participants in the plan?

| 1 | YES | | 5 | NO |

23a. Why do you say that?

_____

_____

_____

_____

24. Do you feel that the plan has been successful from the point of view of physicians and other health professionals?

    | 1 | YES | 5 | NO

    24a. Why do you say that?

    _____

    _____

    _____

25. What about from the standpoint of the community as a whole? Would you say this plan serves successfully as a source, or at least a potential source, of comprehensive care for the entire community?

    | 1 | YES | 5 | NO

    25a. Why do you say that?

    _____

    _____

    _____

26. Finally, what changes would you recommend in the Columbia Medical Plan?

    _____

    _____

    _____

    _____

Overall Evaluation

27. Overall, how good would you say health care facilities and services are for people who live in (NAME OF COMMUNITY) - excellent, good, average, below average, or poor?

    | 1 | EXCELLENT | 2 | GOOD | 3 | AVERAGE | 4 | BELOW AVERAGE | 5 | POOR

28. Are there any features of the health care system of (NAME OF COMMUNITY) which are unique or which might serve as a model for other communities?

    | 1 | YES | 5 | NO

    28a. Which ones? _____

    _____

    _____

Planning of Health Care Facilities

29. I'd like to ask you several questions about the planning of health care facilities for (NAME OF COMMUNITY). First, do you feel that adequate attention has been given to the provision of health care services, facilities, and programs in the planning of (NAME OF COMMUNITY)?

| 1 | YES | 5 | NO

30. INTERVIEWER: CHECK ONE

| 1 | NEW COMMUNITY -- ASK Q. 31

| 5 | CONTROL COMMUNITY -- GO TO Q. 33

31. What services, facilities, or programs were initially planned or encouraged by (NAME OF NEW COMMUNITY DEVELOPER)?

| 0 | NONE -- GO TO Q. 32

_____

_____

_____

31a. What role, if any, did medical or social service professionals play in the planning process?

| 0 | NONE

_____

_____

31b. In your opinion, has (NAME OF NEW COMMUNITY DEVELOPER) shown sufficient initiative in implementing these plans?

| 5 | NO | 1 | YES -- GO TO Q. 32

31c. Why do you say this?

_____

_____

_____

32. Does (NAME OF NEW COMMUNITY DEVELOPER) currently evaluate health care facilities and assess the health care needs of (NAME OF COMMUNITY)?

| 1 | YES | | 5 | NO |

32a. How do they do this?

_____

_____

_____

33. Does any (other) organization monitor the health care needs of (NAME OF COMMUNITY)?

| 1 | YES | | 5 | NO |

33a. How is this function performed?

_____

_____

_____

34. Is there a comprehensive health planning agency for the area in which (NAME OF COMMUNITY) is located?

| 1 | YES | | 5 | NO |

34a. What is the name of this agency?

NAME OF COMPREHENSIVE HEALTH PLANNING AGENCY: _____

_____

34b. In what ways, if any, has it influenced the planning and development of health care facilities in (NAME OF COMMUNITY)?

| 0 | NONE |

_____

_____

_____

35. Are there any ways by which residents of (NAME OF COMMUNITY) can participate in the planning of health care facilities for the community?

| 1 | YES | 5 | NO |

35a. What are they?

_____

_____

_____

35b. How effective have they been -- very effective, somewhat effective, effective, not very effective, or not effective at all?

1	Very effective
2	Somewhat effective
3	Not very effective
4	Not effective at all

36. Has the planning of health care facilities in (NAME OF COMMUNITY), either initially or since development, taken into consideration the needs of people in the surrounding areas?

| 1 | YES | 5 | NO |

36a. In what respects?

_____

_____

_____

37. Has there been any unnecessary duplication of facilities and services within (NAME OF COMMUNITY) and outside the community?

| 1 | YES | 5 | NO |

37a. In what ways?

_____

_____

_____

38.   Before turning to a few questions about your own background, could you
      describe the most important issues or controversies in the area of health
      care currently facing (NAME OF COMMUNITY), including those concerning
      aspects of health care not dealt with in this questionnaire? I would be
      happy to have you elaborate on these as fully as you wish in order to give
      us a more complete picture of health care in (NAME OF COMMUNITY).

Background

Finally, I have some general questions about your present position and background.

39. In what year did you assume your present position?

   YEAR: _____

40. Have you held any other positions with (NAME OF ORGANIZATION)?

   | 1 | YES | 5 | NO

   40a. What were these?

   _____

   _____

   40b. In all how many years have you worked for (NAME OF ORGANIZATION)?

   YEARS: _____

41. What were the most important reasons you (first) came to work here?

   _____

   _____

   _____

42. Do you live in (NAME OF COMMUNITY)?

   | 1 | YES | 5 | NO

   42a. In what year did you move to (NAME OF COMMUNITY)?

   YEAR: _____

43. How do you feel about (NAME OF COMMUNITY) as a place to live? From your own point of view, would you rate this area as an excellent place to live, good, average, below average, or poor?

   | 1 | EXCELLENT | 2 | GOOD | 3 | AVERAGE | 4 | BELOW AVERAGE | 5 | POOR

   43a. Why do you say that?

   _____

   _____

   _____

THANK YOU VERY MUCH, YOU'VE BEEN MOST HELPFUL.

44. Race of respondent.

| 1 | WHITE | 3 | ORIENTAL |

| 2 | BLACK | 4 | OTHER |

45. Sex of respondent.

| 1 | MALE |

| 2 | FEMALE |

Bibliography

Abernathy, W.J. and Schrems, E.L. 1971. *Distance and Health Services: Issues of Utilization and Facility Choice for Demographic Strata.* Research Paper No. 19. Graduate School of Business, Stanford University.

Advisory Commission on Intergovernmental Relations. 1968. *Urban and Rural America: Policies for Future Growth.* A Commission Report (A–32). Washington, D.C.: U.S. Government Printing Office, April.

Alonso, William. 1969. *What Are New Towns For?* Working Paper No. 18. Berkeley: Center for Planning and Development Research, Institute for Urban and Regional Development, University of California, Berkeley, October.

———. 1970. "The Mirage of New Towns," *The Public Interest*, No. 19 (Spring), pp. 3–17.

Altman, Isidore. 1954. "Distances Traveled for Physician Care in Western Pennsylvania," in *Medical Service Areas and Distances Traveled for Physicians Care in Western Pennsylvania*, Public Health Monograph 19. Antonio A. Ciocco and Isidore Altman (eds.). Washington, D.C.: U.S. Public Health Service.

American City Corporation. 1971. *City Building: Experience, Trends and New Directions.* Columbia, Md.: The Corporation.

American Hospital Association. 1972. *Guide to the Health Care Field 1972.* Chicago: The Association.

American Institute of Architects. 1972. *First Report of the National Policy Task Force*, second edition. Washington, D.C.: The Institute, May.

American Public Health Association. 1960. *Planning the Neighborhood.* Chicago: Public Administration Service.

Andersen, Ronald. 1968. *A Behavioral Model of Families' Use of Health Services.* Research Series No. 25. Center for Health Administration Studies. Chicago: University of Chicago Press.

Andersen, Ronald and Anderson, Odin W. 1967 *A Decade of Health Services.* Chicago: University of Chicago Press.

Anderson, J.G. 1973. "Demographic Factors Affecting Health Services Utilization: A Causal Model," *Medical Care*, Vol. II (March-April), pp. 104–120.

Anderson, Odin W. 1963. "The Utilization of Health Services," in *Handbook of Medical Sociology*, Howard E. Freeman, *et al.* (eds.). Englewood Cliffs, N.J.: Prentice-Hall.

Arnold, Mary F. 1971. "Evaluation: A Parallel Process to Planning," in *Administering Health Systems*, Mary F. Arnold, L. Vaughan Blankenship and John M. Hess (eds.). Chicago: Aldine-Atherton, pp. 263–282.

Barry, Mildred and Sheps, Cecil. 1969. "A New Model for Community Health Planning," *American Journal of Public Health*, Vol. 59 (February), pp. 226–236.

Bashshur, Rashid L., Shannon, Gary W. and Metzner, Charles A. 1970. "Some Econological Differences in the Use of Medical Services," Paper presented at the Annual Meeting of the American Sociological Association, Washington, D.C.

Belloc, N.B., Breslaw, L. and Hochstim, J.R. 1971. "Measurement of Physical Health in a General Population Survey," *American Journal of Epidemiology*, Vol. 93.

Bice, Thomas W. and Eichorn, R.L. 1972. "Socio-Economic Status and Use of Physicians' Services: A Reconsideration," *Medical Care*, Vol. 10 (May-June), pp. 261–271.

Bice, Thomas W. and White, K.L. 1969. "Factors Related to the Use of Health Services: An International Comparative Study," *Medical Care*, Vol. 10 (April), pp. 124–133.

Bice, Thomas W. *et al.* 1973. "Economic Class and Use of Physicians' Services," *Medical Care*, Vol. 11 (July-August), pp. 287–296.

Brown, D.R. 1972. "Community Health Planning or Who Will Control the Health Care System?" *American Journal of Public Health*, Vol. 62 (October), pp. 1336–1339.

Bruhn, J.G. 1973. "Planning for Social Change: Dilemmas for Health Planning," *American Journal of Public Health*, Vol. 63 (July), pp. 602–606.

Burby, Raymond J., III and Weiss, Shirley F. with Donnelly, Thomas G., Kaiser, Edward J., Zehner, Robert B., and Lewis, David F., Loewenthal, Norman H., McCalla, Mary Ellen, Rodgers, Barbara G. and Smookler, Helene V. 1976. *New Communities U.S.A.* Lexington, Mass.: D.C. Heath and Company, Lexington Books.

Campbell, Angus, Converse, Phillip E. and Rodgers, Willard L. 1976. *The Quality of American Life: Perceptions, Evaluations, and Satisfactions.* New York: Russell Sage Foundation.

Ciocco, Antonio A. and Altman, Isidore. 1954. *Medical Service Areas and Distance Traveled for Physician Care in Western Pennsylvania.* Public Health Service Monograph 19. Washington, D.C.: United States Public Health Service.

Clapp, James A. 1971. *New Towns and Urban Policy: Planning Metropolitan Growth.* New York: Dunellen Publishing Company.

Coliver, Andrew A., *et al.* 1967. "Factors Influencing the Use of Maternal Health Services," *Social Science and Medicine*, Vol. 1 (September), pp. 293–308.

Comprehensive Health Survey. 1972. Elk Grove Village, Illinois, September.

Conklin, Paul. 1959 *Tomorrow a New World: The New Deal Community Program.* Published for the American Historical Association. Ithaca, N.Y.: Cornell University Press.

Daniels, R.S. 1972. "An Example of Sub-regional Health Planning: A Further Report," *Inquiry*, Vol. 9 (September), pp. 57–63.

Dornblasser, Bright M. 1968. "A Suggested Approach to the Organization and Delivery of Health Services," in *MXC, Minnesota Experimental City*, Vol. 1, Minnesota Experimental City Project. Minneapolis: University of Minnesota, pp. 147–175.

Durbin, R.L. and Antelman, G. 1964. "A Study of the Effects of Selected Variables on Hospital Utilization," *Hospital Management*, Vol. 98 (August), pp. 57–60.

Eichler, Edward P. and Kaplan, Marshall. 1967. *The Community Builders.* Berkeley and Los Angeles: University of California Press.

Eichler, Edward P. and Norwitch, Bernard. 1970. "New Towns," in *Urban America: The Expert Looks at the City*, Voice of America Forum Lectures, Daniel P. Moynihan (ed.). Washington, D.C.: Voice of America, U.S. Information Agency, May, pp. 336–347.

Elwood, Paul M. 1969. "Planning Medical Care for an Experimental City," in *MXC, Minnesota Experimental City*, Vol. 1, Minnesota Experimental City Project. Minneapolis: University of Minnesota, pp. 189–198.

Ernst and Ernst. 1972. "Assessment of Health Care Needs of the Northwest Cook County Area," Prepared for Northwest Cook County Health Needs Study Committee, December 22.

Erskine, Hazel. 1973. "The Polls: Hopes, Fears and Regrets," *The Public Opinion Quarterly*, Vol. 37 (Spring), pp. 132–145.

Feldstein, P.J. and German, J.J. 1963. "Predicting Hospital Utilization: An Evaluation of Three Approaches," *Inquiry*, Vol. 2 (June), pp. 13–36.

Fischer, Linda A. 1971. *The Use of Services in the Urban Scene—The Individual and the Medical Care System.* Chapel Hill, N.C.: Center for Urban and Regional Studies, The University of North Carolina at Chapel Hill.

Fonaroff, Arlene. 1970. "Identifying and Developing Health Services in a New Town," *American Journal of Public Health*, Vol. 60 (May), pp. 821–838.

Freeman, Mark H. 1974. "Letter from Mark H. Freeman," *Update: New Community Digest*, reprinted from *Systems Building News*, August-September 1974. Chicago: Barton-Aschman, Inc., unpaged.

Fuller, B.F. 1969. "Health Manpower and the Delivery of Services," in *MXC, Minnesota Experimental City*, Vol. 1, Minnesota Experimental City Project, Minneapolis: University of Minnesota, pp. 177–182.

Gaus, Clifton. 1971. "Who Enrolls in a Prepaid Group Practice: The Columbia Experience," *Johns Hopkins Medical Journal*, Vol. 128 (January), pp. 9–14.

Gleeson, Geraldine A. and White, Elijah L. 1965. "Desirability and Medical Care among Whites and Nonwhites in the United States," *Health, Education and Welfare Indicators*, (October), pp. 1–10.

Harrelson, E. Frank and Donovan, Kirk M. 1975. "Consumer Responsibility in a Prepaid Group Health Plan," *American Journal of Public Health*, Vol. 65 (October), pp. 1077–1086.

Herman, Harold and Joroff, Michael I. 1967. "Planning Health Services for New Towns," *American Journal of Public Health*, Vol. 57 (April), pp. 633–640.

Heyssel, Robert M. 1971a. "Causes of Retarded Growth in Pre-Payment Plans," *Johns Hopkins Medical Journal*, Vol. 71 (January), pp. 4–8.

———. 1971b. "The Columbia Medical Plan and the East Baltimore Medical Plan," *Hospitals*, Vol. 45 (March 16), pp. 68–71.

———. 1971c. "Summary Comments," in *Audio Proceedings of a Conference on Community-Centered Health Plans*, Sponsored by the American City Corporation, The Urban Life Center, Columbia, Maryland, September 8–10, 1971. Columbia, Md.: The Corporation.

Hoffer, Charles, *et al.* 1950. *Health Needs and Health Care in Michigan.* Special Bulletin 365. East Lansing, Mich.: Section of Sociology and Anthropology, Agricultural Experiment Station, Michigan State College, June.

Hoppenfeld, Morton. 1967. "A Sketch of the Planning-Building Process for Columbia, Maryland," *Journal of the American Institute of Planners*, Vol. 33 (November), pp. 398–409.

Hostetler, Frank C. and Prueske, Eleanor C. 1973. "Health Study Report to the Health Council," Village of Park Forest, Illinois, April.

Jehlik, Paul J. and McNammara, Robert L. 1952. "The Relation of Distance to the Differential Use of Certain Health Personnel and Facilities and to the Extent of Bed Illness," *Rural Sociology*, Vol. 17, pp. 261–265.

Jonathan Development Corporation. 1971. *Jonathan New Town: Design and Development.* Chaska, Minn.: The Corporation, February.

Kaplan, Marshall. 1973. "Social Planning, Perceptions, and New Towns," in *New Towns: Why—And for Whom?* Harvey S. Perloff and Neil C. Sandberg (eds.). New York: Praeger Publishers, pp. 130–136.

Kauffman, Harold R. and Morse, Warren W. 1945. *Illness in Rural Missouri.* Research Bulletin 391. Columbia, Mo.: Agricultural Experiment Station, University of Missouri, August.

Lee, J. 1972. "Planning at the Local Level—the Key to Integration," *Public Health*, Vol. 86 (September), pp. 248–257.

Lively, C.E. and Beck, P.G. 1927. *The Rural Health Facilities of Ross County, Ohio.* Bulletin 412. Wooster, Oh.: Agricultural Experiment Station, October.

McKinlay, John B. 1973. "Some Approaches and Problems in the Study of the Use of Services—An Overview," *Journal of Health and Social Behavior*, Vol. 13 (June), pp. 115–152.

Meadows, Paul. 1970. "Public Health in the New Community," *American Journal of Public Health*, Vol. 60 (October), pp. 1900–1903.

Mields, Hugh, Jr. 1971. "The Politics of Federal Legislation for New Community Development," in *New Community Development: Planning Process, Implementation, and Emerging Social Concerns*, Vol. 2, Shirley F. Weiss, Edward J. Kaiser, and Raymond J. Burby, III (eds.). Chapel Hill, N.C.: New Towns Research Seminar, Center for Urban and Regional Studies, The University of North Carolina, October, pp. 245–261.

———. 1973. *Federally Assisted New Communities: New Dimensions in Urban Development.* A ULI Landmark Report. Washington, D.C.: ULI—the Urban Land Institute.

Minnesota Experimental City Project. 1969. "Health, Medical and Rehabilitation Services and Environmental Health," in *MXC, Minnesota Experimental City*, Vol. 1, Minnesota Experimental City Project. Minneapolis: University of Minnesota, pp. 135–146.

Monteiro, Lois A. 1973. "Expense is No Object . . .: Income and Physicians Visits Reconsidered," *Journal of Health and Social Behavior*, Vol. 14 (June), pp. 99–115.

National Center for Health Services Research and Development, Public Health Service, Health Services Administration, U.S. Department of Health, Education and Welfare. 1972. *The Utilization of Health Services: Indices and Correlates, A Research Bibliography 1972.* Washington, D.C.: The Center, December.

National Center for Health Statistics, Public Health Service, U.S. Department of Health, Education and Welfare. 1967. "Interview Data on Chronic Conditions Compared with Information Derived from Medical Records," Series 2, No. 4. Washington, D.C.: U.S. Government Printing Office, May.

———. 1968. *Volume of Physician Visits, United States, July 1966–June 1967.* Vital and Health Statistics (data from National Health Survey). Series 10, No. 49. Washington, D.C.: U.S. Government Printing Office.

———. 1971. *Health Resources Statistics.* DHEW Publication No. (HSM) 72–1509. Washington, D.C.: U.S. Department of Health, Education and Welfare.

National Commission on Community Health Services. 1966. *Health Is a Community Affair.* Cambridge, Mass.: Harvard University Press.

National Committee on Urban Growth Policy. 1969. *The New City*, Donald Canty (ed.). New York: Frederick A. Praeger, Inc., Publishers.

National Health Forum. 1970. *Meeting the Crisis in Health Care Services in Communities.* Washington, D.C.: The Forum.

"New Communities Checklist Update." 1974. *Systems Building News*, Vol. 5 (August), pp. 30–32.

New Communities Division, Community Resources Development Administration, U.S. Department of Housing and Urban Development. 1969. "Survey and Analysis of Large Developments and New Communities Completed or Under Construction in the United States Since 1947." Washington, D.C.: The Department, February.

Nicoson, William. 1976. "Foreword," in *New Communities U.S.A.*, Raymond J. Burby, III, Shirley F. Weiss *et al.* Lexington, Mass.: D.C. Heath and Company, Lexington Books, pp. xiii-xvi.

O'Harrow, Dennis. 1964. "New Towns or New Sprawl," *American Society of Planning Officials Newsletter*, Vol. 30 (October), pp. 105–106.

Peterson, M.L. 1971. "The First Year in Columbia, Assessments of Low Hospitalization Rate and High Office Use," *Johns Hopkins Medical Journal*, Vol. 128 (January), pp. 15–23.

"Project Agreement Between United States of America and Jonathan Development Corporation." 1970. October 8.

"Project Agreement Between United States of America and Park Forest South Development Company." 1971. March 17.

Purola, T. *et al.* 1968. *The Utilization of Medical Services and Its Relationship to Morbidity, Health Resources and Social Factors.* Helsinki: Research Institute for Social Security.

Reps, John W. 1965. *The Making of Urban America: A History of City Planning in the United States.* Princeton, N.J.: Princeton University Press.

The Reston Virginia Foundation for Community Programs, Inc. 1967. *Social Planning Programs for Reston, Virginia*, Reston, Va.: The Foundation, March.

Richardson, Arthur H. *et al.* 1967. "Use of Medical Resources by Spancos: II. Social Factors and Medical Expense," *Milbank Memorial Fund Quarterly*, Vol. 45 (January), pp. 61–75.

Robinson, G.C. *et al.* 1969. "Use of Hospital Emergency Services by Children and Adolescents for Primary Care," *Canadian Medical Association Journal*, Vol. 10 (November 1), pp. 69–73.

Roemer, M.I. 1961a. "Bed Supply and Hospital Utilization," *Hospitals*, Vol. 35 (November 1), pp. 36–42.

————. 1961b. "Hospital Utilization and Supply of Physicians," *Journal of the American Medical Association*, Vol. 178 (December 9), pp. 987–993.

Rome, Howard P. 1969. "Observations on Medical Psychiatric Aspects of the Experimental City," in *MXC, Minnesota Experimental City*, Vol. 1, Minnesota Experimental City Project. Minneapolis: University of Minnesota, pp. 183–187.

Sandberg, Neil C. 1973. "Can the United States Learn from the Experience of Other Countries?" in *New Towns: Why?—And for Whom?* Harvey S. Perloff and Neil C. Sandberg (eds.). New York: Praeger Publishers, pp. 69–77.

Schonfield, H.K., Heston, J.F. and Falk, I.S. 1972. "Numbers of Physicians Required for Primary Care," *New England Journal of Medicine*, Vol. 286 (March 16), pp. 571–576.

Scott, Randall W. 1971. "New Towns as 'Self-Sufficient' Growth Centers—Dream or Feasible Reality?" *Urban and Social Change Review*, Vol. 5 (Fall), pp. 16–19.

Senior, Boris and Smith, Beverly A. 1972. "The Number of Physicians as a Constraint on Delivery of Health Care: How Many Physicians Are Enough?" *Journal of the American Medical Association*, Vol. 222 (October 9), pp. 178–182.

Shain, M. and Roemer, M.I. 1959. "Hospital Costs Relate to Supply of Beds," *Modern Hospital*, Vol. 92 (April), pp. 71–73.

Shannon, Gary W., Bashshur, Rashid L. and Metzner, Charles A. 1969. "The Concept of Distance as a Factor in Accessibility and Utilization of Health Care," *Medical Care Review*, Vol. 26 (February), pp. 143–161.

Shannon, Gary W., Skinner, J.L. and Bashshur, Rashid L. 1973. "Time Distance: The Journey for Medical Care," *International Journal of Health Services*, Vol. 3 (Spring), pp. 237–244.

Sigmond, Robert M. 1967. "Health Planning," *Medical Care*, Vol. 5 (May-June), pp. 129–141.

Smith, John and Marshall, Douglas. 1970. *Retirement and Migration in the North Central States*. Population Series 23. Madison, Wis.: Department of Rural Sociology, College of Agriculture and Life Sciences, University of Wisconsin, June.

Smookler, Helene V. 1976. *Economic Integration in New Communities: An Evaluation of Factors Affecting Policies and Implementation*. Cambridge, Mass.: Ballinger Publishing Company.

Somers, Anne R. 1967. "An American City and Its Health Problems: A Case

Study in Comprehensive Health Planning," *Medical Care*, Vol. 5 (May-June), pp. 129–141.

Stein, Clarence S. 1957. *Toward New Towns for America.* New York: Reinhold Publishing Corporation.

Stewart, W.H. 1963. "Community Medicine, An American Concept of Comprehensive Care," *Public Health Reports*, Vol. 78, pp. 93–100.

Task Force on Organization of Community Health Services. 1967. *Health Administration and Organization in the Decade Ahead.* Washington, D.C.: Public Affairs Press.

Towle, William F. 1972. "New City, New Hospital," *Hospitals, Journal of the American Hospital Association*, Vol. 46 (January 16), pp. 46–49, 120.

Trevino, Alberto F., Jr. 1974. "New Communities Program: Performance and Promise," *Update: New Community Digest*, reprinted from *Systems Building News*, August-September 1974. Chicago: Barton-Aschman, Inc., unpaged.

Twentieth Century Fund Task Force on Governance of New Towns. 1971. *New Towns: Laboratories for Democracy.* Report of the Twentieth Century Fund Task Force on Governance of New Towns. New York: The Twentieth Century Fund.

U.S. Congress, House of Representatives, Committee on Banking and Currency. 1970. *The Quality of Urban Life.* Hearings Before the Ad Hoc Subcommittee on Urban Growth, Ninety-first Congress, First and Second Sessions, on The Quality of Urban Life. Washington, D.C.: U.S. Government Printing Office.

――――. 1973. *Oversight Hearings on HUD New Communities Program.* Hearings Before the Subcommittee on Housing of the Committee on Banking and Currency, House of Representatives, Ninety-third Congress, First Session, May 30 and 31, 1973. Washington, D.C.: U.S. Government Printing Office.

U.S. Congress, House of Representatives, Committee on Banking, Currency and Housing. 1975. *Oversight Hearings on the New Communities Program.* Hearings Before the Subcommittee on Housing and Community Development of the Committee on Banking, Currency and Housing, House of Representatives, Ninety-fourth Congress, First Session, September 23, 29 and 30, 1975. Washington, D.C.: U.S. Government Printing Office.

U.S. Department of Health, Education and Welfare, Office of Human Development, Administration on Aging. 1973. *New Facts About Older Americans.* DHEW Publication No. (SRS) 73–20006. Washington, D.C.: U.S. Government Printing Office.

U.S. Department of Housing and Urban Development, New Community Development Corporation. 1972. "Instructions for Loan Guarantee Assistance, Urban Growth and New Community Development Act of 1970," Memorandum to Title VII New Community Developers, April 20.

U.S. Department of Housing and Urban Development, Office of the Secretary. 1971. "Assistance for New Communities: Notice of Proposed Rule Making," *Federal Register*, Vol. 36 (July 31), pp. 14205–14214.

Weaver, Robert. 1964. "Testimony of Robert Weaver," in *Housing Legislation of 1964.* Hearings Before a Subcommittee of the Committee on Banking and Currency, Eighty-eighth Congress, Second Session on S. 2468 and other bills to amend the Federal Housing Laws. Washington, D.C.: U.S. Government Printing Office.

Weiss, James E., Greenlick, Merwyn R. and Jones, Joseph F. 1971. "Determinants of Medical Care Utilization: The Impact of Spatial Factors," *Inquiry*, Vol. 8 (December), pp. 50–57.

Wirick, Grover C., Morgan, James N. and Barlow, Robin. 1962. "Population Survey: Health Care and Its Financing, Hospitalization," in *Hospital and Medical Economics*, Vol. 1, Walter J. McNerney *et al.* (eds.). Chicago: Hospital Research and Educational Trust, pp. 122–155.

Index

About the Authors

Norman H. Loewenthal is program coordinator of State Wide Independent Study by Extension, at The University of North Carolina at Chapel Hill. He was a research associate with the NSF/RANN New Communities Project. Mr. Loewenthal received the M.Ed. from The University of North Carolina at Chapel Hill.

Raymond J. Burby, III is Assistant Director for Research, Center for Urban and Regional Studies, The University of North Carolina at Chapel Hill. He was co-principal investigator and deputy project director of the NSF/RANN New Communities Project. He received the M.R.P. and Ph.D. in planning from The University of North Carolina at Chapel Hill. Dr. Burby is the author of numerous articles and monographs including *Planning and Politics: Toward a Model of Planning-Related Policy Outputs in American Local Government*. He is co-author of *New Communities U.S.A.* and co-editor of *New Community Development: Planning Process, Implementation, and Emerging Social Concerns*.